# Advanced Sciences and Technologies for Security Applications

Indexed by SCOPUS

The series Advanced Sciences and Technologies for Security Applications comprises interdisciplinary research covering the theory, foundations and domain-specific topics pertaining to security. Publications within the series are peer-reviewed monographs and edited works in the areas of:

- biological and chemical threat recognition and detection (e.g., biosensors, aerosols, forensics)
- crisis and disaster management
- terrorism
- cyber security and secure information systems (e.g., encryption, optical and photonic systems)
- traditional and non-traditional security
- energy, food and resource security
- economic security and securitization (including associated infrastructures)
- transnational crime
- human security and health security
- social, political and psychological aspects of security
- recognition and identification (e.g., optical imaging, biometrics, authentication and verification)
- smart surveillance systems
- applications of theoretical frameworks and methodologies (e.g., grounded theory, complexity, network sciences, modelling and simulation)

Together, the high-quality contributions to this series provide a cross-disciplinary overview of forefront research endeavours aiming to make the world a safer place.

The editors encourage prospective authors to correspond with them in advance of submitting a manuscript. Submission of manuscripts should be made to the Editor-in-Chief or one of the Editors.

More information about this series at http://www.springer.com/series/5540

J. Martín Ramírez · Bartolomé Bauzá-Abril
Editors

# Security in the Global Commons and Beyond

With a Prologue by Former Minister of the Kingdom of Spain Dr. Josep Piqué

Springer

*Editors*
J. Martín Ramírez
Universidad Antonio de Nebrija
Campus de la Berzosa
Madrid, Spain

Bartolomé Bauzá-Abril
Madrid, Spain

ISSN 1613-5113 ISSN 2363-9466 (electronic)
Advanced Sciences and Technologies for Security Applications
ISBN 978-3-030-67972-9 ISBN 978-3-030-67973-6 (eBook)
https://doi.org/10.1007/978-3-030-67973-6



This Springer imprint is published by the registered company Springer Nature Switzerland AG
The registered company address is: Gewerbestrasse 11, 6330 Cham, Switzerland

*In memoriam*

*Prof. Adam Frączek*

*Rector, Academy of Special Education, Warsaw*

*Chair, Polish CICA International*

*President, International Society of Research on Aggression*

*(1 November 1935–18 October 2020)*

# Introduction

*NON OMNIS MORIAR!*

**to Professor Adam Frączek**
Rector, Academy of Special Education, Warsaw
Chair, Polish CICA International
President, International Society of Research on Aggression

We want to dedicate this book to Prof. Adam Frączek. Graduated in psychology at the University of Warsaw in 1958, he obtained a doctorate in humanities in the field of psychology at this university in 1965, and his habilitation at the University of Warsaw in 1977. He worked at the Faculty of Pedagogy of the University of Warsaw, heading the Department of Educational Psychology. In 1971 he became a member of the Committee of Psychological Sciences of the Polish Academy of Sciences (PAN), working at its Institute of Psychology from 1981 to 1993. In 1987 he was awarded the title of professor.

Professor Adam Frączek worked for the Academy of Special Education Maria Grzegorzewska since 1972, at the then State Institute of Special Education Maria Grzegorzewska of the Department of Psychology, by transforming it into the Institute of Psychology of the PAN, establishing its Faculty of Applied Social Sciences, and assuming the highest function of the Rector of this University for three terms (in the years 1991–1994 and 2002–2008), bringing it to full academic status. After the end of the university management period, Prof. Adam Frączek became the Curator of the UNESCO Janusz Korczak Chair of the Interdisciplinary Studies on Child Development and Well-being, heading this Department until his well-deserved retirement in 2015.

Adam Frączek tried to introduce his colleagues and students to the European world of science, being active in Polish and international scientific, social and publishing societies, and becoming a member of several editorial boards of scientific journals, such as *Aggressive Behavior, Polish Psychological Bulletin,* and *Studia Psychologiczne.*

It is impossible to list all Professor Adam Frączek's contributions in the field of science, organizational and educational activities. An expression of these merits are his many awards and honorary diplomas: Order of Merit for Physical Culture (1978), Gold Cross of Merit (1979), Medal of Maria Grzegorzewska (2004), Children's Friend Society Diploma of the Children's Friends Society (2005), *Pro Publico Bono* Smile for Smile (2005), Medal of the National Education Commission (2006), Merit for Warsaw (2008), and finally, in 2011, the Knight's Cross of the Order of *Polonia Restituta* "for outstanding achievements in research and teaching, for achievements in charity and social activities". He was also involved in social and charity activities, as chairman of the program board of the Foundation for Children's Development Jan Amos Comenius and a member of the board of the National Children's Fund.

His scientific work mainly dealt with the issues of aggression and other phenomena in the field of social pathology and psychopathology, with a particular focus on researching and preventing these phenomena among young people. Among his many publications, we will mention only two of them: *Aggression and Behavior Change: Biological and Social Processes* (1979), and *Socialization and Aggression* (1992). Adam Frączek was elected President of the International Society for Research on Aggression (ISRA) for the period 1990–1992.

Our common interest on research on aggression was what brough us together during the last four decades: attending many ISRA world and European meetings together, sharing the managing of this society as officers, having one of us (JMR) as guest professor in his Warsaw Academy, and starting with full of illusion a series of Conferences on Conflict and Aggression all over the world, in what is today the CICA International Foundation. What started as good scientific colleagues, became a deep friendship for four decades, staying in our respective homes, during our visits to Warsaw and Madrid.

Adam's intellectual strengths and broad knowledge captivated all his research colleagues. But what every person who met him remembers most is his warmth, friendliness, gentleness, and beautiful manners.

We will miss him greatly.

May he rest in peace!

*****

The present book is the product of some selected contributions to the LV CICA, organized by CICA International Foundation and Nebrija University in Madrid, on the Global Commons with the addition of some contributions related to security, which made us rename this book as Security in the Global Commons and Beyond.

The 21 international researchers and leading thinkers who contribute to the book come from three different continents—Europe, America, and the Middle East in Asia, and their background is quite diverse: academics—law, security and conflict studies, humanities—, politicians, diplomats, military—senior officers from all three services—, and professionals working in prestigious companies related to Security. This rather eclectic group of authors approaches the main topic from an interdisciplinary methodology, providing a broader perspective; a stimulating thought process; trans-discipline and global collaboration and cooperation; and an integrated synthesis of knowledge.

Global Commons have always been relevant. It was Mahan who argued that "the first and most obvious light in which the sea presents itself from the political and social point of view, is that of a great highway; or better, perhaps, of a wide common...".

Under this wide title, Global Commons, understood as those natural spaces beyond national appropriation or claim of sovereignty, we deal with sensitive areas and issues in the Artic Ocean; in the high seas, down to the ocean depths to the non-jurisdictional waters, where explotation of resources, such as minerals, fishery, and the seaborne migrations in the Mediterranean Sea or in the Indian Ocean take place; also both, the Airspace and the Outer Space, are dealt with, including very interesting ethical aspects. Cyberspace presents also some characteristics that may facilitate its consideration as a Global Common, particularly with the risk posed by its non-peaceful use by state and non-state actors. Pandemics, like the present SARS CoV-2, remind us of how fragile are such concepts as frontiers and globalization. Our prayers and thoughts are with the victims and families of those affected by this virus and with those who need to migrate in search of better living conditions and a safer future for them and their families.

As it will be found in this book, in addition to the unique legal implications that the Global Commons possess, they are viewed, more and more intently, as a common pool of resources. Or perhaps, not that common... Resources, one of the key words in this book, but also: access and security. And still, another one: data! the cyberspace contribution to the Security equation.

For Security to be comprehensive, it has to be approached from a global perspective, acknowledging the jurisdictional borders of countries, but facilitating an integrated action, encompassing the core themes in a multidisciplinary approach, bringing an inclusive and enriching intellectual exchange to reach a better understanding of the dynamics of society in the world today.

This book deals with these two areas: Global Commons (but not only) and Security, inextricably melted together and more relevant than ever in a world which is ever globalized and... with an incognita looming on the horizon: the effects of the Coronavirus pandemic upon the International Relations and a Globalization we were starting to get used to.

This book is divided in two parts. The first part includes eleven chapters, dealing directly with the Global Commons.

The first four chapters are related to the High Seas and resources and trade. We start with two chapters dealing with the Arctic. Formally not a Global Common but whose melting may provide access to untapped resources and new trade routes. Adm del Pozo, Spanish Navy (Ret), discusses these new trade routes and the opportunities, and threats as well, and what they represent to seafarers, though not exclusively. This view is supplemented by Lt García Estrada, Spanish Navy, who understands that the melting in the Arctic and the exploration for resources may result in another scenario for great power competition. Dr. Abad, from the Nebrija University, deals with another hot spot: the South China Sea (SCS), a usual ground for rivalry. She proposes the management of the SCS, and its riches, as a Global Common. Finally, Dr. Maestro, researcher at the Spanish Geologic & Mineral Institute, plunges into the mineral-related activities in the international seabed area, and particularly on some implications of the exploitation of rare metals.

Then, chapters 5 to 7, discuss the particularities of the Outer Space. Dr Yániz, who is a Spanish Air Force retired General, puts the background for the next two chapters, claiming that Space exploration and its use should be for the benefit and in the interests of all countries, while stressing some considerations related to its importance for the future of humanity. The Canadian Ambassador Dr. Meyer, argues that we are witnessing a revival of confrontational approaches on the part of leading powers which points the evolution of Outer Space as a "war-fighting domain". Rector Cayón and the Irani researcher Saloome Yousefian (Nebrija University), consider the ethical-legal considerations related to outer space's political and strategic *statu quo*.

The eighth to tenth chapters deal with Cyberspace, whose characteristics and vulnerabilities make us vulnerable and fragile. MGen (Ret) Spagnol, Italian Army, discusses cyberspace as an advantageous terrain for war that will create new forms for international relations. Three researchers from the University of Granada—Moreno-Mercado, Luengo and García Marín—use the Lybian War as a case study to analyze some characteristics of cyberspace. From Israel, Dr. Boulos, currently at Nebrija University, investigates the foreign cyber intervention in electoral processes, focusing on central principles of international law.

Finally, Dr. Priego, from the Comillas University, dissects in the eleventh chapter the situation of the Old City of Jerusalem, and suggests a solution based on its consideration as a Global Common with no possibility of being dominated and or exploited by any State.

The second part two of the book, the twelfth to fifteenth chapters, is dedicated to Security beyond the Global Commons, and deals with areas related to Environment, Conflict and Aggression.

Dr. García Gascó-Romero, Data Protection Officer at Airbus, discusses the added value of the so-called new black gold in the age of digitalization: personal data in the context of international security. Justice Dr. García Sedano, Deputy Magistrate at Madrid Provincial Court, weighs the financial dimension of Security using the case study of human trafficking in Spain. Morón Elorza, Head Veterinarian at the Biodomo Zoo and Aquarium, Science Park of Granada, discusses one of the main threats to humanity: the growing demand of food linked to the rapid increase in global population and the need to achieve food security. The final chapter of the book, written by Dr. Martínez-Otero, Director of the Complutense Research Group on Psychosociobiology of Violence: Education and Prevention, addresses the serious global phenomena of violent and antisocial behavior in school, and proposes co-existence at school, as a path to its solution.

Last but not least, we have been honoured by an excellent prologue by Former Minister of the Kingdom of Spain, Dr. Piqué. His wit and insight is a great contribution to this book. The book is completed by an Introduction and an Epilogue by both co-editors. Needless to add that this book reflects personal opinions of the authors.

We hope that this volume may contribute to achieving a more secure social system, and a better understanding of security in the global commons… and beyond. Hopefully, these areas, usually under the realm of discussion among specialists, would become the subject of a broader social discussion, as they concern each of us, both in the spheres of obligations and entitlements. Past and current crises, illegal migration and military build-up, indicate that there is a lot to be improved in these areas.

Madrid, Spain<br>December 2020

J. Martín Ramírez<br>Bartolomé Bauzá-Abril

# Prologue

## Global Commons: A Concept at Risk

According to conventional International Public Law, the "Global Commons" or "Common Spaces" are those spaces that are not under the sovereignty of any particular political subject (the States recognized by the United Nations), and which are usually identified with open seas (not included in territorial waters), air (beyond the airspace of each State), outer space and cyberspace. Arctic and Antarctic Polar zones are also usually included. They do not belong to anyone in particular and are available to all, as long as the International Treaties relating to each case are complied with.

Although they are sometimes identified, and overlap, with the so-called "global public goods", we are talking about something different.

For example, freedom of navigation through straits and the free trade associated with it; peace and security within United Nations' multilateral framework (with a Security Council establishing binding positions to Member States; International Justice through the International Criminal Court in cases of genocide or crimes against humanity; the non-proliferation of nuclear weapons; or, at present, now in 2020, the fight against pandemics, only possible within a multilateral institutional framework where reporting, coordination of actions, and related protocols compulsions are met, as well as common criteria about their impact on the population).

Not forgetting, of course, the conservation of the planet and the environment that has led to major international agreements such as the Kyoto Protocol, in 1997, or the Paris Agreements in 2015, from which, unfortunately, the United States has withdrawn. The problem is already very real and the problems arising from climate change very worrying. But there are worrying too those generated from both atmospheric and maritime pollution. The accumulation of plastics and micro-plastics in the oceans, to give a specific example, is a real global tragedy.

But it is clear that all this is intimately intertwined and, obviously, such concepts are not always peaceful in legal and political terms, or even military ones. And so it is, because their interpretation results in substantial geopolitical consequences.

In fact, disputes over territorial waters and continental platforms are very frequent. Or in the scenario that opens with the melting of the Arctic Ocean, as a product of climate change. Not to mention the growing struggle for space (and its use, theoretically forbidden, for war purposes) and, of course, the open battle for control of cyberspace and its impact in geopolitical terms. Something strictly linked to the great struggle for the dominion of new digital technologies and, in particular, artificial intelligence and all its extraordinary derivations (transmission networks—the different Gs—of all kinds of data between people and things or "Internet of Things", "machine learning", "blockchain", and a long etcetera…).

It is becoming increasingly clearer that the geopolitical scenario of this century is being defined around who will consolidate the required technological superiority (and, consequently, military) in all fields, but also and in a very special way, those that, so far, we have called "Global Commons". This is, undoubtedly, the context in which the growing struggle for global hegemony between the so-far dominant power, the United States, and the emerging (or, rather, re-emerging) power, China, must be interpreted. Not forgetting, of course, other relevant actors, such as Russia, Turkey, Iran, India, Brazil or the European Union itself.

The risk of falling into a new Thucydides Trap is increasing, and not necessarily in the conventional military terrain. The battle theatre is largely going to be the global common spaces and goods field, although they can be recognized in specific geographical scenarios, such as the South China Sea, the Arctic Ocean or the Western Indian Ocean Straits. And we also find it in the context of the so-called "hybrid war" in which the influence on shaping public opinions—one's own and the adversaries'—is increasingly decisive and which, again, is totally determined by the new communication and information technologies. We already have multiple examples of all this.

In other words, confrontation does not have to be of a "traditional" military nature (even if it necessarily contains such elements), but increasingly of technological dominance over the adversary's defensive systems. And that inevitably includes space and cyberspace.

However, this being inevitably the case, it is complemented by repositioning on land, sea, and air, in which United States' undisputed hegemonic position, after the West's victory in the Cold War in the second half of the last century, is recently questioned. Hegemony that has also manifested itself about the "Global Commons", by somehow becoming its guarantor and guardian, for the benefit of its own dominion strategy.

Something that not only China, but also very clearly Russia and, to some extent, countries like Iran, Turkey or North Korea are openly questioning. Paradigmatic examples are the new trade routes that are opening up in the Arctic. In fact, for the first time in a long time, these routes will not be controlled by the United States, and Russia's role is going to be decisive, not only in economic and commercial terms, but as regards access to vital raw materials and, of course, from a military point of view.

Not forgetting the role of the European Union, particularly at a time when the concept of the West, as a space of solidarity in defence of common values, is in a manifest crisis, with a clear weakening of the Atlantic bond between Europe and the United States.

We're talking about the defence and commitment (Western, but with a universal vocation) to values such as representative democracy, market economy and private initiative, an open society based on individual freedom and equality and the rule of law, or what we know as an international liberal order and its multilateral institutions, which arises from the end of World War II.

The European Union is a clear product of multilateralism, cooperation, subjection to rules and commitment to International Law, and respect for human rights. And consistently in the defence of free trade, the renunciation of the use of force not subject to shared norms, or support for institutional, economic and social development anywhere on the planet that meets such standards.

Therefore, with much to say regarding common and global spaces and goods, they indeed should remain as peaceful areas of cooperation.

In any case, we must not call on self-deception or fall into sterile "do-goodisms" that inevitably end up crashing with the harsh reality of life. We must be aware that there is only an effective defence of all these concepts if it is expressed in terms of power. And with its language and expressions, and its real credibility. As the proverb says, "you can't be a vegetarian in a world of carnivores". Especially when the United States withdraws not only from its global responsibilities, but also from defending values so far shared by the West as a whole.

But, let's go back to the "Global Commons" and the battle to turn them into spaces that consolidate old or new hegemonies. In order to do so, strengthening one's own military capabilities is absolutely essential. We are witnessing a phase of rearmament of enormous proportions, with great budgetary efforts to increase these capacities, regarding both conventional and nuclear weapons. These are being developed in the traditional scenarios (land, sea and air) and increasingly, in space and cyberspace.

Bad times, then, for the Global Commons, again.

A2/AD[1] is probably a key concept for explaining what is happening in this field. China has developed this approach—and continues to expand it—in South and East China Seas. The goal is to counter United States' hypothetical military superiority in the area (and in the access to the Strait of Malacca or Taiwan) through a complex military deployment strategy (combat aircraft, warships, submarines, mining, ballistic and anti-missile systems…) to deter, due to its high costs, any attack on the mainland or adjacent—natural or artificial—islands. It is in this context where the expansion and increasingly aggressive Chinese claims on enclaves in these seas that affect almost every country, from Japan, to the Philippines, Vietnam, Brunei or Indonesia, can be explained. The ultimate goal is to prevent a hypothetical action by North American aircraft carriers in that area that would end their mission of ensuring freedom of navigation in the area and the non-appearance of alternative powers.

[1] A2/AD means "Anti Access/Area Denial".

In the nineteenth century, the great Alfred Mahan[2] said that whoever dominated maritime trade would dominate the world. The ruling of the seas explains the Spanish and Portuguese empires and also the Dutch or, of course, the British ones. And to this day, those of North America.

But, in the twenty-first century, this is not enough in itself. As we have seen in the case of the A2/AD concept, it is impossible to exercise control over the seas without controlling the rest of "Global Commons". The safety of warships is inseparable from satellite navigation systems and, therefore, from being present in space and cyberspace. Otherwise, they may end up being more vulnerable. This was seen when China showed its ability to destroy its own satellite from its territory in 2007, despite an informal moratorium period on the development of that capacity. Both China, Russia or the United States (and probably others, such as Iran, Turkey or Israel) have launched anti-satellite systems that contrast with the commitments regarding the Outer Space Treaty, signed in 1967. This treaty, in accordance with the meaning of the concept "outer space" as a common space, prohibited the installation and eventual use of weapons of mass destruction in space, as well as any claim of sovereignty over it and the militarization of any celestial body.

However, the development of all kinds of satellites, both public and private (with special focus on the increasing and very worrying phenomenon of space junk), their use for espionage and counter-espionage, and for the on-the-spot identification of military targets and their eventual destruction by guided missile systems, as well as to counter potential attacks is an undeniable and deeply disturbing reality.

This is as disturbing as the fight to control the Internet and cyberspace. Western countries have believed the Internet would help to exercise freedom, since it is available to everyone and allows a global free flow of ideas and values. A common space, to sum up, not compartmentalizable and available to everyone.

Nothing further from the truth. The control over its contents has become a key tool for undermining individual freedom and enabling increasing suffocating control of societies by political powers. 1984, 5.0 version. Quite the opposite to the great goal of liberal democracy: the safeguarding of individual freedom from the arbitrariness of political power.

In the end, whoever controls cyberspace (protecting themselves from outside influences that can destabilize their political, economic and social systems, or by allowing, on the contrary, destabilizing attacks on other people's systems) will dominate the rest of "Global Commons" and, consequently, exercise its hegemony at the global level. The integration of space and cyberspace as a new dimension over traditional land, sea and air is already a remarkable reality. This is the new "Great Game" of this century.

And the victim of it is the very concept of "Global Common".

---

[2]Mahan, Alfred Thayer (1892). *The Influence of Sea Power upon the French Revolution and Empire*, 1793–1812. Little, Brown & Co, Boston.

I cannot stress this enough: these are bad times for peaceful, cooperative and inclusive globalization. The logic of force over reason has brazenly returned.

September 2020

Dr. Josep Piqué
Minister for Foreign Affairs of the Kingdom of Spain (2000–2002)

**Dr. Josep Piqué** has a degree in Economics and Business Studies with an Outstanding Merit. He is also a Ph.D. in the same subject-matter with an Outstanding Cum Laude as well as a degree in Law, all the title above at the University of Barcelona. Academically, he has been lecturing Economic Theory since 1984. He also worked as Economist in the Studies Service Department of La Caixa from 1984 to 1985.

During his public stage, he has been Minister of Industry and Energy (1996–2000), Government Spokesman (1998–2000), Minister of Foreign Affairs (2000–2002) and Minister of Science and Technology (2002–2003). He has also been Deputy and member of the Spanish Parliament.

He was Chairman and CEO of Ercros Group from 1992 to 1996, Chairman of Vueling from 2007 to 2013, Director of Airbus Group from 2011 to 2014, Vice-Chairman and CEO of OHL Group from 2013 to 2016 and independent Director of Aena from 2017 to January 2019, among others. Currently, he is the Chairman of ITP aero, independent Director of SEAT, S.A. and independent Director in ABENGOA, S.A, AMADEUS, ATRYS and ALANTRA.

In the field of civil society, Piqué is member of the Board of Trustees in several foundations and associations. He is the President of the Spanish–Japanese Forum and Foundation, The Spanish–Korean Chamber of Commerce, the Association for the Searching for Excelence, CITpax (Toledo International Center for Peace) and the Iberian-American Business Foundation. He has been Vice President of the Círculo de Empresarios (Business Forum) and President of the Círculo de Economía (Economics Forum).

# Acknowledgments

This book has been a scientific fruit of a CICA (International Conference of Conflict and Aggression), organized in Madrid by the Nebrija-Santander Chair for Risks and Conflicts Management (Center for Conflict Studies), in collaboration with CICA international Foundation and the Spanish Pugwash National Group. The academic cooperation of the CESEDEN (Spanish Center of Studies on National Defence), EuroDefense-Spain and the Harvard Kennedy School Spanish Alumni Network is also appreciated, as well as its financial sponsorship by the Spanish Ministry of Defence, throughout its *Secretaría General de Política de Defensa* and, last but not least, by the *Banco de Santander*.

Finally, we would like to finish these words of acknowledgment expressing our explicit thanks to Annelies Kersbergen, our *liaison* with the Springer *Series of Advanced Sciences and Technologies for Security Applications*, in recognition of the continuous and essential support during the edition of our books.

# Contents

# About the Editors

**J. Martín Ramírez** was born in Madrid. Currently, he is Chair of the Center for Conflict Studies at Universidad Nebrija; of the CICA International Foundation; and of the Spanish Pugwash Movement (Peace Nobel Laureate, 1995). He studied Medicine, Humanities, and Law, obtaining a Ph.D. degree in Medicine and Surgery (Neurosciences) and in Philosophy (Education) as well as three Diplomas and a Master in National Defence at the Spanish MoD Center for Advanced Studies for Defence (CESEDEN). He is a Humboldt & Fullbright Fellow, in Ruhr Universität and Stanford, respectively. Dr. Martín Ramírez is also Research Fellow of International Security Program of the Harvard University and Visiting Fellow of the Hoover Institution on War, Revolution and Peace, Stanford University, probably the two most important left-leaned and right-leaned American think-tanks, respectively. He also served as Visiting Professor and Research Fellow at universities in Israel, France, Poland, Wales, Australia, Japan, Canada, Iran, Guatemala, Germany, and the USA. He has been awarded multiple international honours, such as being several times official of the Boarding Counsel of the International Society for Research on Aggression (ISRA), on the Advisory Board of the Society for Terrorism Research (STR) and of the Professors World Peace Academy (PWPA), as well as Fellow of the World Academy of Art and Sciences and of the New York Academy of Sciences, and a Professional Award on Aggression and Inter-ethnic Conflicts by the East-West Center, established by the United States Congress, among others. Dr. Martín Ramírez is author of more than 500 scientific publications, books and articles, in more than ten languages. He has also been Head of the Universidad Complutense Research Group on Sociopsychobiology of Aggression, Head of the Departments of Psychobiology at the Universities of Seville and Complutense, and Director of the Cabinet of the Rector at the Universidad Autónoma de Madrid.

**Rear Admiral (R) Bartolomé Bauzá-Abril** joined the Spanish Navy in 1975 and retired after over 35 years of experience on board ships (both as a crewmember and Commanding Officer) and staffs (Navy, Joint, NATO and EU). He has been Commanding Officer of the gunboat *Mouro*, the corvette *Cazadora*, the frigate *Baleares* and the amphibious assault ship *Galicia*. He has been part of the Academic Staff (Strategy) in both the Spanish Navy War College and the Joint Staff College.

As Flag Officer he has been commissioned twice to the EU EUNAVFOR HQ (Op. Atalanta) at Northwood as Deputy Commander (2010 and 2014); and has served as Director Operational Preparation (OPD) for the evaluation of the NATO Response Forces Joint HQ readiness (2010–2012). His last assignment was Director CIS Spanish Navy HQ. When he retired, he founded Outrospection SL, a Business Development Support company based in Madrid, Spain, with presence in the UK (via Outrospection Ltd, co-founded as well by Bauzá-Abril) and France. Outrospection SL and Outrospection Ltd have provided customised business support to organisations and companies across the EU. Bauzá-Abril has written a number of articles on Defence issues and is a member of the Scientific Committee at CICA International.

# The Global Commons

# The Declaration of the South China Sea as a Global Common: Conflict Management and Environmental Protection

**Gracia Abad-Quintanal**

**Abstract** The concept of Global Commons refers to areas or resources outside the control of any particular nation state (UNEP), but on which many may depend or at least benefit. The existence of such spaces can be enormously favourable for trade, communication, governance and, in short, the functioning and stability of the international order. In view of the successive definitions of the concept of Global Common, there is clearly no reason not to consider the South China Sea as such. It is so not only because of the "High Sea" nature of much of the area, but also because of its value in terms of the biosphere and the physiosphere. It is therefore not surprising that since 1945 the South China Sea has been considered a Global Common without question. However, over time, China's rise, its growing interests in the area and its increasing competition with other regional and extra-regional players would eventually alter this situation. The conflict in the South China Sea is therefore a conflict with many sides as, far from being merely a territorial conflict, it is also a fishing and energy conflict and, perhaps most important of all and, as we pointed out earlier, a geostrategic conflict. So far, all avenues for resolving the conflict, both jurisdictional and negotiated, have proved unsuccessful. Thus, we see how the tyranny of the commons continues in the area we are dealing with, as competition for resources continues to reach levels that make sustainable use of them impossible. In this regard, we are witnessing a rapid deterioration of the area's coral reefs and an increasingly serious risk of military escalation with consequences that are difficult to measure and anticipate. As a result, and since it is increasingly urgent to find a solution to the problem, we believe that perhaps the best option, which has not been sufficiently considered until now, is to return to the consideration and management of the area as a global common, making it possible for all states with claims on the area to manage and exploit it jointly. However, it should be borne in mind that the main

In: Security: the Global Commons and Beyond, Edited by J. Martin Ramirez, and Bartolomé Bauzá-Abril. © 2021 Springer International. Submitted: October 21, 2020; Accepted: November 26, 2020.

G. Abad-Quintanal (✉)
International Relations Department, Faculty of Social Sciences, Nebrija University, Madrid, Spain
e-mail: gabad@nebrija.es

 
J. M. Ramírez and B. Bauzá-Abril (eds.), *Security in the Global Commons and Beyond*,
Advanced Sciences and Technologies for Security Applications,
https://doi.org/10.1007/978-3-030-67973-6_1

challenge to be overcome in order to enforce this solution is China's own position and its wish to consolidate its exclusive control over the area.

**Keywords** Concept of Global Common · High sea · South China Sea · Competition for resources

## 1 Introduction: The South China Sea as a Global Common

The concept of Global Commons refers, as defined by the United Nations Environment Programme (UNEP), to areas or resources outside the control of any particular nation state, but on which many may depend or at least benefit. The existence of such spaces can be enormously favourable for trade, communication, governance and, in short, the functioning and stability of the international order.

From the general definition just mentioned, it is possible to identify different types of Global Commons. Specifically, the first four spaces recognised as belonging to this category by international law were the high seas, Antarctica, the atmosphere and outer space.

Over time, other entities are being recognised which may also form part of this category of Global Commons, among which cyberspace should undoubtedly be highlighted (Jasper 2012, p. 1).

For their part, other authors contribute another approach that we could consider more specific. Thus, Quilligan (2009, p. 37) refers to three sets of elements that can be considered in this way:

- The noosphere (Culture, traditions, communities, associations, rights of certain groups …)
- The biosphere (Fishing, agriculture, land, forests …)
- The physiosphere (Minerals, energy, water …).

On the base of these definitions, there is clearly no reason not to consider the South China Sea as a Global Common. It is so not only because of the "High Seas" nature of much of the area we are concerned with, but also because of its value in terms of the biosphere and the physiosphere. It is therefore not surprising that since 1945 the South China Sea has been considered a Global Common without question.

However, the existing literature on the Global Commons also explains that the inappropriate or excessive use of such areas can lead to conflict in them, a conflict that will materialise, among other things, in disputes over sovereign claims, competing national interests, etc. (Jasper 2012, p. 31).

Thus, it seems clear that this is what has happened in the South China Sea since the Chinese rise eventually altered the situation described above. Indeed, the People's Republic of China does not hesitate to challenge free access to areas it considers to be of vital strategic importance and to undermine the alliances that have existed since the Second World War in the Pacific, alliances on which stability has rested in the area ever since.

Along these lines China has even dared to reinterpret the law of the sea by trying to seek support for its territorial claims (Jasper 2012), when in 2009 it submitted a 1947 map—the so-called Cow's Tongue map (Mitchell 2016, p. 14)—to the United Nations Commission on the Limits of the Continental Shelf where, by drawing a dashed line composed of nine lines, it established the area it considers its own, which covers practically the entire South China Sea. This claim makes it somewhat easier to understand why it has repeatedly declared its sovereignty over the area under consideration (Pant 2011, p. 16), calling into question not only the UNCLOS (1982) but also the Global Common character previously accepted for the area.

Competition for fishing resources and territorial disputes thus appear in the area, since, leaving aside the imprecision of the claims (Huaigao 2019, p. 231), we must keep in mind that Taiwan also claims its historical right over the entire South China Sea, while Vietnam, the Philippines and Malaysia claim 20–24, 8–9 and five islands and/or reefs respectively, and Brunei demands respect for the two hundred miles of its exclusive economic zone (Thayer 2011; Steffens 2013, p. 92).

At the same time, misgivings also arise from other actors, including extra-regional ones—the United States in particular—who see how Chinese movements could call into question the military preponderance Washington had held in the region since 1945 (Mitchell 2016, p. 18), something they does not seem willing to accept (Steffens 2013, p. 88; Jasper 2012).

In short, China's attitude and behaviour appear to have distanced us from the management of the area we are concerned with as a Global Common. However, it is no less true that the conflict triggered by this attitude and behaviour does not call into question the nature of the area considered as global common, in other words, the applicability of the concept to the case in hand, as indeed, among the causes that can give rise to conflicts in areas considered as global commons, mention is usually made precisely of disputes over claims to sovereignty or the existence of competing national interests (Jasper 2012).

## 2 The South China Sea Conflict

Although conflict is a constant in the Asian seas, the South China Sea stands out particularly in this respect (Cole 2013, p. 166). The South China Sea covers an area of some 350,000 km$^2$, which includes the archipelagos of the Paracelsus and Spratly (Collins 2003, p. 189), as well as the Macclesfield strip (Cole 2013, p. 174) and is home to one of the richest and most biologically diverse marine ecosystems in the world (Pejsova 2014, p. 1). The problem is its control, which most of the coastal states want, totally or partially, thus giving rise to conflict over this area which, although not new, has intensified in recent years.

## 2.1 The Nature of the Conflict

The conflict, far from being univocal in its nature, has many aspects, as it is not only a territorial conflict but also a fishing and energy conflict (Collins 2003, p. 191) and, perhaps most importantly of all and as we pointed out above, a geostrategic conflict.

Indeed, while the states that are parties to the conflict (People's Republic of China, Republic of China, Vietnam, Philippines, Malaysia and Brunei) are claiming all or part of the islands, islets, atolls and reefs in the South China Sea, they are also clashing over the rights to exploit the fishing resources and hydrocarbon deposits—oil and natural gas—existing on the continental shelf. With respect to the latter, it should be said that although they are uncertain in volume (Steffens 2013, p. 91), similar to Mexico's according to US data, and lower only to Saudi Arabia's if we pay attention to the People's Republic of China's data, we could be talking, in the case of oil, of some 11 billion barrels of oil that are not being exploited.

Furthermore, beyond the territory and the resources it contains, what makes this area important is its location which, according to some, would make it the most important sea route of the twenty-first century. In this sense, we should not forget that up to 80% of oil imports circulate through it or, even more seriously, that it is an area that makes it possible for the naval forces of different states, including those of the United States and the People's Republic of China to move and Project power.

Indeed, as far as the PRC is concerned, the South China Sea, the *Chinese Caribbean* or the *Asian Mediterranean* (Kaplan 2014, p. 49), is crucial for both its New Silk Road project as well as its efforts to add maritime power to its status as a continental power (Huaigao 2019, p. 221) on the basis of the development of a deep blue Navy (Kaplan 2014, p. 37) which would allow China to should control the *Rimland*, according to the geopolitical concept coined by Spykman (Kaplan 2013, p. 211).

For its part, the United States is clear that the defence of freedom of navigation and, with it, free access to the Asian high seas area and the application of international law in the area are in line with their national interest and are therefore they are entitled to defend its interests in the conflict (Thayer 2011). As if this were not enough, the United States' ability to project force both from the sea and from its bases in Asia has been the key to its action as guarantor of security in the region since the Second World War (Abad-Quintanal 2016, p. 236). A guarantee that would disappear if the strategy of access denial (Abad-Quintanal 2016, p. 243) deployed by the PRC in recent years to prevent US penetration (Kaplan 2013, p. 216) beyond the first chain of islands (Abad-Quintanal 2012)—a strategy recognised even by some high-ranking Chinese officials and in which the South China Sea plays a leading role—was to succeed (Steffens 2013, p. 103).

In short, this is a key area in the struggle for both regional and global hegemony, which explains why the different actors, but especially the People's Republic of China, are determined to fight for it (Steffens 2013, p. 88).

## 2.2 *The Strategies of the Actors and Their Impact*

At least as complex as the nature of the conflict are the strategies of the actors. A complexity that, to a large extent, is a consequence of both the diversity and the changes that are taking place. In this sense, it is worth noting a wide range of strategies that range from merely claiming historical rights to the flights and crossings of ships and aircraft, to the occupation of islands through the use of military and/or paramilitary troops and the construction of platforms, structures and islands.

Special attention should be paid to the approach of the People's Republic of China, which has covered this whole spectrum, clearly increasing its presence in the area since the beginning of this century. Thus, for example, it has combined the expansion of its economic activities in the area (Pejsova 2014, p. 1), with the sending of coastguard ships on reconnaissance missions in equal parts. It should be said that this greater Chinese assertiveness has led, as expected, to repeated clashes with other states with claims in the area, especially the Philippines and Vietnam (Cole 2013, p. 175), thereby damaging at certain times the *charm offensive*deployed by the People's Republic of China towards Southeast Asia (White 2012, p. 43).

Probably aware of this reality, the PRC has striven, since the middle of the past decade, to portray itself as a facilitator for a negotiated management of the South China Sea. All in all, such negotiation would always be limited to the coastal states and would exclude extra-regional states with interests in the area, chiefly the United States (Desert 2016), seeking once again to achieve the dual objective of strengthening its presence in the area and simultaneously weakening that of its rival.

These efforts should not overshadow the PRC's opposition to dealing with all the ASEAN states that are parties to the dispute jointly, in a multilateral way. On the contrary, as in many other issues, it has frequently insisted on addressing the problem bilaterally with each of the ASEAN states involved, thus clearly taking advantage of its status as a major power. It should be said that in many cases, if the ASEAN states have been able to resist the Chinese pressure it has been because they have felt supported by the USA (Cole 2013, p. 176), even though this support can only be described as fluctuating.

In any event, as we pointed out earlier, there is no doubt that the United States, although not a party to the South China Sea conflict and therefore not a primary actor in the conflict, is a secondary actor of great importance, as it has clear interests both in the peace and stability of the region and in ensuring that it does not end up being dominated by another power: the PRC. Indeed, in 2012, through the State Department, it did not hesitate to state that its national interest made it important to "maintain peace and stability, respect for international law, freedom of navigation and legal trade in the South China Sea" while calling on the states of the region to settle disputes peacefully without resorting to intimidation or force.

And the fact is that, although Washington has remained fairly on the sidelines with respect to the various sovereignty claims, the growing desire shown by China over the past two decades to dominate the area—even changing the prevailing rules (Cole 2013, p. 176)—challenging the balance of power in the struggle for regional and global primacy, has led the US to take a clearer position on the conflict (Steffens 2013, p. 90). This involvement could not be welcomed by China, which has not hesitated to regard it as interference in matters that should not concern Washington.

Beyond all that has been pointed out so far, the problem with many of the strategies deployed is that they are based on (or at least involve) an abusive use of the resources in the area considered, contributing to their deterioration and aggravating the conflict itself (Jasper 2012). Thus, for instance, abusive fishing and fishing outside existing regulations have become sadly common—bringing the area's fisheries to the brink of collapse (Steffens 2013, p. 90), pollution of the sea and degradation of unique habitats in the world, likely to cause serious problems for a long period of time and leading the FAO to warn that this is one of the most overexploited systems in the world (Pejsova 2014, p. 1).

## 3 Attempts at Conflict Resolution

### *3.1 International Law*

Among the attempts to solve the conflict we should mention first, perhaps because it is the most elementary, the repeated calls made to the People's Republic of China to respect the United Nations Convention on the Law of the Sea (UNCLOS), entered into force on 16 November 1994 upon deposition of the 60th instrument of ratification. Among other things, states in article 123 that "coastal States of semi-enclosed maritime areas shall cooperate in the management, conservation and exploitation of the living resources therein", something that clearly applies to the South China Sea. However, the PRC has systematically disregarded these calls despite being a signatory to the aforementioned convention, arguing that the United Nations' maritime management codes are incompatible with its own internal regulations and that, in fact, they are just another element in the West's efforts to limit it.

However, beyond the attitude displayed by the PRC, it is undeniable that both the vagueness of some of its prescriptions and the difficulty of their application in the specific geographical context of the South China Sea, as well as the interested interpretations of the rule made by the different states—and not only by the PRC—have contributed to undermining the possibilities of a successful application of the Jamaica Convention in the area under consideration (Steffens 2013, p. 94).

### *3.2 Negotiated Solutions*

As opposed to solutions derived from the application of existing international law or even those that could be reached through multilateral negotiation, China prefers, as mentioned above, bilateral negotiation with each of the other parties involved (Thayer

2011), something that is seen as unfair by most of them given the difference in size between each of them and the PRC itself. However, even in those cases in which some progress has been made along these lines, like in 1995 when a bilateral code of conduct was agreed with the Philippines, it has also failed to prevent subsequent incidents even between the two parties to that code of conduct.

In any case, there are continuous efforts to find a way to manage the area in question and avoid confrontation. Since 2002, attempts have been made to promote the adoption of a code of conduct between the parties involved. The first advances in this sense were the 1992 South China Sea Declaration (Steffens 2013, p. 94) and the Declaration of the Code of Conduct of the Parties in the South China Sea agreed between ASEAN and the PRC in 2002 (Pejsova 2014, p. 3; Thayer 2011). In a further step, it must be said that, at least since the 1980s, there have been proposals to promote the joint development of the South China Sea, proposals in which the PRC itself has often been a protagonist. However, such efforts have so far been unsuccessful, and while China went so far as to say that there could be an agreement in this sense by 2017 (Huaigao 2019, p. 220), the truth is that it is has not been achieved yet. Beyond all this, it is important to remember that codes of conduct and exploitation agreements are not necessarily legally binding—the states considered that at some point a binding code of conduct would be adopted, but this has never materialized—nor, more importantly, do they have the capacity to solve the sovereignty conflict.

Similarly, in the framework of the ASEAN Regional Forum, an attempt has been made to promote a cooperative solution to the problem. As the ASEAN itself, the ARF has been incapable of leading any attempt to reach an agreement or negotiation in relation to this conflict (Steffens 2013, p. 101). Perhaps the most noteworthy effort in this framework is that made by the United States in 2010 in the context of the ARF (ASEAN Regional Forum) meeting held in Hanoi. This was a notable effort for at least two reasons: it was led by the United States and was in response to an increasingly assertive Chinese attitude which, in fact, has not been reversed.

Thus, it remains clear that it is difficult to reach a negotiated solution as that requires two conditions—benign bilateral relations and political will (Huaigao 2019, p. 221)—which are doubtful to exist right now, to say the least.

### *3.3 Jurisdictional Solutions*

Of course, there has been no lack of attempts to find a jurisdictional solution to the conflict, or at least to part of it. The most relevant example in this respect was the decision by the Philippines to take it to the Court of Arbitration. Before the Court, the Philippines invoked the United Nations Convention on the Law of the Sea, to which we referred above.

The Court ruled in favour of the Philippines, noting that China had violated international law, while rejecting almost all of China's claims. The People's Republic of China, for its part, after trying to boycott the process, chose not to recognise the ruling.

Instead, it counterattacked through the Supreme People's Court by promulgating a regulation that would allow the PRC to "establish a clear legal basis for China to safeguard the maritime order". On those bases, the PRC insisted that it would "prosecute any foreigner found fishing or prospecting in the waters in dispute".

Moreover, in this specific case, the Philippines would also end up abandoning its initial claims in the context of the changes derived from the so-called *Independent Foreign Policy* launched by President Duterte. In that framework they developed an approach according to which "the area in dispute has never belonged to anyone".

## 4 The Return of the Area to the Situation of Global Common: A Proposal for an Alternative Solution

Whereas, as we see, no solution has been achieved so far either through jurisdictional means or in a negotiated manner, in the area under discussion we see the continuing *tragedy of the commons*, as competition for resources continues at levels that make sustainable use of resources impossible (Jasper 2012, p. 30). In this regard, we are witnessing a rapid deterioration of the area's coral reefs and an increasingly serious risk of military escalation with consequences that are difficult to measure and anticipate.

As a result, there is an increasingly urgent need to find a solution that will slow down or at least limit these processes, and perhaps the best option, which has not been sufficiently considered, is to return to the consideration and management of the area as a global common.

This option would involve the joint management and exploitation of the area by all the states with claims to it, using the instruments provided by the multilateral processes present in the área: East Asian Summits (EAC), ASEAN + 3 or ARF.

The area's return to the situation of global common would undoubtedly make it possible to respond to the environmental situation while helping to prevent an escalation, which would be an ideal solution. However, there is at least some doubts as to the feasibility of this possibility, not only because similar frameworks and options have not worked in the past but also because it seems clear that the problem in the area we are dealing with is not so much competition for resources but chiefly and above all a territorial conflict and, probably, and this is the most problematic, hegemony in the Asia–Pacific region. Indeed, the latter is the most complicated aspect, as although a kind of "regional sovereignty" (Steffens 2013, p. 102) over the islands aimed at allowing them to be exploited jointly could provide a response, at least temporarily, to the territorial conflict, the same cannot be said of the struggle for hegemony.

Specifically, it is considered that in order for a global common to be recognised and respected as such all the powers with interests in the area under consideration need to feel that a regime of this kind protects their interests. That is the only manner to ensure responsible, sustainable and cooperative use of the shared spaces (Jasper

2012, p. 7) and this, which can be fulfilled in the case of the other parties to the conflict, does not appear to be so clear in the case of the People's Republic of China.

Indeed, while a return to the situation of global common could make it possible to manage and alleviate the environmental problems arising from the conflict and accommodate the energy, economic, territorial and sovereignty interests that motivate it, it would not serve as a response to the struggle for hegemony, as a solution to the conflict of the major powers.

In other words, in this case the so-called *problem of the global commons*is clearly present, as while everyone has incentives to benefit from them, the different parties have a different level of motivation to contribute to their creation, maintenance and sustainability (Jasper 2012, p. 28).

## References

Abad-Quintanal, G. (2012). La Política Exterior y de Seguridad o la Búsqueda del Poder Integral. *Atenea, 37*, 12–18.

Abad-Quintanal, G. (2016). Doble Reaseguro o Doble Inestabilidad. El papel de Estados Unidos en Asia y el Conflicto por las Islas Senkaku Diaoyu. *Revista UNISCI, 41*, 235–245.

Cole, B. (2013). *Asian maritime strategies: Navigating troubled waters*. Naval Institute Press.

Collins, A. L. (2003). *Security in Southeast Asia. Domestic, regional and global issues*. Singapore: Institute of Southeast Asian Studies.

Desert, D. (2016). The internationalization of maritime disputes in the South China Sea: Environmental destruction in the high seas and threats to the Global Commons. *EJIL: Talk!*, 28 Apr. Available at https://www.ejiltalk.org/.

Huaigao, Q. (2019). Joint development in the South China Sea: China's incentives and policy choices. *Journal of Contemporary East Asia Studies, 8*(2), 220–239.

Jasper, S. (Ed.). (2012). *Conflict and cooperation in the Global Commons. A comprehensive approach for international security*. Washington, DC: Georgetown University Press.

Kaplan, R. D. (2013). *The revenge of geography*. New York: Random House.

Kaplan, R. D. (2014). *Asia's Cauldron: The South China Sea and the end of a stable Pacific*. New York: Random House.

Mitchell, M. D. (2016). The South China Sea: A geopolitical analysis. *Journal of Geography and Geology 8*(3), 14–25.

Pant, H. V. (2011). *China's rising. Global profile*. Brighton: Sussex Academic Press.

Pejsova, E. (2014). The South China Sea's commons: Behind and beyond sovereignty disputes. *Alert, Issue 30*, June 2014.

Quilligan, J. B. (2009). People sharing resources toward a new multilateralism of the Global Commons. *Kosmos* (Fall–Winter), 36–43.

Steffens, A. W. (2013). Scramble in the South China Sea: Regional conflict and US strategy. *Strategic Studies Quarterly* (Fall), 88–107.

Thayer, C. A. (2011). South China Sea: A commons for China only? *Yale Global Online*, 7 July 2011. Available at https://yaleglobal.yale.edu/content/south-china-sea-commons-china-only.

United Nations. (1982). *United Nations Convention on the Law of the Sea (UNCLOS)*. 10 Dec 1982, Jamaica.

White, H. (2012). *The China choice. Why we should share power*. Oxford: Oxford University Press.

**Gracia Abad-Quintanal** holds a Ph.D. in International Relations (Honours), a M.Phil. in International Relations and a B.A. in Political Science from Universidad Complutense de Madrid. Dr. Gracia Abad is Associate Professor in International Relations, Research Coordinator at the Social Sciences School and Coordinator of the Ph.D. Programme on Security and Risks and Conflicts Managemente, at Nebrija University. She has also taught undergraduate, graduate and specialisation courses at Comillas University, Saint Louis University, Complutense University of Madrid and University of Salamanca, among others.

# The Exploitation of the Sea for Trade and Communication: The New Arctic Routes, Challenges, Conflicts and Prospects

**Fernando del Pozo**

**Abstract** The steady reduction of the Arctic ice, owing to complex phenomena usually summarised as global warming, is opening large tracts of land, but especially of ocean waters, to exploitation. This suggests new possibilities, such as fisheries, mining, oil extraction, scientific research, and many others, of which the new routes of navigation are in the first place a necessary component of all these new exploitations, and also by themselves seem to offer a promise to shorten traditional routes. Here we examine the prospects offered by this hitherto nearly unknown area, and the difficulties posed by its desolation, the harsh climate, and the limited support, even absence of it, for accurate position, navigation and timing, for modern communications, aids to navigation, and other safety elements.

**Keywords** Arctic · Arctic ice · Communications · Ecotourism · Fishing · Fossil fuel · Global warming · Liquid natural gas · Mining, · Navigation · Satellite navigation systems

## 1 Introduction

When we talk about the exploitation of the sea what we first think of is the riches that the sea offers and have to be extracted with the opposition of the waters and the obstacles presented by distance and depth: fish, oil, minerals, even wind and tides energy. But we tend to forget that the main gift of the sea, and the factor that makes all of that possible, is a means to transport goods far more efficiently than across land, not to mention air. The law of physics that so nakedly proclaimed Archimedes

In: Global Commons and Beyond, Edited by J. Martin Ramirez, and Bartolomé Bauzá-Abril. © 2021 Springer International. Submitted: August, 03, 2020; Accepted: September, 14, 2020.

Fernando del Pozo, Admiral (Ret.) of the Spanish Navy; Fellow of the Spanish *Academia de las Artes y Ciencias Militares*; Director of Wise Pens international.

F. del Pozo (✉)
Padriñán 63A, 36960 Sanxenxo, Pontevedra, Spain
e-mail: fernando.delpozo@gmail.com

 
J. M. Ramírez and B. Bauzá-Abril (eds.), *Security in the Global Commons and Beyond*, Advanced Sciences and Technologies for Security Applications,
https://doi.org/10.1007/978-3-030-67973-6_2

of Syracuse allows us to move efficiently and at a time many thousands of tons of the most varied, heavy or voluminous cargo, and to proceed directly from the departing point to the destination without crossing barriers or having to previously build bridges or tunnels. Not surprisingly, 90% of the world traffic of goods is seaborne. And this has not changed from the most remote history.

The initial trade routes changed radically a few times: first when, in the quest to improve on the Portuguese route to the Far East, a full continent was found obstructing the way to the East through the West, which created a host of new routes; later when the routes imposed by the wind were shortened by the near-simultaneous—in historical terms—appearance of mechanical propulsion and the building of the Suez and Panama canals. The wool and tea races, the galleon of Acapulco, and other wind-dependant routes were replaced by more direct, frequent and regular routes.

Today we are again in the threshold of new transformations with as much potential impact on the global trade as mechanical propulsion, Suez or Panama. Autonomous ships, in search of savings in a business line where 30% of the running costs are in manpower, will reinforce transport of flammable or otherwise unsafe cargo in lines away from chokepoints, somewhat reproducing the ancient routes marked by the aptly called *trade winds*; the possible construction of new canals in Nicaragua, Istanbul, or the Kra peninsula, may shorten again and alleviate bottlenecks in the routes with the East, especially the last one, as the congested and dangerous—not only because of the traffic density, but also because of endemic piracy there and in the South China Sea–Malacca Strait, which the Kra canal may allow to bypass, is the conduit through which travels 28% of the world's soy, 20% of rice, 8% wheat, 15% corn, and 32% of ammonium sulphite, the main fertilizer, besides a variable but sizeable part of the seaborne oil and gas.

But the biggest potential to change the pattern of the world's maritime traffic is the Arctic ice melting, which not only will open new alternative routes but will also create its economic dynamics. Of the modalities of the new routes that the ice withdrawal allows, the trans-Arctic ones are capturing the imagination of North American and European shipowners, as it promises both a more convenient alternative to Panama for North American countries, and for Europe to bring the Far East closer. We will have a look at how this may transform the exploitation of the sea for trade and communication, and the many challenges this presents.

## 2 The Arctic Melting

Global warming has in a short time gone in public perception from incredulity, through sceptic acceptance, to undeniable reality. One of the irrefutable pieces of evidence of this reality, because a temperature rise of ¼ °C every 20 years is hard to perceive from personal experience—hence the sceptic's ignorance of the impact in ocean currents and climate—is the rapid melting of the Arctic ice. Global warming is not uniform: while in Antarctica it is barely measurable, in the Arctic it is as much as four times the global average, owing to two perverse feedback phenomena,

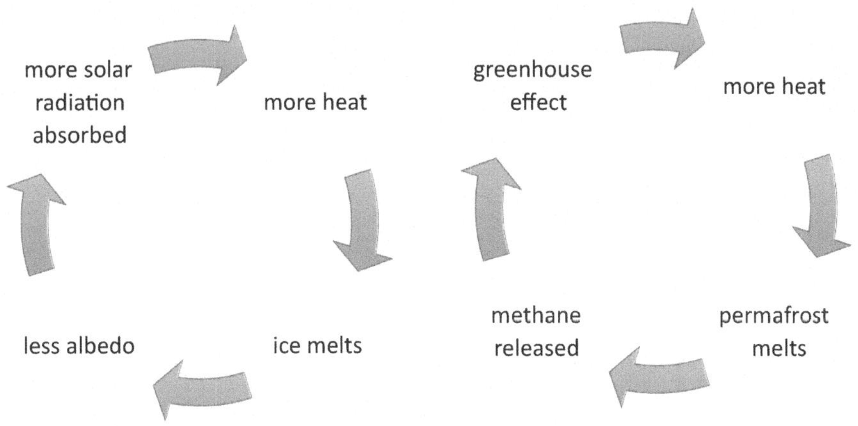


**Fig. 1.** The perverse cycles of Arctic warming

independent of each other but working in the same direction, and which do not happen in Antarctica owing to its being a continent, instead of an ocean. One is: less ice, less albedo, more heat, less ice; and the other is: permafrost melts, releases methane, greenhouse effect, more permafrost melts (Fig. 1). These feedbacks make irrelevant the debate whether global warming is anthropogenic (which is the scientific consensus) or not, because these cycles once initiated have a life of their own.

Methane, in particular, 25 times more efficient than $CO_2$ in the greenhouse effect, and of which it is estimated that 250,000 MT (Metric Tons) are liberated every year, has another source besides permafrost, which is the sublimation of methane hydrates present in the Arctic Ocean and Siberian lakes. This has been documented, and in such quantities that sizeable bubbles have been observed in the surface of the lakes.

The first of the two cycles might be reversed (Fig. 2), but only a catastrophic event could provoke it, like a gigantic volcanic eruption originating a global winter, which has already happened in the remote past, or alterations in the eccentricity of the Earth orbit and equinox precession, which caused the Pleistocene glaciations. In any case, as we cannot speculate with phenomena of which the probability of occurrence is unknown, we will be content to analyse what will happen in the coming decades, or even centuries (Fig. 3), which is a steady reduction of the volume and extension of the Arctic ice. Large tracts of the Arctic Ocean that were permanently iced over are becoming seasonably free, and zones that were iced only seasonably now are free the whole year-round.

As a result, the Arctic has become a subject of growing attention in hope of the riches that the withdrawing ice may uncover, or at least make more accessible, thus freeing routes so far unpassable, even joining the Atlantic with the Pacific, something very much sought after historically, and on the search of which many explorers lost their lives.

Fig. 2 A hypothetical feedback cycle for Arctic cooling

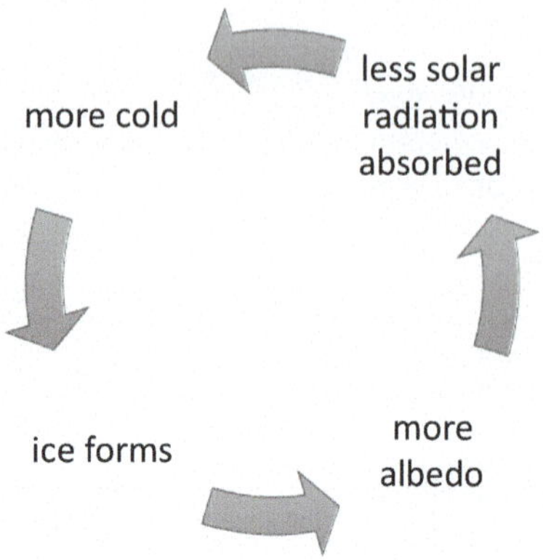


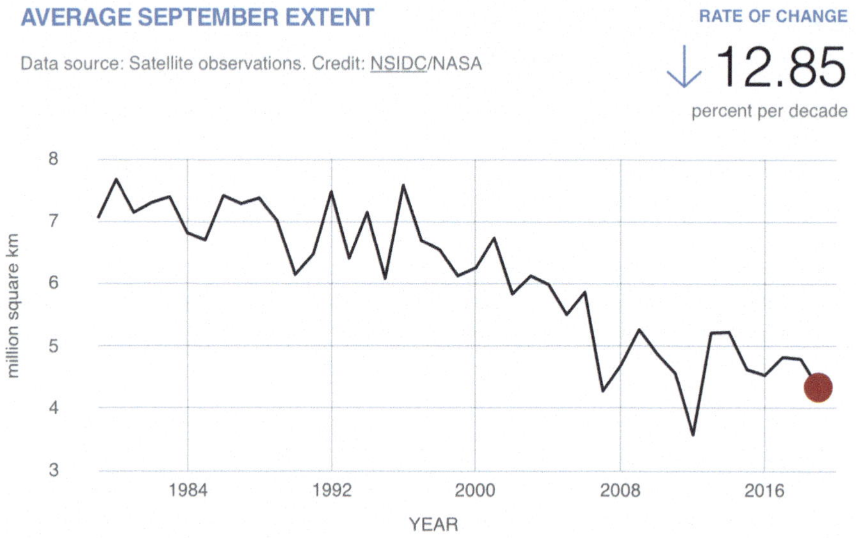


**Fig. 3** The diminishing extent of Arctic ice

## 3 Arctic Traffic

There are three classes of traffic in the Arctic, which are affected in different ways by the changing conditions: destinational, intra-Arctic and trans-Arctic.

## 3.1 Destinational Traffic

Destinational traffic, which proceeds to a destination to eventually return the same way is made of a variety of navigators: the quickly growing influx of eco-tourists and adventurers, scientific or industrial researchers, and fishermen.

Mining exploitation is the prime mover of intra-Arctic traffic, as centres of mining exploitation, singularly in Siberia, trade intensely with each other, although in the final instance it also generates destinational traffic.

Finally, the trans-Arctic traffic between Bering and either Baffin Bay through the Northwest Passage (NWP), or the Barents Sea through the Northern Sea Route (NSR), is the biggest object of speculation as its possibilities are only becoming apparent now (Fig. 4).

All of them generate economic activity, which attracts people in search of gains, and unfortunately many of them with scarce experience in the harsh Arctic environment.

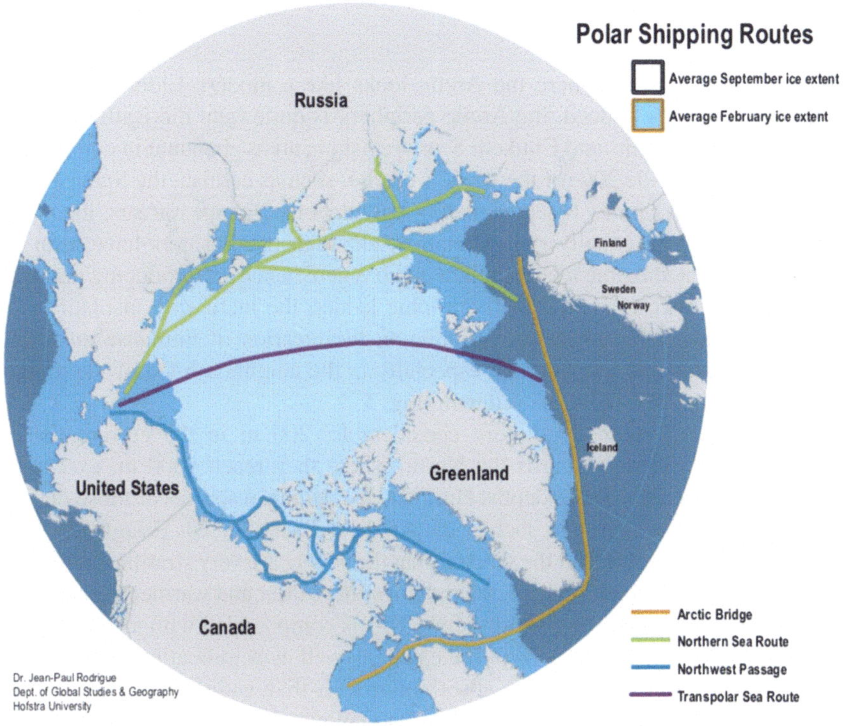


**Fig. 4** The Polar shipping routes

### 3.1.1 Ecotourism

Ecotourism, in particular, is a cause of great concern, in no small measure because curiosity impels them to reach farther than what prudence should allow, but especially because an accident in one of these ships places in grave danger perhaps several thousands of people, most of them unprepared for Arctic conditions, and search and rescue services (SAR) are practically absent because of enormous distances to any habitation. How to fight pollution in ice, also, is still something unresolved.

In June 1989 the Russian cruiser *Maxim Gorkiy* crashed against solid ice near Svalbard and started to sink. As luck would have it, a Norwegian coastguard cutter was "only" five hours away, and weather was unusually fair. This experience, and other more recently such as the *Clipper Adventurer*, which went aground in the desolate Nunavut coast with 128 passengers in 2010, and had to wait for two days until passengers and crew were rescued, have moved the local countries to require these touristic companies to undertake the trips in pairs.

### 3.1.2 Fisheries

Fishing is another area where the Arctic looks like a modern Eldorado, holding wonderful promises. Indeed, the Arctic periphery is quite rich: the Baffin Bay, the Bering area, the Barents and Chukchi Seas are fishing areas abundant in commercial species—they provide 20% of the world's catch—such as codfish, the Spanish fishermen's target in Barents. It seems therefore evident that, as ice retreats, the newly open waters will be equally rich. Certainly, although these waters have been for millennia separated by the ice from light and oxygen, hence not producing plankton and algae, the lowest echelon of the trophic ladder, the increasing insolation and exposition to the atmosphere are stimulating the creation of immense quantities of phytoplankton and zooplankton, especially in the neighbourhood of the mighty Siberian rivers, which induces optimism (Fig. 5).

Unfortunately, Arctic depths are considerable, 200 m in the current fishing grounds, but deepening towards the North, where they reach 4000 m, except for the Lomonosov Ridge. These depths eliminate the demersal species or those that are so in some period of their life, such as the Arctic codfish, which is pelagic as young and demersal as an adult. But the worst is that the waters are very stratified, with cold and fresh water from melting ice remaining over the saltier and warmer water, which inhibits upwelling of the bottom nutrients. This is compounded with a lack of ports to unload, process and shipment of the catch, as well as acidification of the Arctic because paradoxically cold waters absorb more $CO_2$ than warmer ones, and the not very well understood phenomenon of an anomalous abundance of contaminants, especially mercury, with the result that the apparent promise of bountiful catches has weak support (Fig. 6).

### 3.1.3 Mining

In respect to mining, the riches of the Arctic area are considerable, and in general they are in an advanced grade of exploitation, which positively impacts maritime traffic.

In Alaska, the Red Dog Mine is the biggest producer of zinc in the world. Canada produces gold, coal, quartz, nickel, iron, diamonds and uranium. Greenland has deposits of diamonds, gold, niobium, tantalite, uranium, iron and rare-earths (Fig. 7).

Siberia, in particular, has mines of practically any commercially valuable mineral, and its production is concentrated along their mighty rivers.

Dudinka by the Yenisey river serves the mining complex of Norilsk, the main world producer of nickel and palladium; Yamburg, Noviy Port and Sabetta in Ob river, also in Siberia, and in the European Russia Varandey, serving the Pechora

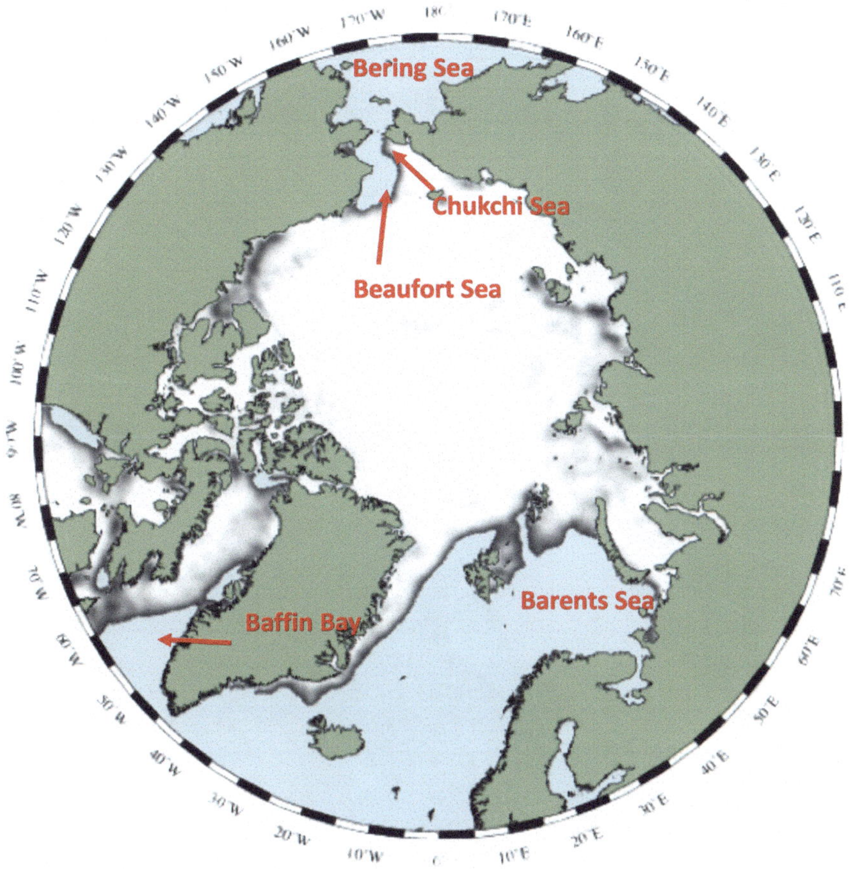


**Fig. 5** Main Arctic fishing areas

basin, have an intense activity, especially as a link to Murmansk, which is the gate to the Atlantic.

### 3.1.4 Fossil Fuels Extraction

As for fossil fuels, known reserves hypothetically accessible, estimated as around 13% of the world fuel and 30% of gas, seem to justify the optimism. But exploration and exploitation activities, which have been growing until recently, have begun to diminish owing to the evolution of oil prices, the pressure of ecologist organisations, and practical difficulties. The important trans-Alaska pipeline turned out to be much costlier and difficult than estimated, because in winter the terrain is hard as a rock, and in summer it is so soft that the pipeline sinks in the peat. Shell Oil ceased operations in the Chukchi Sea in September 2015 after having invested more than $7 billion

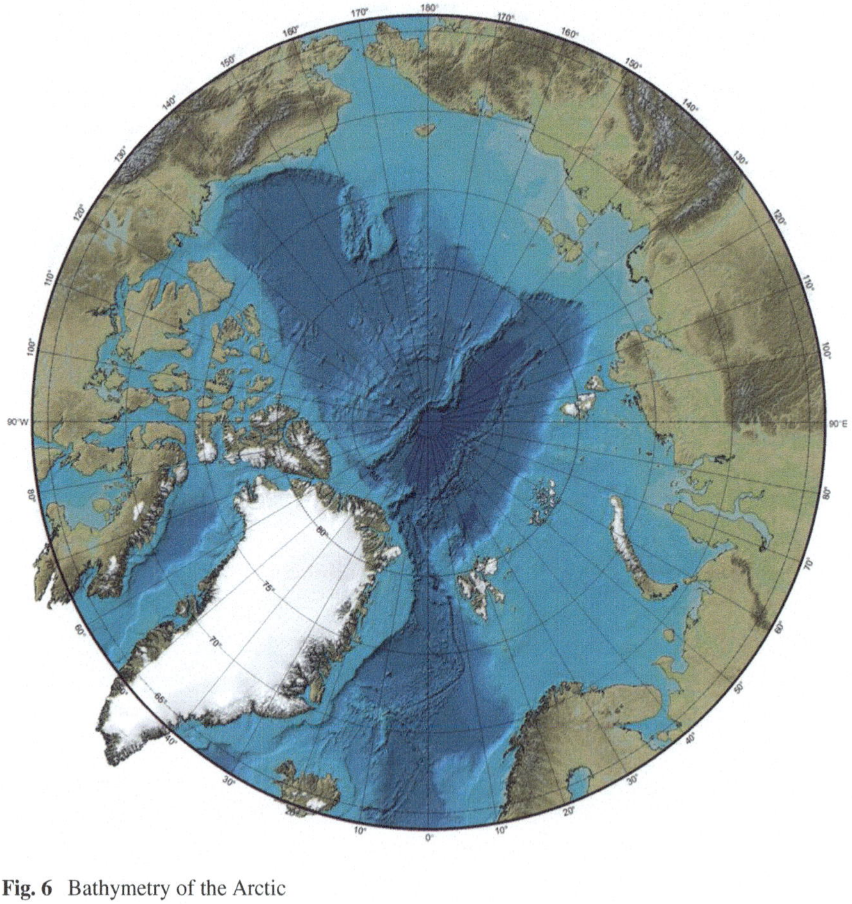


**Fig. 6** Bathymetry of the Arctic

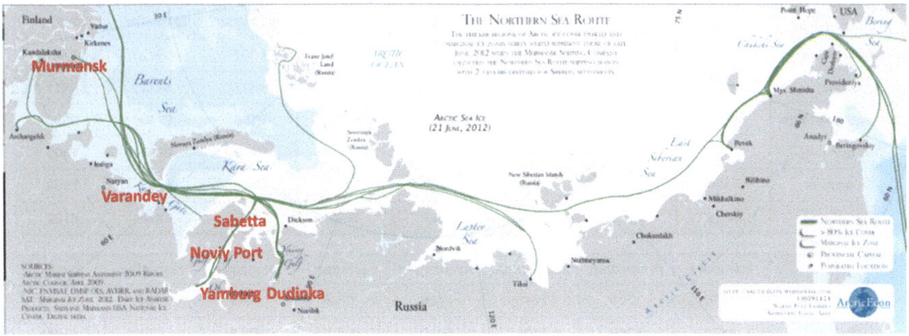


**Fig. 7** Mining exploitations along the Northern Sea Route

in exploration, and in December 2016 a joint Canada-US decision has banned new drillings in Chukchi and Beaufort Seas, a decision difficult to revert because of its binational character.

A different kind of fuel, methane hydrates, can be found in depths over 300 m and temperatures between 0 and 2 °C, or in sedimentary rocks in Alaska or Siberia, therefore, while not privative of the Arctic it seems that in this area it should be plentiful. The methane contained in the hydrates is one of the cleanest fuels known, but recovering it is a serious problem because as soon as it is freed from those conditions it sublimates and gets lost in the atmosphere. Attempts are being made at the industrial exploitation of this fuel with a procedure that avoids adding greenhouse gas to an already polluted high atmosphere, which may succeed in the next few years.

## 3.2 *Intra-Arctic*

Intra-Arctic traffic is therefore basically what joins the Siberian and Russian ports between them. There is just one international intra-Arctic line, joining Murmansk (Russia) with Churchill (Canada). The intention is to develop the province of Manitoba and the Northern territories. Churchill is not connected by road with the rest of Canada, but it is the port where grain arriving by rail from the great prairies can be exported to Europe. Now, this new line extends the season to four months and allows Churchill to receive Russian fertiliser.

## 3.3 *Trans-Arctic*

The North-West Passage and the Northern Sea Route, although of similar length, have certain important differences. For the US the Northwest Passage is a potential alternative to Panama Canal, especially for its northernmost ports, which could

| Suez Route | Hamburg | Rotterdam | Amsterdam | Antwerpen | London | Algeciras | Marseille | Venice |
|---|---|---|---|---|---|---|---|---|
| Yokohama | 11488 | 11229 | 11208 | 11184 | 11141 | 9867 | 9442 | 9241 |
| Busan | 11458 | 11199 | 11178 | 11154 | 11111 | 9837 | 9412 | 9211 |
| Shanghai/Ningbo | 10806 | 10547 | 10526 | 10502 | 10459 | 9185 | 8760 | 8559 |
| Hong-Kong | 10053 | 9794 | 9773 | 9749 | 9706 | 8432 | 8007 | 7806 |
| Singapore | 8599 | 8340 | 8319 | 8295 | 8252 | 6978 | 6553 | 6352 |
| Port-Klang | 8369 | 8110 | 8089 | 8065 | 8022 | 6748 | 6323 | 6122 |

| Arctic Route | Hamburg | Rotterdam | Amsterdam | Antwerpen | London | Algeciras | Marseille | Venice |
|---|---|---|---|---|---|---|---|---|
| Yokohama | 7378 | 7355 | 7376 | 7436 | 7463 | 8689 | 9382 | 11552 |
| Busan | 8402 | 8379 | 8400 | 8460 | 8487 | 9713 | 10406 | 11511 |
| Shanghai/Ningbo | 8129 | 9419 | 8127 | 8187 | 8214 | 9440 | 10133 | 10859 |
| Hong-Kong | 8963 | 8940 | 8961 | 9021 | 9048 | 10274 | 10967 | 10106 |
| Singapore | 10267 | 11557 | 10265 | 10325 | 10352 | 11578 | 12271 | 10652 |
| Port-Klang | 10497 | 11787 | 10495 | 10555 | 10582 | 11808 | 12501 | 10882 |

**Fig. 8** *Source* Own elaboration. In this table, distances between some Asian and European ports have been compiled comparing the NSR and Suez routes. Where one of the two is significantly shorter than the alternative it has been highlighted.

benefit from a shorter route, although differences with Canada as to the interpretation of international Law are an obstacle, while for Europe it has a scant interest.

Besides, they do not open at the same time. While in the Siberian coast the influx of the powerful Siberian rivers facilitates the maritime ice melt, in Canada the strong interaction with landmasses prevents it in a great measure, with the result that it opens later and closes earlier. Besides, navigation in those straits with blocks of old and hard ice adrift is very dangerous at all times. This effectively rules out reliable exploitation of the NWP for the time being.

The question, therefore, is whether for Europe in general, and Spain in particular, the eventual opening of the Northern Sea Route is advantageous for commerce with Asia, as not only it is seasonably practicable, but its permanent opening seems to be within reach. The answer is that only the ports of northern Europe and northern Asia benefit from a shorter distance. A similar distance for the two routes, NSR and Suez, occurs approximately between Algeciras and Shanghai. Any route with terminals further south from one or the other port cannot be improved by northern Siberia, except for the factor of the absence of piracy, something unheard of in the cold Arctic climate (Fig. 8).

But distance is not everything. What the shipowner is looking for when considering the possibility of using the Northern Sea Route is not to reduce the distance, but rather the time, and that is quite a different proposition. The traffic speed in the north is slower because even in the best conditions, which usually happen in September, there are drifting ice blocks; they are also rapidly changing, the reason why Russia forces ships making the route to be accompanied by icebreakers; and the administrative procedures before undertaking the transit can be very long. For all these reasons, it does not seem that even routes between ports as far north as Rotterdam or Hamburg and Busan (Korea) are currently competitive with Suez.

### 3.3.1 Northern Sea Route Trials

In the summer of 2009 the German company Beluga Shipping sent two general cargo ships, the *Beluga Fraternity* and the *Beluga Foresight*, of 12,744 Tm, making the line from Yangpu to Rotterdam, by the Northern Sea Route instead of the usual Suez Canal, partly to check the possible savings, and partly to avoid the risks of piracy, then rampant in the Aden area, in addition to the more "traditional" piracy of Malacca and the South China Sea. They also took the opportunity to enter Noviy Port, Yamburg and Archangel to load and unload cargo. The trip was made without incident, but the administrative processes that cost the *Beluga* expedition almost a month of paperwork in Vladivostok, and the obligation to be accompanied by a Russian icebreaker, who in the Beluga case was not one, but two the required ones, the *50 Let Pobedy*, the largest in the world, and the not much smaller *Rossia*, both nuclear powered, made the trip much longer than estimated.

Although reportedly they did not find ice in noteworthy amounts during the 22 days of the transit, the lack of reliable forecasts of the presence of ice was considered an important negative factor for regular use of the route.

More recently, the shipping company TeeKay has sent an LNG carrier, the *Eduard Toll*, in the middle of winter to cross the Northern Sea Route. It has managed to do it without icebreaker company, but it must be taken into account that it is a recently built ship with full polar navigation specifications. In other words, it is practically an icebreaker in addition to its role as LNG carrier.

And in this list of examples of trials by big shipping companies, the giant shipping company Maersk has decided to experiment with the Northern Sea Route for its container ships. It has chosen for this a relatively small vessel, of only 3 600 TEU (the largest Post-Panamax are up to 21 000 TEU), most of which carry, appropriately enough, frozen fish.

### 3.3.2 The Trans-Polar Route Prospects

The situation is forecast to improve in the second half of the century when the transpolar route becomes practicable. A table similar to the previous ones has been compiled in Fig. 9, which shows a certain, but not decisive, improvement over the NSR. Nevertheless, this will not happen until at least 30 or more years from now, and in any case only by vessels qualified for polar navigation. The conventional ones, however, will not only have by then the Northern Route regularly open but maybe seasonably also the Northwest Passage.

## 4 Legal Disputes

With the retreating ice not only uncovering new routes but also making erstwhile forbidden areas more accessible, it is not surprising that there are a respectable number of disputes before the International Seabed Authority and the International Tribunal for the Law of the Sea for delimitations of Exclusive Economic Zones, continental platforms and extended continental platforms, some of them affecting the navigation routes, most with significance in the rights of exploitation of the seabed. The most important ones are:

- Canada considers that the restrictions of the Art 38 United Nations Convention for the Law of the Sea (UNCLOS)[1] apply to the passage of the NW, and has established baselines around its islands. While the US (and the EU) profess that the exception does not apply, and they see the Northwest Passage as a new shipping route, Canada sees its thaw as an opportunity for the development of its Northern territories and Inuit communities, hence reserved to Canada's national goals.
- Russia (2001, 2015) and Denmark on behalf of Greenland (2014) claim the Lomonosov Ridge as an extension of their respective continental shelves. Canada is also expected to claim the Lomonosov Ridge as an extension of its continental shelf.
- The US claim an extended continental shelf, based on Art 76 UNCLOS, but this is not recognized by others as the US is not part of the UNCLOS (so far it has failed to ratify it).
- Canada and the US are disputing the rights over a part of the Beaufort Sea, rich in oil, citing historical reasons that date back to the United Kingdom-Russia Treaty of 1825.

But not everything is unresolved disputes. Happily:

| Polar Route | Hamburg | Rotterdam | Amsterdam | Antwerpen | London | Algeciras | Marseille | Venice |
|---|---|---|---|---|---|---|---|---|
| Yokohama | 6478 | 6455 | 6476 | 6536 | 6563 | 7789 | 8482 | 10652 |
| Busan | 7502 | 7479 | 7500 | 7560 | 7587 | 8813 | 9506 | 10611 |
| Shanghai/Ningbo | 7229 | 8519 | 7227 | 7287 | 7314 | 8540 | 9233 | 9959 |
| Hong-Kong | 8063 | 8040 | 8061 | 8121 | 8148 | 9374 | 10067 | 9206 |
| Singapore | 9367 | 10657 | 9365 | 9425 | 9452 | 10678 | 11371 | 9752 |
| Port-Klang | 9597 | 10887 | 9595 | 9655 | 9682 | 10908 | 11601 | 9982 |

**Fig. 9** *Source* Own elaboration. The trans-polar route

[1]Article 38 Right of transit passage: In straits referred to in article 37, all ships and aircraft enjoy the right of transit passage, which shall not be impeded; *except that, if the strait is formed by an island of a State bordering the strait and its mainland, transit passage shall not apply if there exists seaward of the island a route through the high seas or through an exclusive economic zone of similar convenience with respect to navigational and hydrographical characteristics.*

- Russia and Norway amicably agreed on the division of waters in the Barents Sea (2011).
- Canada and Denmark (acting on behalf of Greenland) are negotiating the partition of Hans Island in the Kennedy Canal.

## 5 Navigation

### *5.1 Global Navigation Satellite Systems (GNSS)*

Difficulties for navigation in the Arctic are not just restricted to ice. The ubiquitous Global Positioning System (GPS), although its satellites are low on the horizon, is marginally sufficient for navigation, but insufficient for scientific or prospecting work and air navigation.

The new European *Galileo* system somewhat improves it (higher altitude and 56° instead of 55° of inclination) and the Russian GLONASS improves a bit more (64.8°). But the different datums used by each system give as consequence differences in the positions that differ by up to 6 miles from those provided by the GPS.

There are other satellite navigation systems, such as the Chinese BeiDou, the Indian Navigation Constellation (NavIC), or the Japanese Quasi-Zenith Satellite System, but they have only local coverage for the time being, and while in time they may become global (China has declared such ambition for their BeiDou) it remains to be seen their eventual impact in the Arctic.

The general problem is that these orbits need to have a sizeable inclination away from 90° to be stable, with which coverage in the Arctic will always de deficient, at least until there is a redefinition of the parameters used by navigation satellites or a technological breakthrough.

GNSS have enhancements, in the form of a broadcast of situational errors found in a local station, and assumed to be valid for the area surrounding the station. GPS and Galileo have such enhancements (the WAAS and EGNOS systems, respectively). Unfortunately, suitable local stations do not abound in the Arctic, and, worse, the broadcast cannot be implemented there because they rely on communications geostationary satellites, which are below the horizon beyond approximately 70° latitude (Fig. 10).

Regretfully, two global navigation systems that preceded GPS were decommissioned despite their usefulness in the Arctic: *Transit*, the first satellite system used low polar orbits which ensured full Arctic coverage, disappeared in 1996; *Omega*, a VLF hyperbolic system that with just eight stations gave full global coverage, was switched off in 1997.

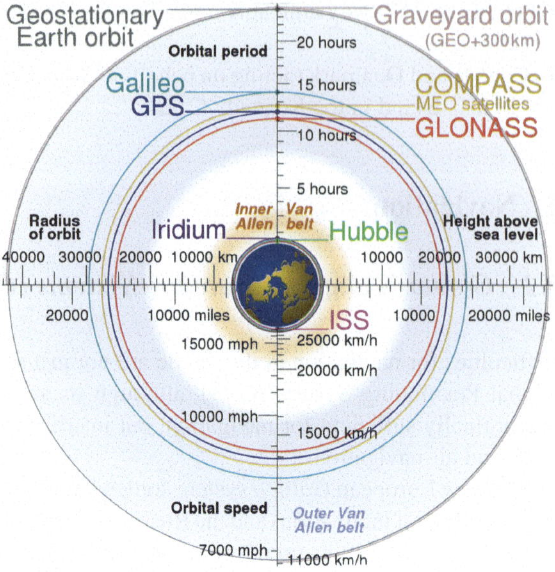


**Fig. 10** Orbits of main communications and navigation satellite systems

## 5.2 *Non-satellite Electronic Navigation Systems*

Of the several non-satellite navigation systems, Loran-C has been the most successful, but it was decommissioned in 2009 by the US Government, despite wide acceptance and strong advice against its disappearance.

The main reason for the desire to keep it was the development of eLoran, which uses in part Loran-C infrastructure. This modern derivative of the traditional hyperbolic systems is extremely well suited for the Arctic needs, as it relies on a short number of ground stations, and is able to provide Virtual Aids to Navigation (VAtoN) in addition to its excellent native Position, Navigation and Timing (PNT). It could also replace the WAAS/EGNOS functions by broadcasting errors locally instead of via geostationary satellites. Unfortunately, it needs considerable investment which nobody seems eager to provide.

## 5.3 *Navigation Support*

Of greater significance, the crucial aids to navigation (AtoN), such as lighthouses, radar beacons, lateral and danger markers, AIS transponders, etc., do not exist along the routes. Only the crowded Siberian rivers have a comprehensive AtoN system.

There is the possibility of replacing the non-existing AtoN by VAtoN, but this would need a supporting system, such as the eLoran alluded to above.

But worst, and central to it all, charts are so poor that cannot be relied upon for reasonably safe navigation, and it will take many decades to bring charting up to the level of quality used in most parts of the world (it is estimated that only about 11% of the Arctic Ocean is adequately charted).

It is widely believed that the US and Russian navies, which extensively used those waters during the Cold War to deploy their ballistic missile submarines, possess valuable hydrographic information, but it remains classified today, except the data obtained by sonar of the thickness of the ice sheet, which have been disclosed for scientific purposes and have helped to quantify its reduction, but which do not help navigation at all.

## *5.4 Communications*

Communications is another of the weak points for Arctic development. Geostationary satellites in the Clarke Belt (35 786 km of altitude, 0° inclination) which carry most global communications, especially the maritime ones, are very low and even below the horizon for most of the Arctic, making them useless beyond 70°, even less if the user is not at the same longitude as the satellite, which is usually the case.

Submarine cables, of which at least two cross the Arctic, have no nodes in the area, which prevents internet communication. Conventional HF, the standard resource, provided a very narrow bandwidth, and it is subject to propagation problems.

All this leaves us very few possibilities. *Iridium* is a commercial system designed to provide a service similar to that of GSM telephones (voice, SMS, narrowband e-mail and internet) but incapable of contending with the broadband communications required by naval, SAR, scientific and industrial operations. It consists of 66 satellites in 86.4° inclination orbits, hence much closer to polar than the other systems. But besides its poor standard capabilities (maximum data rate of 2400 baud and latencies up to 1800 ms) it uses compression techniques that degrade signal quality, acceptable for voice, SMS or e-mail, but unacceptable for even not much demanding data communications.

Russia, always concerned with communications with its extensive Arctic areas, developed the *Molnya* (Lightning) system. This uses elliptical and highly eccentric orbits (12 h period, perigee 500 km, apogee 40,000 km) which spend more than two-thirds of the satellite period well above the Arctic horizon. With three satellites per orbit and two or three equally spaced orbits, it manages to provide continuous coverage at the price of the need to use tracking, instead of static, antennas. It is fully operational, and it looks like the best option to develop a communications system for the Arctic in a short time.

# 6 The Shipowner's Decision

The shipowner confronted with the decision to start exploiting the Northern Sea Route in preference to the traditional route Suez Canal–Indian Ocean–Malacca Strait, must weigh all these factors, some positive, some negative, before entering a business which may not be as advantageous as it appears. This process could be summarised in a list of strengths, weaknesses, opportunities and threats, in the line of the standard SWOT processes.

## *6.1 Strengths*

- It is a shorter route, which may mean less time and fuel (but this must be assessed).
- No risk of piracy.

## *6.2 Weaknesses*

- Only North-Europe/North-Asia routes are shorter. As shown in Fig. 8, not all combination of ports of departure and arrival yield distance advantage.
- Slower transit (reduces the distance advantage).
- Unpredictable ice conditions (but this should improve over time).
- Seasonal exploitation. This will probably last until well into the 2050s.
- Extra expenses in crews training and personal equipment.
- Extra expenses in ship's polar fitting and special equipment. This may include some expensive items, such as screws and water inlets protection, which must be done in dry dock.
- Russian close supervision, including icebreakers. This involves time and expenses, but it may improve over time as traffic increases.
- Inaccurate PNT; the *eLoran* promising alternative lacks a good sponsor for the time being, although the UK has shown interest, partly for reasons unconnected with the Arctic (backup of GNSS in case of hostile jamming or otherwise catastrophic failure).
- Inaccurate and incomplete cartography, which will not be remedied any time soon.
- Almost non-existent aids to navigation (AtoN). eLoran could be a remedy, but, again, not soon.
- Deficient communications (geostationary satellites below the horizon, no cable nodes, faulty HF). Potential alternatives (*Molnya*, *Tundra* or *Iridium*) need development, but it is not yet in sight.

### *6.3 Opportunities*

- Commerce with busy Siberian mining centres along the route (e.g., *Beluga* expedition).

### *6.4 Threats*

- Two or more years of limited ice reduction may force abandonment of a route and with it a line of business, which may incur losses.
- In case of an accident or other emergency, SAR is unavailable along most of the route. This is linked to geography and the desolation of the surrounding coasts, hence not easy to fix.
- Bad meteorology (up to 15 low-pressure systems a month, with 70 kts winds and persistent fogs).

## 7 A Forecast

The biggest change to commercial routes over the coming years will be as a consequence of Arctic melting (followed far behind in influence by the autonomous ships and the hypothetical opening of the Kra Canal). But not all components of the Arctic traffic will be equally important.

### *7.1 Destinational and Intra-Arctic Traffic*

The biggest contributors to the traffic flow will be the intra-Arctic and destinational routes serving the mining—and to a lesser extent agricultural—centres, followed by scientific, exploratory and touristic. The current fishing banks will continue to be exploited, but the opening of new ones doesn't seem probable.

### *7.2 Trans-Arctic Traffic*

Trans-Arctic routes will take time, probably decades, to fully develop. Even then, competitivity with traditional routes (Suez, Panama) will be limited. However, an eventual increase of piracy, or closure of the Suez Canal—caused by either a war or an accident—could alter this forecast.

### 7.3 Aids to Navigation

Cartography, aids-to-navigation (virtual or physical) and communications require big investments and a long time. Currently, they are very deficient.

### 7.4 Search and Rescue

SAR enormous shortcomings will continue to be an important obstacle to all kinds of navigation in the Arctic for the time being.

## 8 In Summary

The sea still offers more than what we have been taking so far, not only in the areas of mining, oil extraction, fishing and energy but also in the well-exploited field of the trade routes, in which regard the Arctic looks like a firm promise. However, the remaining obstacles will need time and heavy investment to be solved, and risky decisions will have to be taken against other priorities (except perhaps by a Russia already heavily committed to the development of her Arctic regions). As a consequence, the new "gold rush" that its melting seems to suggest to many will not be the explosive phenomenon they expect. We must temper the enthusiasm and exercise patience for still a few decades to come.

## References

Caputi, C. (2013). *The wider north, opportunities and challenges.* European Union Institute for Security Studies.

Chatham House International Law Discussion Group. (2008). *The Arctic and climate change.* A summary of the Chatham House International Law discussion group meeting held on 14 February 2008.

Economist. (2013). *The Arctic. Tequila sunset: Global warming may make the northernmost ocean less productive, not more so.* The Economist, 9 Feb 2013.

Feldt, Lutz. *Security dialogue on the maritime domain. The importance of the Artic region: Implications for Europe and Asia.* German Maritime Institute/Wise Pens International Limited, September 2013.

Foreign Policy. (2020). *Think again, the Arctic.* Lawson W. Brigham, 6 Aug 2010.

Humpert, M. (2013). *The future of Arctic shipping: A new Silk Road for China?* The Arctic Institute Center for Circumpolar Security Studies, Nov 2013.

IALA. (2017). *Report of the IALA seminar on Arctic navigation,* 9–10 Nov 2017. IALA Headquarters, Saint Germain en Laye.

Lin, R. L. C. (2008). *Crisis or opportunity: The impact of melting ice on the northwest passage.* Wenzao Ursuline College of Languages.

O'Rourke, R. (2011). *Changes in the Arctic: Background and issues for congress*. Congressional Research Service, 23 Dec 2011.
USSR Minister of Merchant Marine. (1990). *Rules of navigation. Regulations for navigation on the seaways of the Northern Sea route*. Approved by the USSR Minister of Merchant Marine, 14 Sept 1990.
Wise Pens International. (2013). *Naval challenges in the Arctic region*. A study by Wise Pens International. In response to EDA contract, ref. No 12.CAP.OP.405, 9 Sept 2013.
Wise Pens International. (2017). *The return of anti-submarine warfare: How the changing nature of the undersea domain requires Europe to reconsider a fundamental naval mission*. Wise Pens International Food for Thought Paper, Commissioned by the European Defence Agency, Mar 2017.
Wise Pens International. (2017). *Arctic training. A study by Wise Pens International*. In response to EDA contract, ref. No 16.CAT.OP092, 9 Sept 2013, Mar 2017.

**Admiral Fernando del Pozo** was born in Barcelona in 1944, joined the Spanish Naval Academy in 1961, was commissioned in July 1966, and achieved three-star rank in December 2003. As a junior officer he had assignments onboard destroyers, frigates, and squadron staffs. He specialized in naval electronics and obtained the Naval War College diploma in 1978. At sea, he commanded FPB *Cadarso*, corvette *Diana*, frigate *Victoria* and the 41st Frigate Squadron, which he left to take command of NATO's Standing Naval Force Mediterranean (September 1997–September 1998). He had the distinction of being the first Spanish officer ever in command of a NATO force, achieving flag rank during this command. Ashore he has served in the Spanish Navy Mission in Washington D.C. (1980–85). From 1993 until 1997 he directed the Strategic Plans Branch in the Navy Staff. In October 1998 he was appointed Deputy Representative of SACLANT in NATO's Military Committee until October 2001, when he became Deputy CinC Southern Atlantic, in Oeiras (Portugal). In June 2004 he was elected by the NATO Chiefs of Defence as Director, International Military Staff, the first Spanish officer to be appointed to this post. He exercised this responsibility until June 2007. Having reached the end of his active naval career, Admiral del Pozo has been a project director in the think-tank *Royal Institute Elcano* on matters related to the EU and NATO, having published many articles and papers on defence and security-related subjects in the Institute's publications, in *Politica Exterior, Panorama Estratégico, Atenea, Instituto Español de Estudios Estratégicos* and other publications, as well as lecturing in various fora. Since July 2009 he has been a Director of Wise Pens International, working in maritime security affairs, mostly on commission of the European Defence Agency, several Directorates-General of the EU Commission, and the European External Action Service.

# Climate Change and Great Power Competition in the Arctic

Ángel García Estrada

**Abstract** Global warming and climate change are causing a progressive reduction in the extent of Arctic ice, altering living conditions and significantly increasing access to resources banned to humans so far. This has caught the attention of great powers and a critical race has begun to try to extend their influence in this region, where control of sea routes and exploitation of mineral and living resources will lead to unexpected international relations. China, Russia, and the United States are developing strategies to achieve a preeminent position in this region, considering the Arctic is warming twice as fast as the global average and holds approximately 90 billion barrels of undiscovered oil—about 13% of global estimates—and 30% of the Earth's undiscovered natural gas reserves.

**Keywords** Arctic · Climate change · Arctic competition · Arctic geopolitics

## 1 Global Warming: The Case of the Artic

Climate change and global warming are causing polar caps to melt and permafrost[1] shrinkage. According to data from National Snow and Ice Data Centre (NSDIC 2020), the extent of sea ice at the North Pole has been rampantly decreasing since records started in 1979, being the fall of 2012 the all-time low (see Figs.1 & 2).

The extent of ice increases during the fall and winter, whereas it decreases during the spring and summer. This regime causes the greatest extension in March and in September the ice formation is the least of the year. Besides, the rise of temperature

[1] *Permafrost* refers to the permanently frozen layer of subsoil, which may or may not be covered with ice or snow and which contains a large amount of carbon dioxide and methane.

In: Security in the Global Commons and Beyond, Edited by J. Martin Ramirez, and Bartolomé Bauzá-Abril. © 2021 Springer International. Submitted: September, 03, 2020; Accepted: October 13, 2020.

Á. G. Estrada (✉)
Spanish Navy, C/ Santiago 37, Piso 7, 41003 Sevilla, Spain
e-mail: agares4@fn.mde.es



J. M. Ramírez and B. Bauzá-Abril (eds.), *Security in the Global Commons and Beyond*, Advanced Sciences and Technologies for Security Applications,
https://doi.org/10.1007/978-3-030-67973-6_3

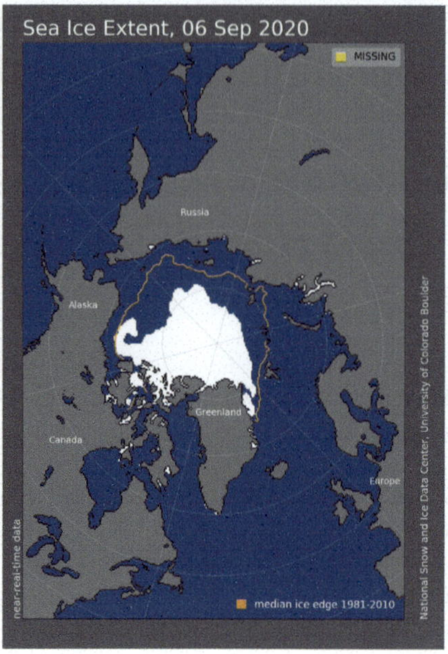


**Figs. 1 & 2** Maximum-minimum March–September 2020 ice extent. *Source* National Snow and Ice Data Centre

has recently reached unprecedent levels in the Arctic. The remote Siberian city of Verkhoyansk registered 38 °C (100.4 °F) during a heatwave this summer, setting a new record in the Arctic Circle (Reuters 2020).

According to data from Arctic Monitoring and Assessment Program (AMAP 2017), the Arctic Ocean could be fully navigable starting in 2050 or even in the late 2030s. Leveraging the summer thaw conditions, several shipping companies have carried out shipments using the passages of the Arctic Ocean. Although there is evidence that other vessels had previously crossed the Northeast Passage, the first to complete the navigation between Taicang and Rotterdam in the maritime trade domain was, in 2013, the*Yong Sheng*, a vessel chartered by COSCO.

The *Yong Sheng*, a vessel fitted for navigation in polar waters holding an B1 Ice Class qualification from the CCS (ARC 4 in the Russian equivalent or IA according to Lloyd's criteria),[2] sailed on August 15 from Taicang, and after crossing the Barents Sea on September 1 arrived in Rotterdam on September 10. A similar journey through the Strait of Malacca and the Suez Canal extends up to 10,600 miles and 36 days of

[2]To navigate through polar waters (Arctic and Antarctic), ships must meet the requirements established by the IMO (International Maritime Organization), which vary depending on the conditions and type of ice it can support. The classification varies between PC1 and PC7. There are other organizations with their own standards such as Lloyd's, the China Classification Society (CCS) or the Russian Maritime Registration of Shipping. Available at: https://www.imo.org/es/MediaCentre/HotTopics/polar/Documents/A%2026-Res.1024.pdf#search=clasificaci%C3%B3n%20de%20buques.

navigation, meaning savings up to 2800 miles and 9 days. Since then, COSCO has deployed up to ten vessels to the Arctic and completed 14 voyages along the Arctic routes (Jiang 2018).

Danish shipping company Maersk has also taken steps to bring in the Arctic as one of its major shipping routes. The *Venta Maersk*, an icebreaker-container ship with a capacity of 3200 TEU,[3] carried out the transit between Vladivostok and Saint Petersburg during the summer of 2018.

Another navigation milestone in the Arctic was reached in January 2018 by the *Eduard Toll*, an icebreaker-gas carrier that transported Liquefied Natural Gas (LNG) from the Russian terminal of Sabetta to the French port of Montoir, conducting the winter transit autonomously, without the assistance of icebreakers. The *Eduard Toll*is a modern gas tanker of almost 300 m in length, built in Daewoo's Korean shipyards and whose Arc 7 class rating has allowed it to navigate waters with ice up to 1.8 m thick. This vessel is the fourth in a series of fifteen gas carriers contracted by Russia to transport LNG on the Northeast Passage (Maritime Executive 2019b).

The emerging shipping routes in the Arctic are the following:

(1) The Northwest Passage, which runs along the Canadian coast and Alaska from the Atlantic Ocean to the Bering Strait.
(2) The Northeast Passage or the Northern Sea Route, throughout the Russian coast, from the Strait of Bering to the Barents Sea.
(3) The transpolar route, not open yet to navigation, will be the shortest route from the Bering Strait to Europe.
(4) The Arctic Bridge, that links Hudson Bay (Canada) with the Kola Peninsula (Fig. 3).

## 2 The Northeast Passage: The Russian Stance

In 2014, Russian President Vladimir Putin defined the Arctic as a traditional Russian area of interest, since it concentrates each and every aspect of national security: military, political, economic, technological, environmental and resources (Putin 2014).

Russian interest in the Arctic is not new, but it only remained latent due to the economic and social crisis that Russia suffered during the crumble of the Soviet Union. Subsequent to the arrival of Vladimir Putin to power, Russia's booming economy allowed to increase its spending on defence and state policies, being the presence and expansion in the Arctic one of the main goals.

In 2008 it was published the roadmap of Russian policy in the Arctic (Government of the Russian Federation 2008), where four basic national interests were identified:

---

[3] TEU stands for Twenty-Foot Equivalent Unit which can be used to measure a ship's cargo carrying capacity. The dimensions of one TEU are equal to that of a standard 20′ shipping container.

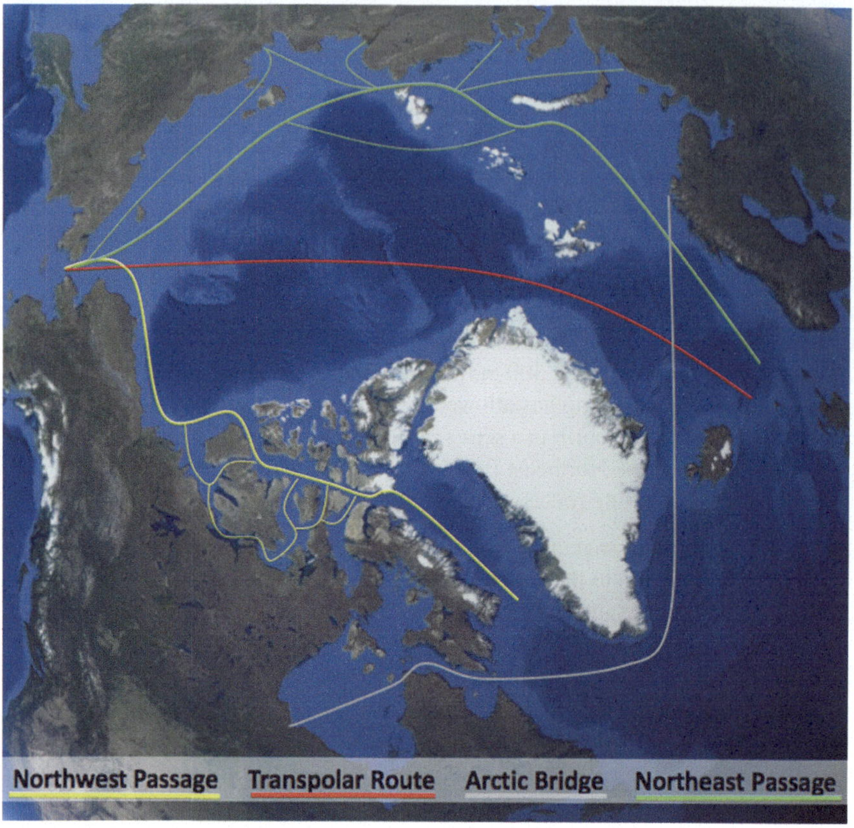


**Fig. 3** Arctic shipping routes. *Source* Self-made with Google Earth ©

(1) The Russian Arctic as a basic source of resources.
(2) Maintaining the Arctic as a zone of peace and cooperation.
(3) Preserving the unique Arctic ecosystem.
(4) Using the Northern Sea Route (NSR) as a main route of communication for Russia.

This document was followed by others such as *The Strategy for the Development of the Arctic Zone of the Russian Federation and Provision of National Security to 2020* (Government of the Russian Federation 2013), the *State Program of the Russian Federation—Socioeconomic Development of the Russian Arctic Zone to 2020* (2014), or the *State Program of the Russian Federation—Socioeconomic Development of the Russian Arctic Zone to 2025* (2017), updating the Russian program of 2014. And, on March 2020 Vladimir Putin approved the *Basic Principles of Russian Federation State Policy in the Arctic to 2035* (Government of the Russian Federation 2020), an update on the *2008 State Policy Principles*.

An overview of these strategies shows the evolution of the Russian approach to the Arctic. In the beginning, the development of infrastructures and exploitation of resources were considered in a cooperative environment, while in later documents is clearly stated the need to ensure security is above the exploitation of resources.

The key aspects of the Russian policy to reinforce sovereignty in the Arctic are:

(a) Its jurisdiction over the NSR (Fig. 4).
(b) The expansion of the EEZ as a continuity of its continental shelf, for the right of exploitation of resources beyond 200 miles.

The Russian assertiveness proclaiming its jurisdiction of the NSR is accompanied by policies that include the creation of infrastructures to make the route attractive and profitable, improvements in aids to navigation and communications, the construction of high-power icebreakers and self-propelled extraction platforms, as well as scientific research. Should not go unnoticed the expeditions sent to gather evidence that the Lomonosov and Mendeleev ridges are extension of the Russian continental shelf, culminated in 2007 when Russia planted a flag in the Arctic seabed. Another aspect highlighted by President Putin is the reinforcement of the presence of the Russian Armed Forces to ensure infrastructures and the exploitation of resources, refurbishing abandoned airfields and building military bases such as Kotelny, in the New Siberian Islands archipelago (Fig. 5).

The expansion of Russia's Exclusive Economic Zone (EEZ) in the Arctic would grant the right to exploit the vast living and mineral resources found in it, which along with the use of the NSR to transport oil and gas to China, would bring Russia into the fight for being the world's largest supplier of crude oil, currently in the hands of the US and Saudi Arabia, according to the U.S. Energy Information Administration data (EIA 2018). In July 2018 Russia shipped LNG to China for the first time using the NSR (Ilyushina and Pleitgen 2019), and during the autumn of that same year, icebreakers escorted a Chinese convoy in transit from the Bering Strait to Europe, confirming that the use of this route is now possible.

The Northern Sea Route Authority (NSRA), established in 2013, aims to regulate the transit of ships through the NSR, providing the necessary icebreaker and

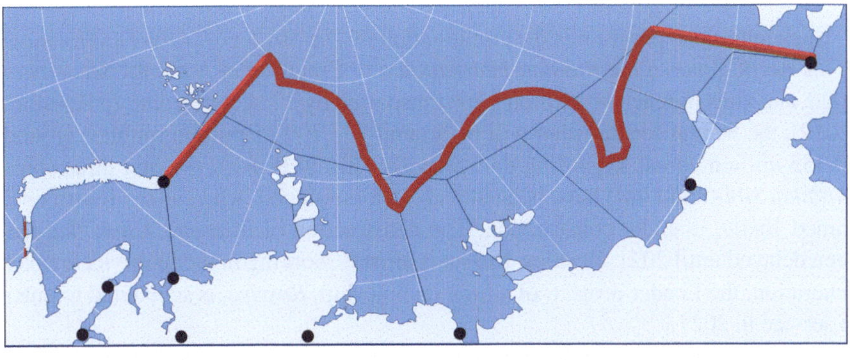

**Fig. 4** NSR limits. *Source* Northern Sea Route Authority (NSRA)

pilotage services for navigation and implement aids to navigation and communications systems. Until 2019, to conduct the transit through the NSR it was required to submit an application to the NSRA no less than fifteen days in advance; however, since the French Navy ship Rhône transited through the NSR, the Moscow regime heightened its demand up to 45 day notice to authorize the transit of any non-Russian military vessel (Maritime Executive 2019c).

On December 21, 2019, President Dimitri Medvedev signed the *NSR Infrastructure Development Plan for the 2035 Horizon* (Government of the Russian Federation 2019). Its objective is the construction of infrastructures to promote maritime trade and the extraction of fossil fuels in the Arctic. Vertebrated around 84 relevant actions, it assigns the state corporations of nuclear energy (Rosatom), crude oil (Rosneft), maritime and river transport (Rosmorrechflot), the LNG Company Gazprom and Novatek the responsibility of reaching the following milestones:

(1) The construction of 40 vessels until 2035, including 5 nuclear icebreakers of 60 MW (Project 22220), 3 of 120 MW corresponding to the "Leader" project (also known as project 10510), 13 hydrographic vessels and 16 rescue and support vessels. Besides, it is planned to extend the operational life of the three nuclear icebreakers currently in operation and of three other special purpose vessels.
(2) The refurbishing of four airports in the polar region (Amderma, Pevek, Chersky and Keperveen).
(3) The construction of infrastructures in the ports of Chaika and Severny, both on the Taymyr peninsula, and the dredge of the port terminal of Utreny, on the coast of Ob.
(4) The building of a railway network to connect the port of Murmansk with different sites.
(5) Putting into orbit 12 satellites to ensure communications and meteorological observation capacity.
(6) The creation of a Search and Rescue network.
(7) The building of or acquisition of transport aircrafts capable of operating autonomously in extreme conditions (3 units) and helicopters with the capacity to operate on existing and future icebreakers (5 units).

Such ambitious program is the continuation of *The Strategy for the Development of the Arctic Zone of the Russian Federation and Provision of National Security to 2020*, and aims to reach 80 million tons transported by 2024. According to Rosatom (2019), the budget for this plan will be around 737,700.35 million roubles, around 10,355 million euros. Regarding the icebreaker 22220 Project, the first three ships (*Arktika*, *Sibir* and *Ural*) have been already commissioned, whereas the fourth one, named *Yakuti*, is under construction. The construction of fifth one, *Chukotka*, has been delayed until 2021. Besides, Russia is already working in the future icebreaker generation, the Leader project, of which its first ship, *Rossiya*, is scheduled to enter in service in 2027.

The Basic Principles of Russian Federation State Policy in the Arctic to 2035 (State policy) and the NSR Infrastructure Development Plan for the 2035 horizon

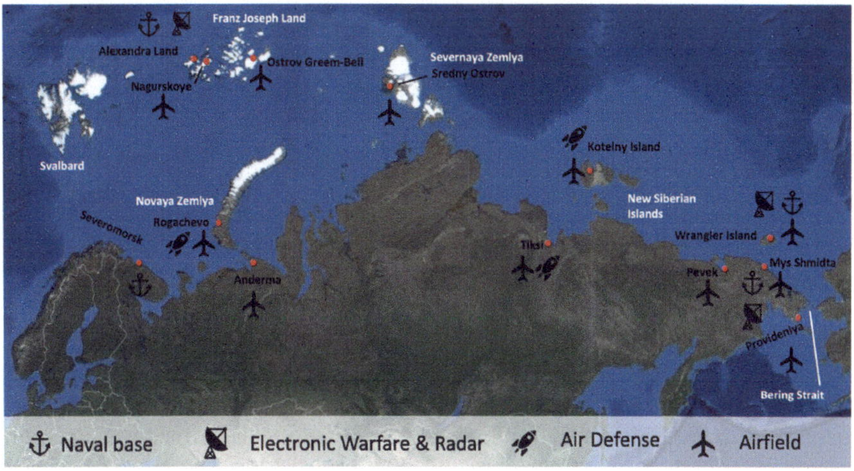


**Fig. 5** Russian military facilities in the Arctic. *Source* Self-made with Google Earth ©

should be understood as two parts of the same plan. On the one hand, the newly State Policy shows few differences with its predecessor, underlining the importance of the Arctic for Russia since it is its main source of economic growth, providing a 10% of the GDP and accounts for 20% of Russian exports and, on the other hand, the NSR as a global competitive national transport corridor. However, it points out that security, sovereignty and territorial integrity are above resource development.

The military agenda is to be focused on building defensive capabilities to ensure Moscow's ability to deter any foreign military aggression in the Arctic. Besides, this State policy update emphasizes the prosperity of the Russian Arctic population. In terms of threats and challenges in the 2035 horizon, Russia assesses as domestic threats the declining population in the Arctic, the inadequate transportation and communications network and the low rates of geological resource exploration. The external threats are treated as challenges to overcome, as for example the non-explicit reference to the US efforts to designate the NSR as an international passage or the unsolved overlapping in sovereignty claims with Canada and Denmark (Buchanan 2020).

In combination with this infrastructure construction plan and to boost business volume, the Duma passed last March a law to significantly reduce taxation on resource exploitation activities in the Arctic, with the objective of promoting extraction activity (Arctic 2020). There are three activities that will benefit the most from this tax reduction: (1) the extraction and production of LNG, (2) the petrochemical industry, and (3) the extraction of minerals. Specifically, taxes on the extraction of maritime crude oil will be reduced by 5% during the first fifteen years, it will be reduced by 50% on new prospects and the industry of production of LNG and petrochemical products will be exempt from taxes during the first 12 years for new oil extraction projects on the coast. According to Government estimates, the investment attracted to the Arctic in the next fifteen years will be 216 million euros. In addition, Vladimir

Putin approved on July a package of federal laws on tax relief on business in order to support entrepreneurial activity in the Russian Arctic (Arctic 2020).

## 3 China, the Polar Silk Road and the NSR

The evolution of the thaw of the Arctic and the new opportunities it offers have not gone unnoticed by China, in continuous search for the expansion of its economy and influence. The ambition to materialize the new Polar Silk Route, along with the publication of the first China Arctic Policy are much more than a declaration of intent.

Despite not being an Arctic state, without territorial sovereignty or rights over existing resources, China calls itself a *near-Arctic*state and has earned its admission as an observer in the Arctic Council (Arctic 2020) since 2013. The AC was founded in 1996 by the Ottawa Declaration and comprises Canada, Denmark (by virtue of Greenland), Finland, Iceland, Norway, Sweden, Russia and the United States of America, in addition to organizations representing indigenous populations. It was established as a forum to promote cooperation between the Arctic states, specifically excluding any military aspect.

China's relationship with the Arctic began with scientific research conducted by the *Polar Research Institute of China* (PRIC), responsible for managing the infrastructure and means for research programs such as the icebreaker *Xue Long* (Snow Dragon). Scientific research has been used by China as a vector for strategic projection; however, in its Arctic White Paper it is already established that its interest in the Arctic is not exclusively limited to research but extends to trade, although it disguises its ambitions in good intentions.

In political terms, in China's eyes the Arctic situation exceeds the competences of the bordering countries and advocates for international governance (Arctic 2020). This is how the government led by Xi Jinping aims to make its approach to the Arctic, arguing globalization and the direct impact of alterations in the Arctic on China, as the major argument for its claim. The English version of the Arctic Policy (Xinhua 2018) emphasizes the "cooperation to open the door to participate in the affairs of the Arctic", dressing it with respect, development and sustainability, specifically:

(a) Protecting the Arctic and its environment, addressing climate change and deepen understanding of the Arctic.
(b) A rational use of Arctic resources such as oil, gas and minerals.
(c) Participation in the development of the Arctic maritime routes, respecting the jurisdiction of the Arctic countries in accordance with international maritime law.
(d) Cooperation to develop the Polar Silk Route.

The aforementioned English version is outlined to show the China's kindest face and not to unveil its alleged real intentions, since it does not develop any strategy to reach planned milestones nor does it refer to the relationship of Arctic politics with its national security (Maritime Executive 2018). This absence of tangible objectives makes the international community distrust the intentions of Beijing.

For Brady (2017), China's interests in the Arctic can be clustered into three categories: security, resources and technology. Access to polar regions is essential to develop the Chinese global positioning system, the Beidou project, as well as weather forecasting systems. The emerging resources reachable only once the permafrost had disappeared are a candy coveted by the Arctic states, of which the executive led by Xi Jinping hopes to obtain benefits by negotiating bilateral exploitation agreements with members of the Arctic Council.

The Arctic shipping lanes are one of China's major interests. On the one hand, because it receives the oil and gas supply necessary for its industry by sea, and, on the other hand, as a mean of exporting its products, the Polar Silk Road. The Sabetta gas terminal on Russia's Yamal Peninsula is expected to supply four million tons of LNG to China per year, according to Chinese authority's data. Ensuring its energetic supply is only one of China's initial steps, since its ambition is to establish a Polar Silk Route that would slash times of transport of goods to Europe, apart from avoiding piracy areas such as the Strait of Malacca and the Sulu-Celebes Sea. To reinforce this will, the Government is urging Chinese companies to undertake projects and make investments to create infrastructures to enhance the Polar Silk Route (Nakano 2018).

Regarding its Arctic capabilities, China currently has two icebreakers, the *Xue Long* and *the Xue Long 2*, launched in September 2018 and in service since July 2019. In 2016 there was speculation on whether China could be planning to build a nuclear icebreaker (Nielsen 2016) and rumours were later confirmed, since Chinese Nuclear Energy Group (CGN) has put out to tender offers of contracts to build a nuclear icebreaker of 30,000 tons of displacement and 160 m in length. Currently only Russia has nuclear icebreakers, operated by civilian crews. This construction would multiply China's capacities in Arctic waters, as they offer greater autonomy by not depending on fuel and greater power that allow them to navigate at higher speeds on thicker ice. Besides, at Marintec fair held in Shanghai in December 2019, two ship designs earmarked for operations in polar conditions were presented. Hudong-Zhonghua, a major shipyard based in Shanghai, subsidiary of the China State Shipbuilding Corporation, exhibited a model of an ice-capable LNG carrier which meets the requirements for an Arc7 ice class notation, able to break ice up to 2.1 m thick. China is seeking to develop its own technology to build polar ships to boost the Polar Silk Road.

In terms of technology, China launched in September 2019 the first satellite of its polar observation constellation Ice Pathfinder. In June 2020 the satellite sent back its first pictures of the Arctic region and provided full coverage in the following days. Once all 24 satellites are in orbit, the network will operate around the clock, delivering hourly tracking data about iceberg drifts and the collapse of ice shelves. Fitted with Automatic Identification System (AIS) receiver, it can monitor shipping traffic in real time (Zhou 2020). There is no doubt about this space-based technology will reinforce existing ground sensors and augment China's Arctic understanding and knowledge. Such meteorological, hydrographical, magnetic and acoustic data would be useful to both military and non-military Chinese agencies.

Another vector of Chinese presence in the Arctic is its investments in Iceland since they signed a trade agreement in 2013 (Government of Iceland, Ministry for Foreign Affairs 2013). This alliance has its origin in 2007 when Iceland was excluded from the*Arctic Five* initiative promoted by Denmark, consisting of the US, Russia, Denmark, Norway and Canada, which aimed to solve the problems related to the Arctic. The extraction of minerals and rare earths are the main Chinese interests in these territories, although its move has not been limited to this area. The construction of a modern embassy and Huawei's agreement with Icelandic communications operator Nova reinforce China's presence in Iceland.

Greenland is also a China's investments target, both in infrastructure and in mining industry. China attempted to acquire an abandoned US naval base in 2016 or, more recently, Chinese company CCCC (China Communications Construction Company) was participating in the race for the construction of two airfields and the modernization of the airport in Nuuk, Greenland's capital, which was finally prevented by Denmark, perhaps motivated by the suggestion of the then Secretary of State for Defense James Mattis (Auerswald 2019).

## 4 The Northwest Passage. Canada and the US

Canada has claimed its sovereignty over the territory between the 81st and 141st meridians West since 1925. Although the continental territory is not a matter of dispute, certain archipelagos, such as the Ellesmere, have sparked debate between Canada and Denmark. To reinforce its sovereignty over these territories, Canada has carried out moves to artificially inhabit lands in 1953 and 1955 (Morrison 2006).

The thaw associated with global warming has caught the attention of several states on the Arctic, but not exclusively from Arctic states. Thus, Canada has detected the critical need to reinforce its presence in the channels constituting the Northwest Passage. Nevertheless, the US does not recognize as Canadians the Arctic waters that bathe the islands of Canada, claiming and executing the right of free navigation through international waters. In turn, Canada is conducting scientific research to prove the extension of the continental shelf and thus be able to claim the extension of the right to exploit the underlying resources on the seabed.

The Canadian approach to the Arctic is framed in the *Canada's Arctic and Northern Policy Framework* (Government of Canada 2019). Developed in collaboration with indigenous populations and other stakeholders, this plan aims to address the challenges posed by climate change, poverty, food insecurity and the lack of infrastructure and transportation. The defence deserves an exclusive document (Government of Canada 2017).

This directive gives Canada's Armed Forces a crucial role in demonstrating and enforcing sovereignty over its territories in the Arctic and projecting a credible image of security. In this regard, the construction of six Arctic offshore patrol vessels, the acquisition of amphibious vehicles operable in the Arctic and the improvement of the infrastructures for surveillance and communications systems are the priorities established by the Canadian government.

The international approach of Canadian Arctic policy involves bilateral relations with other Arctic states. Canada has signed agreements with Russia and Norway and, what is more, it is currently collaborating with the US Coast Guard in the construction of the new North American icebreakers (Canada National Research Council 2018).

Another point that highlights the relevance of the Arctic for Canada is its Oceans Protection Plan (Government of Canada 2016), document that outlines the roadmap to reinforce Canadian dominance in its part of the Arctic. Its key policies are the following:

(1) The Search and Rescue capacity.
(2) The ability to respond to environmental emergencies.
(3) An Icebreaker fleet.
(4) To improve its knowledge of the Arctic maritime environment and surveillance capabilities.
(5) To strengthen the military presence in the Arctic to prevent and respond to security-related incidents.
(6) To increase collaboration and cooperation with neighbours and allies in matters of maritime security, security and defence.

The Coast Guard provides the icebreaker service with two heavy icebreakers (arctic class 4), five medium-sized (arctic class 3) and nine multitasking ships (arctic class 2) (Canadian Coast Guard 2020), which is key to ensure maritime traffic in these waters, as well as advice on maritime routes depending on the current ice conditions (Fig. 6).

## 5 US Stance. 10 Years Behind Russia?

The access of the US to the Arctic is granted by virtue of Alaska, the 49th state that was bought from Russia in 1867 for 7.2 million dollars. The US has been a member of the Arctic Council since its foundation in 1996 and held its presidency for two biannual terms, 1998–2000 and 2015–2017. During the last chairmanship, Barack Obama became the first President to visit the Arctic of Alaska, a sign that sought to visualize the growing relevance of the region to the United States and to show its commitment to climate change.

During Obama's administration, the *National Strategy for the Arctic Region* (U.S. Government 2013) and the *Executive Order Enhancing Coordination of National efforts in the Arctic* (Obama 2015) were published. Under this Executive Order, a specific structure for the Arctic—the *Arctic Executive Steering Committee*—was created to centralise the direction of the different working groups, improve the coordination of federal Arctic activity and thus optimize resources.

The National Strategy for the Arctic was focused on three lines of action: (a) the US security interests; (b) a responsible administration of the Arctic region; and

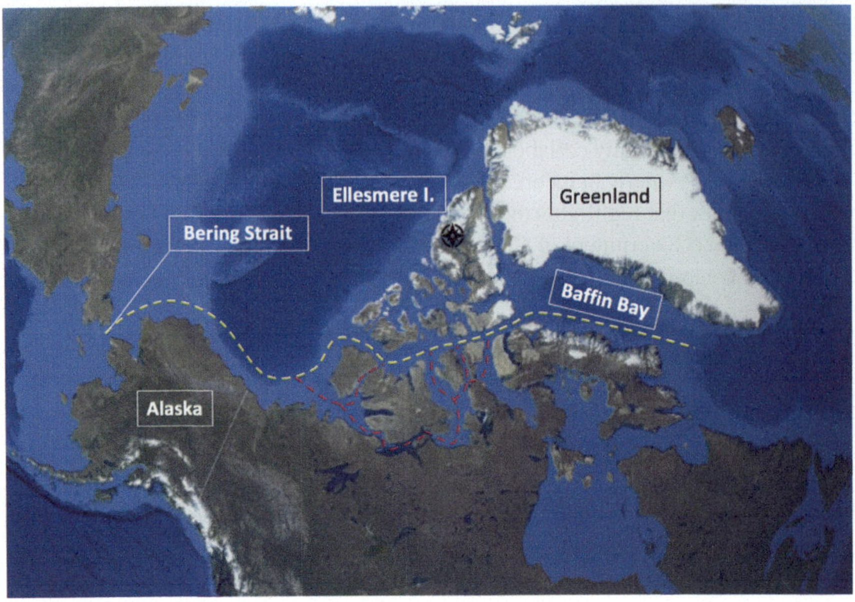


**Fig. 6** Maritime routes of the Northwest Passage. *Source* Self-made with Google Earth ©

(c) strengthening international cooperation, while at the same time placing special emphasis on addressing the climate change and minimize the impact on the ecosystem of the region.

US security is understood as the protection of the US population, US sovereignty and rights, as well as its natural resources and interests. To ensure security, the executive identified several aspects to be specifically developed:

(1) To build Arctic infrastructures and strategic capabilities.
(2) To strengthen awareness over the Arctic.
(3) To preserve freedom of navigation in the Arctic region.
(4) To ensure the energy independence of the US.

The reality shows today's US capabilities in the Arctic are notably inferior to its near-peer competitors China and Russia. The Coast Guard has only two old icebreakers since the Polar Sea went out of service in 2010. Both ships are based in Seattle, Washington state, 2250 miles from the Bering Strait, gateway to the Arctic. The closest American berth to the Arctic is Dutch Harbour, located at 710 miles on Unalaska Island where Dutch Harbor is located (Axe 2019).

To mitigate this disadvantage, the Congress initially approved in April 2019 the spending of 750 million dollars to build a heavy icebreaker that could be expanded to a total of three, raising spending to 1.9 billion dollars (Maritime Executive 2019a). The contract was assigned to the VT Halter Marine shipyard and included engineering, design and construction expenses for the first icebreaker, which is scheduled to begin its construction in 2021 and enter service in 2024. If the expansion up to three icebreakers finally materializes, they would be delivered in a rate of one per year since 2025. The Joint Program of the Coast Guard and the US Navy Polar Security Cutter (PSC) aims to expand the initial acquisition to three medium-sized icebreakers (United States Naval Institute 2019).

In June 2020, President Trump signed *The Memorandum on Safeguarding U.S. National Interests in the Arctic and Antarctic Regions* (U.S. Government 2020) in order "to develop and execute a polar security icebreaking fleet acquisition program that supports our national interests in the Arctic and Antarctic regions" to be ready by 2029. It aims to "retain a strong Arctic Security presence", to which is needed a ready and capable icebreaker fleet. In addition, it requires to identify at least two optimal basing locations in the US and two optimal basic locations abroad, taking into account the final dimension of the designed fleet.

Despite no official statements have been made in relation to this, icebreaker fleet bases could be allocated in several spots notably closer than Dutch harbour:

- St. Michael, a village located 360 nautical miles (nm) away from Bering Strait and well sheltered from westerly swells and winds.
- Wales, in the Bering Strait. It has an airfield but offers no shelter to swells and the ice concentration could be a major drawback.
- Hooper Bay, 270 nm from the Bering Strait and fitted with an airfield but offers little shelter.
- St. Lawrence Island, 130 nm from the Bering Strait, fitted with an airfield and offers good shelter from Westerly swells and winds (Fig. 7).

During the first year of Trump's administration the US chairmanship of the Arctic Council ended, after which the administrative structures created by President Obama,

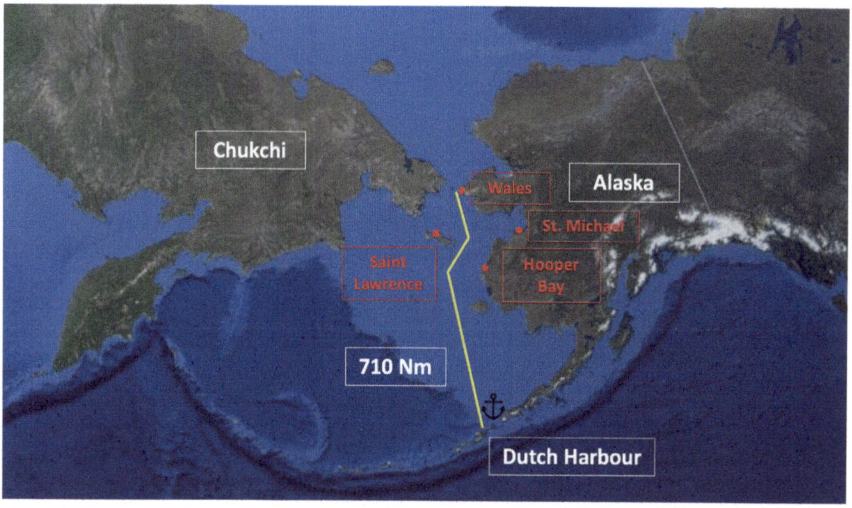


**Fig. 7** US infrastructures in the Arctic and possible icebreaker fleet bases locations. *Source* Self-made with Google Earth ©

the *Arctic Executive Steering Committee* and the U.S. Special Representative for the Arctic were relegated to the background and Arctic-specific structure was disassembled (Conley 2019). In fact, it was not until July 2020 when Donald Trump decided to restore the role and James DeHart was appointed as U.S. Coordinator for the Arctic Region (US Department of State 2020).

The current Trump's foreign policy is more assertive and less persuasive than his predecessor Obama, but his failure to buy Greenland is one indicator that the position of US in the Arctic is far from ideal. Its interest in Greenland is no other than controlling the exit of the Northwest Passage, in addition to blocking the Chinese advance and its growing investments in mining in the autonomous territory belonging to Denmark (Lanteigne and Shi 2019). Fewer media coverage had the failed acquisition by China of a former US base in 2016, which was prevented by Denmark, still in control of Greenland's foreign and defence policy.

A dramatic shift in the US posture took place in May 2019 when the Secretary of State, Mike Pompeo, pronounced his speech in Finland during an Arctic Council meeting, where he stated "the region (i.e. the Arctic) has become an area for power and competition, and the eight Arctic states must adapt to this new future" (Pompeo 2019).

The *Department of Defense (DoD) Arctic Strategy* was updated in 2019 (U.S. Department of Defense 2019), renewing the US strategic objectives in the Arctic. It pointed out the need of building the capability to promptly identify threats in the Arctic, ensuring an accurate and flexible response and taking actions to mitigate those threats in the future, with the ultimate goal of projecting credible deterrence in the Arctic.

However, despite the recent interest shown by the White House and the steps taken, the miscalculation and the stagnation of the US foreign policy in the Arctic for the last two decades has put the country in a critical situation.

## 6 Conclusions

1. The Arctic has become a chessboard where great powers are developing their strategies to achieve a preeminent position to control the access to emerging resources. In this game, several bilateral alliances are being forged:
   - The approach of China and Russia for the mutual use of the Northern Sea Route or the Northeast Passage for the transport of energy and to promote the Polar Silk Route.
   - US natural allies should be Norway, Denmark and Canada. Nevertheless, the US diplomacy abruptness towards Greenland and the Freedom of Navigation Operations (FONOPs) in waters of the Canadian Arctic only hinder the chances of winning for its side these countries.
   - China has made huge investments in Iceland and Greenland to gain presence in the Arctic and to exploit the existing mineral resources on these rich territories.

2. It has taken the US a decade to provide a response to China and Russia in terms of an Arctic strategy. The stagnation of US policies in the last decade places the country in a dangerous position vis-à-vis its strategic competitors, especially China. The Asian country has published its Arctic Policy and has made powerful investments to ensure the import of fuels and minerals, in addition to developing infrastructure in the Arctic that will underpin its economic growth. The situation of the US icebreaker fleet is a clear example of the disadvantage that the United States government has to face in the short term in order not to be definitively surpassed by China and Russia.
3. Russia intends to develop its power in the Arctic through the jurisdiction of the NSR by imposing stiff conditions for its use. Once it has made the route profitable, it will allow it to take a more aggressive stance by requiring the presence of Russian pilots onboard of ships transiting the northern route, in addition to imposing the contracting of icebreakers to ensure safety in navigation. In this way, exhaustive control of the route is ensured and episodes such as the French Navy ship free transit would be avoided. The United States will push to make the Northeast Passage an international waterway with the same status as the Straits, where coastal countries cannot prevent the innocent passage[4] of ships. However, the US is not a signatory to UNCLOS (1982), an inconsistency that will make it difficult to defend this point.
4. The transpolar route will limit the monopoly that Arctic states have on Arctic routes. The possibility of transit through international waters will reduce the power of Russia, on the one hand, and the influence of the country that comes to exercise authority in the Northwest Passage, on the other hand (see point 5). It seems that China could be preparing the most for this scenario, as it would be the main beneficiary due to its relative proximity to the Arctic and its economic capacity that would allow it to build a fleet designed to operate in these conditions. Its uninterrupted scientific research in the Arctic and the construction of a nuclear-powered icebreaker are indications pointing to the Arctic as one of China's strongest bets in the mid-term.
5. A gloomy landscape looms the Northwest Passage. Will Canada be able to defend its position as sovereign country over the waters of the Northwest Passage or will it give in to the US push? The reality is that only the awkwardness of the diplomacy of the current Trump administration could explain why the US has not proposed a win-win agreement to seduce the executive led by Justin Trudeau. The American soft power is not at its best meanwhile Russia and China continue to seize the opportunity to gain ground that will take the US a great effort to recover it.

The appearance of the Arctic new maritime routes necessarily implies the loss of relevance of the traditional maritime routes and current choke points. The hardest-hit

[4]The right of Innocent Passage is set out in the United Nations Convention on the Law of the Sea (UNCLOS), and subject to this Convention, ships of all States, whether coastal or land-locked, enjoy the right of innocent passage through the territorial sea.

could be the Suez Canal due to the main oil importers will have closer sources of supply and in more politically stable areas.

## References

AMAP. (2017). *Snow, water, ice and permafrost in the Arctic (SWIPA)*. Oslo. Available at https://www.amap.no/documents/doc/snow-water-ice-and-permafrost-in-the-arctic-swipa-2017/1610.

Arctic. (2020a). Putin signs law on excess profits tax and MET in the Arctic. *The Arctic*, 19 Mar 2020. Available at https://arctic.ru/economics/20200319/934004.html.

Arctic. (2020b). Putin signs law on tax relief for business operating in the Arctic. *The Arctic*. Available at https://arctic.ru/economics/20200714/954895.html.

Arctic Council. (2020). About us. Accessed 23 July 2020 at https://arctic-council.org/index.php/en/about-us.

Auerswald, D. (2019). China's multifaced Arctic strategy. *War on the rocks*. Available at https://warontherocks.com/2019/05/chinas-multifaceted-arctic-strategy/.

Axe, D. (2019). 43 years in the making: US Coast Guard finally gets new icebreakers. *The National Interest*. Accessed Aug 2020 at https://nationalinterest.org/blog/buzz/43-years-making-us-coast-guard-finally-gets-new-icebreakers-45572.

Brady, A. M. (2017). *China as a polar great power*. Washington: Cambridge University Press.

Buchanan, E. (2020). *The overhaul of Russian strategic planning for the Arctic zone for 2035*. Russian studies series. NATO Defence College. https://www.ndc.nato.int/research/research.php?icode=641#_ednref9.

Canada National Research Council. (2018). *Canada and US collaborate on icebreakers of the future*. Government of Canada. Available at https://nrc.canada.ca/en/stories/canada-us-collaborate-ice breakers-future.

Canadian Coast Guard. (2020). *Icebreaker operation services*. Accessed 30 July 2020 at https://www.ccg-gcc.gc.ca/icebreaking/home.

Conley, H. (2019). The implication of US policy stagnation toward the Arctic region. *CSIS*. Available at https://www.csis.org/analysis/implications-us-policy-stagnation-toward-arctic-region.

Government of Canada. (2016). *Oceans protection plan*. Available at https://www.tc.gc.ca/media/documents/communications-eng/oceans-protection-plan.pdf.

Government of Canada. (2017). *Canada's defence policy: Strong, secure, engaged*. Accessed on 20 Aug 2020 at https://dgpaapp.forces.gc.ca/en/canada-defence-policy/docs/canada-defence-pol icy-report.pdf.

Government of Canada. (2019). *Canada's Arctic and northern policy framework*. Accessed 12 Aug 2020 at https://www.rcaanc-cirnac.gc.ca/eng/1560523306861/1560523330587.

Government of Iceland, Ministry for Foreign Affairs. (2013). *Free trade agreement between Iceland and China*. Available at https://www.government.is/topics/foreign-affairs/external-trade/free-trade-agreements/free-trade-agreement-between-iceland-and-china/.

Government of the Russian Federation. (2008). *Principles of the state policy of the Russian Federation in the Arctic to 2020 and beyond*. Accessed Sept 2020 at https://static.government.ru/media/files/A4qP6brLNJ175I40U0K46x4SsKRHGfUO.pdf.

Government of the Russian Federation (2013). *The strategy for the development of the Arctic zone of the Russian Federation and provision of national security to 2020*. Accessed Aug 2020 at https://www.research.kobe-u.ac.jp/gsics-pcrc/sympo/20160728/documents/Key note/Russian%20Arctic%20strategy%202013.pdf.

Government of the Russian Federation. (2019). *Infrastructure development plan of the northern route for the horizon 2035*. Available at https://government.ru/docs/38714/.

Government of the Russian Federation. (2020). *Vladimir Putin approved basic principles of state policy in the Arctic*. Available at https://en.kremlin.ru/acts/news/62947.

Ilyushina, M., & Pleitgen, F. (2019). Inside the military base at the heart of Putin's Arctic ambitions. *CNN*. Available at https://edition.cnn.com/2019/04/04/europe/russia-arctic-kotelny-island-military-base/index.html.

Jiang, J. (2018). Cosco to increase Arctic voyages this summer. *Splash 247*. Accessed 24 June 2020 at https://splash247.com/cosco-increase-arctic-voyages-summer/.

Lanteigne, M., & Shi, M. (2019). China steps up its mining interest in Greenland. *The Diplomat*. Available at https://thediplomat.com/2019/02/china-steps-up-its-mining-interests-in-greenland/.

Maritime Executive. (2018). China launches icebreaker Xuelong 2. *The Maritime Executive*, 9 Oct 2018. Viewed at https://www.maritime-executive.com/article/china-launches-icebreaker-xuelong-2.

Maritime Executive. (2019a). VT Halter wins contract for new US Coast Guard icebreaker. *The Maritime Executive*. Available at https://www.maritime-executive.com/article/vt-halter-wins-contract-for-new-us-coast-guard-icebreaker.

Maritime Executive. (2019b). Flashback: LNG tanker makes record Northern Sea Route transit. *The Maritime Executive*, 1 May 2019. Available at https://www.maritime-executive.com/article/flashback-lng-tanker-makes-record-northern-sea-route-transit.

Maritime Executive. (2019c). Russia tightens control over Northern Sea Route. *The Maritime Executive*, 3 Aug 2019. Available at https://www.maritime-executive.com/article/russia-tightens-control-over-northern-sea-route.

Morrison, W. (2006). Canadian Arctic sovereignty. *The Canadian Encyclopedia*. Available at https://www.thecanadianencyclopedia.ca/en/article/arctic-sovereignty.

Nakano, J. (2018). China launches the Polar Silk Road. *CSIS*. Available at https://www.csis.org/analysis/china-launches-polar-silk-road.

Nielsen, T. (2016). China plans to sail nuclear in Arctic. *The Barents Observer*. Available at https://thebarentsobserver.com/en/arctic/2016/08/china-plans-sail-nuclear-arctic.

Obama, B. (2015). *Executive order enhancing coordination of national efforts in the Arctic*. Accessed 5 Sept 2020 at https://obamawhitehouse.archives.gov/the-press-office/2015/01/21/executive-order-enhancing-coordination-national-efforts-arctic.

Pompeo, M. R. (2019). *Looking north: Sharpening America's Arctic focus*. Remarks, Michael R. Pompeo, Secretary of State, Rovaniemi, Finland. US State Department, 6 May 2019. Accessed 10 Sept 2020 at https://www.state.gov/looking-north-sharpening-americas-arctic-focus.

Putin, V. (2014). *Putin at the Security Council meeting on state policy in the Arctic*. Accessed 12 Aug 2020 at https://en.kremlin.ru/events/president/news/20845.

Reuters. (2020). *Russia confirms high temperature record in Siberian town*. Available at https://www.reuters.com/article/us-climate-change-wmo-russia/russia-confirms-record-high-temperature-in-siberian-town-idUSKBN2412SG.

Rosatom. (2019). *Rosatom recounted plans to develop the North Sea Route until 2035*. Accessed 10 Aug 2020 at https://www.rosatom.ru/journalist/smi-about-industry/v-rosatome-rasskazali-o-planakh-po-razvitiyu-sevmorputi-do-2035-goda/.

United Nations Convention on the Law of the Sea. (1982). Available at https://www.un.org/depts/los/convention_agreements/texts/unclos/unclos_e.pdf.

U.S. Department of Defense. (2019). *Report to congress DoD Arctic strategy*. Accessed 08 Sept 2020 at https://media.defense.gov/2019/Jun/06/2002141657/-1/-1/1/2019-DOD-ARCTIC-STRATEGY.PDF.

U.S. Department of State. (2020). *Appointment of the U.S. coordinator for the Arctic region*. Accessed 10 Sept 2020 at https://www.state.gov/appointment-of-u-s-coordinator-for-the-arctic-region/.

U.S. Energy Administration Information. (2018). *The US is now the largest global crude oil producer*. 12 Sept 2018. Available at https://www.eia.gov/todayinenergy/detail.php?id=37053.

U.S. Government. (2013). *National strategy for the Arctic region*. 10 May 2013. Accessed 22 Aug 2020 at https://obamawhitehouse.archives.gov/sites/default/files/docs/nat_arctic_strategy.pdf.

U.S. Government. (2020). *Memorandum on safeguarding U.S. national interests in the Arctic and Antarctic regions.* 9 June 2020. Accessed 5 Sept 2020 at https://www.whitehouse.gov/presidential-actions/memorandum-safeguarding-u-s-national-interests-arctic-antarctic-regions/.
U.S. National Snow and Ice Data Center. (2020). *Quick facts on sea ice.* Available at https://nsidc.org/cryosphere/quickfacts/seaice.html.
U.S. Naval Institute. (2019). Report on congress on polar security cutter program. *USNI*, 20 Sept 2019. Available at https://news.usni.org/2019/09/20/report-to-congress-on-coast-guard-polar-security-cutter-3.
Xinhua. (2018). China Arctic policy. *Xinhua*, 26 Jan 2018. Available at https://english.www.gov.cn/archive/white_paper/2018/01/26/content_281476026660336.htm.
Zhou, L. (2020). China's ice pathfinder satellite sends back first pictures of Arctic region. *South China Morning Post*, 19 June 2020. Available at https://www.scmp.com/news/china/diplomacy/article/3089801/chinas-ice-pathfinder-satellite-sends-back-first-pictures.

**Lieutenant Ángel García Estrada** was born in La Coruña, Spain, in 1985. In 2006 he joined the Spanish Navy and after five years at Spanish Naval Academy he was promoted to Lieutenant JG in 2011.

His first assignments were on board of frigate "Blas de Lezo" and Oceanographic Research Vessel "Hespérides", participating for six months in the 20th Antarctic Campaign. In July 2015 he was promoted to Lieutenant and specialized in naval communications. He served in frigate "Cristóbal Colon" as Head of Department of Navigation and Communications for three years. During 2017 took part in a deployment in Australia, sailing around the world in 210 days.

His interest in geopolitics and geostrategy arose during his Master's degree studies which, along with his Antarctic experience and the natural enthusiasm of a Navy officer for issues related to the sea, woke up his interest in the Arctic, the maritime routes and great powers strategies in the region.

# The Future of Mining: The Exploitation of Marine Geological Resources as Global Commons

**Adolfo Maestro-González**

**Abstract** The increasing demand for minerals and metals by society, together with the depletion of land resources, has generated a peaked interest in marine mineral exploitation. For a global commons such as the oceans, the International Seabed Authority is mandated under the United Nations Convention on the Law of the Sea to organize, regulate and control all mineral-related activities in the international seabed area for the benefit of mankind as a whole. Under the auspices of the International Seabed Authority (ISA), projects exploring seabed mineral resources in the seabed and ocean floor and subsoil thereof, beyond the limits of national jurisdiction, named 'the Area', began in 2001. From then to the present, more and more countries have become involved in such projects. The interest in seabed exploration lies in the extraction of Ni–Cu–Mn from polymetallic nodules, Co–Ni–Mn from ferromanganese crusts, and Cu–Zn–Au–Ag from polymetallic sulphides. Research developed in the last ten years has additionally demonstrated the existence of rare metals and rare earths as possible by-products of the extraction of the main metals of interest. The future exploitation of these metals has implications related to industrial and high-technology purposes, and is also closely linked to the development of renewable energies that enable us to face climate change, secure energy supplies, and promote sustainability and economic competitiveness. Currently, the Legal and Technical Commission of the ISA is finalizing the Regulations for the Exploitation of Mineral Resources in the Area, which will mark the starting signal of deep-sea mining.

**Keywords** Cobalt-rich ferromanganese crusts · Deep-Sea mining · International seabed authority · Polymetallic nodules · Polymetallic sulphides · The area

In: Security in the Global Commons and Beyond, Edited by J. Martin Ramirez, and Bartolomé Bauzá-Abril. © 2021 Springer International. Submitted: August, 28, 2020; Accepted: October, 15, 2020.

A. Maestro-González (✉)
Departamento de Investigación y Prospectiva Geocientífica, Instituto Geológico y Minero de España, C/Calera 1, 28760 Tres Cantos, Madrid, Spain
e-mail: a.maestro@igme.es

 
J. M. Ramírez and B. Bauzá-Abril (eds.), *Security in the Global Commons and Beyond*, Advanced Sciences and Technologies for Security Applications,
https://doi.org/10.1007/978-3-030-67973-6_4

## 1 Introduction

Even before the beginning of civilization, the human species development was linked to the exploration and exploitation of mineral resources. In recent decades, as a consequence of strong global economic growth, the demand for mineral raw materials has increased significantly. This is particularly true of metals whose use is closely linked to high technologies, renewable energies or industrial development. The strategic importance of extractive activity for industrial and technological development has led to a search for new mineral deposits and a greater volume of those metals under increasing demand. In 2017, the European Commission presented a report to the European Parliament, the Council, the European Economic and Social Committee, and the Committee of the Regions with a list of critical raw materials for the European Union. They include cobalt, antimony, beryllium, fluorite, gallium, germanium, graphite, indium, magnesium, niobium, platinum group metals, rare earth elements (REE), tantalum or tungsten. These metals are scarce in European countries, and mostly come from a handful of countries: China, Russia, Democratic Republic of the Congo, Chile and Brazil (Price 2010).

Until today, the planet's emerged land was the sole source of these minerals. This area only accounts for 30% of the earth's surface, the rest being seas and oceans. Half of the sea and ocean areas is at depths greater than 200 m—about 360 million $km^2$. Because the mean value of the water column is around 3800 m, it is not easy to obtain continuous and reliable information about the characteristics of the ocean floor with good resolution. In fact, just 18% of the seabed has been mapped applying modern quality standards (Mayer 2018). In the 1960s, following the publication (in 1965) of the book '*The Mineral Resources of the Sea*' by John L. Mero, interest in minerals in the seabed grew. The book claimed that the seabed could become an important source of mineral supplies to meet the world's needs. But due to the technical difficulties, it was not until the late 1990s that systematic exploration projects were undertaken in sectors of the seabed holding mining potential. Cathles (2013) suggests that the exploitation of the mineral resources of the seabed would allow the recovery of a wide array of elements such as uranium, copper, zinc, cobalt, nickel, lithium, REE and phosphate, under high demand by the industry. At present, three marine mineral resources are under particular commercial demand: manganese nodules in abyssal plains, cobalt-rich ferromanganese crusts found in seamounts, and accumulations of polymetallic sulphides in hydrothermal emission zones. If the metallic tonnages of deep-ocean deposits in the Clarion-Clipperton Zone (CCZ) (ISA 2010) and Prime Crust Zone (PCZ) (Hein and Koschinsky 2013) are compared with global terrestrial reserves (USGS 2012), mineral deposits in the marine zone are found to have 27 times more tellurium, 13 times more cobalt, 12 times more manganese, seven times more yttrium, four times more nickel and arsenic, and twice as much molybdenum and bismuth (Fig. 1).

The oceans contribute in a fundamental way to the development of life on Earth since they are a source of biological food resources and raw materials; they constitute an important energy resource; they act as a climate regulator; they produce most of

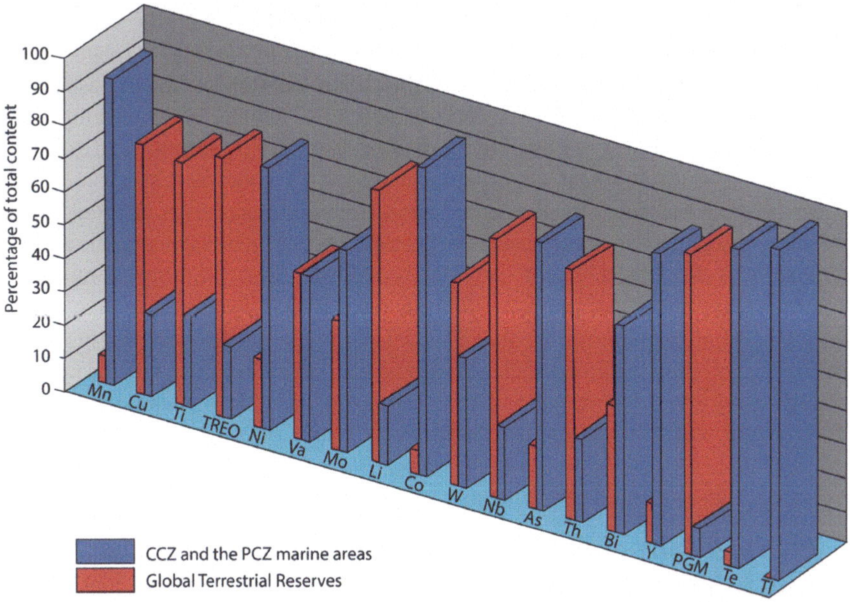


**Fig. 1** Bar diagram showing the comparison expressed as a percentage of total contained of 16 metals and two metal groups (TREO: Total Rare Earth Elements as Oxides, and PGM: Total Platinum Group Metals) from the CCZ and the PCZ marine areas (ISA 2010; Hein and Koschinsky 2013) with the Global Terrestrial Reserves (USGS 2012)

the oxygen in the atmosphere; they are the support of economic activities and of communication thanks to maritime transport. The oceans importance for mankind is so huge that our existence depends on theirs. For this reason, the international community has considered essential the need to conserve and protect the oceans for development and human well-being. In 1994, the United Nations Convention on the Law of the Sea (UNCLOS) came into force, which recognizes the concept of the global commons for the oceans. The UNCLOS recognizes the coastal States a jurisdiction over the maritime sectors close to their coasts and the existence of a marine zone beyond the limits of national jurisdiction of the coastal State, named 'The Area, which is really part of the global commons. In order to manage the mineral resources of the seabed in the Area, an intergovernmental body called the International Seabed Authority (ISA) was created in 1994, whose objective is to organize, regulate and control all mineral-related activities in the Area as a global common or common heritage of mankind. This autonomous organization, which has a relationship agreement with the United Nations, has in recent years carried out detailed regulations for the exploration activities of the mineral resources of the Area, and is currently developing regulations for their exploitation.

Although the analysis of the implications of deep-sea mining in the Area cannot exclude its interaction and impact on the global environment, economy, society and technological development, this chapter does not intend to address them in depth, since this would require the realization of a monographic book on the subject. The purpose of this chapter is mainly to introduce the reader to the aspects related to the typology of the mineral resources of the seabed, their location and the key aspects of the existing regulations for their exploration and those that are being developed for their exploitation. In any case, since in the mineral resources exploration and exploitation regulations development, environmental aspects are addressed, also topics such as: establishing measures for the seabed protection and restoration affected by the exploration/exploitation activities to minimize the impact on biota; economic aspects in relation to the fees payment that will be derived from the mineral resources exploitation by contractors or how the mineral resources exploitation may affect developing land-based producer States; social aspects in relation the benefits distribution to developing countries; and technological aspects in relation with the systems development for the exploitation and minerals treatment for the metals extraction that are respectful with the environment, will also be briefly discussed in this chapter.

## 2 Physiography of the Ocean Floor and Its Relationship with Mineral Resources

Taking into account the morphological features of the seabed, it can be divided into three main physiographic units: continental margins, deep ocean basins, and oceanic ridges. The continental margin is subdivided into the continental shelf, the continental slope and the continental rise (Fig. 2).

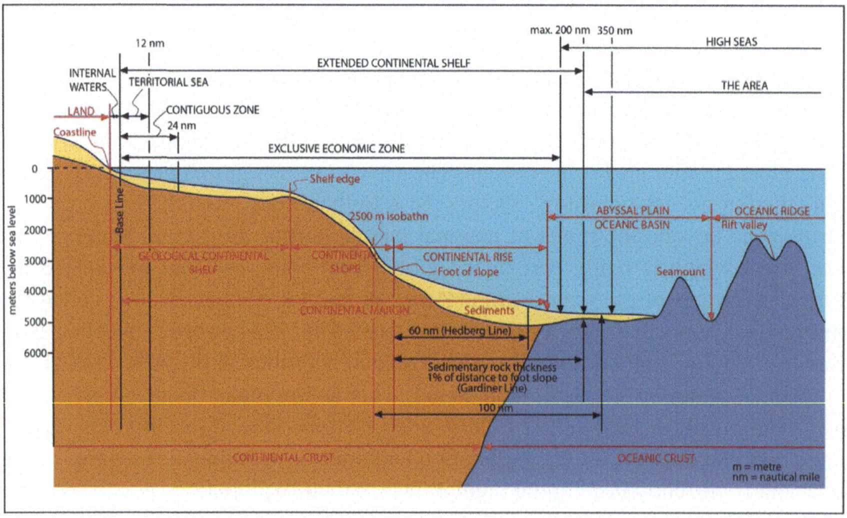


**Fig. 2** Diagrammatic division of the Maritime Zones according to the UNCLOS (in black) and geological and geomorphological physiographic provinces (in red)

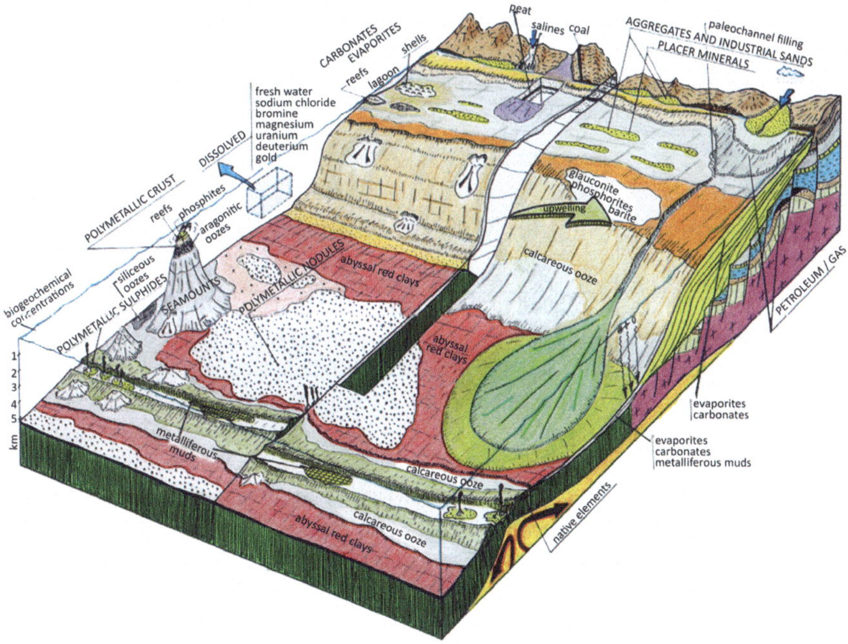


**Fig. 3** Location and types of the main mineral aggregate accumulations on the seabed (courtesy of Professor Francisco J. Hernández-Molina, Royal Holloway University of London)

These physiographic provinces are further characterized by their greater or lesser interaction (due to their proximity) with the sedimentary processes of the continental emerged areas, the activity of marine currents, atmospheric dynamics in the case of surface currents, or variations in temperature and salinity in the case of deep currents, and with volcanic and biological activity that can determine the chemical composition of the water. All these factors control the formation of one type or another of mineral aggregates on the seabed (Fig. 3).

On the continental shelf, there are frequent mineral accumulations owing to decantation processes, forming so-called "placers". These minerals come from the continental area and are transported through river channels, then accumulate and are distributed in the marine area by coastal currents and waves. Gold and diamond placers are perhaps the best known among these types of deposits (Glasby 1979), but there are other types such as cassiterite, ilmenite, magnetite, monazite, rutile, xenotime and zircon. On the upper continental slope, accumulations of glauconite, phosphorite and barite can be found in connection with upwelling currents of cold and nutrient-rich waters that are transported to the surface from depths of less than 200 m (Glasby 1979). Finally, in the deep marine areas we can find important accumulations of polymetallic nodules in the abyssal plains, cobalt-rich ferromanganese crusts in the seamounts, or polymetallic sulphides linked to the hydrothermal activity of the oceanic ridges (Glasby 1979; Hein et al. 2013). The latter will be described in more detail below, since the surface they occupy—the polymetallic nodules covering 38 million $km^2$, the cobalt-rich ferromanganese crusts 1.7 million $km^2$, and the polymetallic sulphides 3.2 million $km^2$—make them mineral reserves of great interest for future exploitation (Levin 2020).

## 3 Management of Seabed Mineral Resources in the Area

The legislative framework related to sovereignty and human activities in the oceans was established in the United Nations Convention on the Law of the Sea (UNCLOS), which is considered one of the most important multilateral treaties in history, referred to as "the Constitution of the Oceans" to govern the ocean, one of the Global Commons. It was approved in April 1982 in New York, signed by the States in December 1982, in Montego Bay, and finally enacted in November 1994. It establishes the limits of maritime zones, navigation rights, safety in the oceans, the conservation and management of marine resources, the protection and preservation of the marine environment, and the guidelines for marine scientific research, among other matters. The UNCLOS sets forth three international institutions to oversee correct compliance with the precepts contained therein: the Commission on the Limits of the Continental Shelf, the International Tribunal for the Law of the Sea, and the International Seabed Authority (ISA).

The maritime zones mark the rights of dominion, sovereignty and jurisdiction of the waters adjacent to countries. From the baseline toward the open sea, the following zones are distinguished: the Internal Waters, the Territorial Sea, the Contiguous Zone, the Exclusive Economic Zone, the Extended Continental Shelf and the Area (the last two zones are included in the High Seas) (Fig. 2).

In the Internal Waters and Territorial Sea, the sovereignty of the coastal State extends into the air space, as well as its bed and the subsoil. The breadth of the Territorial Sea must not exceed 12 nautical miles measured from the baseline. In the Contiguous Zone the coastal State does not have sovereignty; its rights are acknowledged only in customs, sanitary, fiscal and migratory matters, and it may not extend beyond 24 nm from the baselines from which the breadth of the territorial sea is measured. The Exclusive Economic Zone shall not extend beyond 200 nm from the baselines from which the breadth of the territorial sea is measured, while the coastal State has sovereign rights for the purposes of exploration and exploitation, conservation and administration of natural resources, both living and non-living, from the waters overlying the seabed and the seabed and subsoil, and has jurisdiction over facilities and structures, marine scientific research, and the protection and preservation of the marine environment. A request by the coastal States for the Extended Continental Shelf is based on a series of geological or geomorphological criteria related to the location of the foot of the slope or the 2500 m deep isobath, or sedimentary factors related to the thickness of sedimentary rocks (Fig. 2).

The coastal State shall submit information to the Commission on the Limits of the Continental Shelf on the limits of the continental shelf beyond 200 nm from the baselines from which the breadth of the territorial sea is measured, so as to establish the proper justification for the request and await its approval. The coastal State exercises sovereign rights over the extended continental shelf for the purposes of its exploration and the exploitation of its natural resources. Natural resources are mineral resources and other non-living resources of the seabed and its subsoil, as well as living organisms belonging to sedentary species. The rest belongs to the so-called Area that the UNCLOS defines as *the seabed and ocean floor and subsoil thereof, beyond the limits of national jurisdiction*. The mineral resources of the seabed in the Area are common heritage of mankind, because they are located in a Global Common, and their exploration and exploitation are regulated by the ISA. The Area comprises a little over 64% of the entire surface of the oceans (Sterk 2015).

# 4 Mineral Resources of the Area

The Area pays special attention to three types of mineral aggregates: polymetallic nodules, cobalt-rich ferromanganese crusts and polymetallic sulphides. The corpus of knowledge about their formation, composition and extension stems from recent times, although the first information surrounding their existence was gathered at the end of the XIX century.

## *4.1 Polymetallic Nodules*

Oceanic manganese nodules were discovered in 1868 in the Kara Sea (Russia) (Manheim 1965). Later, during the famous oceanographic expedition aboard the HMS Challenger, which circumnavigated the world between 1872 and 1876, nodules of ferromanganese enriched in nickel, copper and cobalt in 1873 were recovered southwest of the Canary Islands Archipelago (Spain) (Murray 1891). Years later, manganese nodules were discovered in different sections of the ocean floor, and around 1960 these mineral aggregates were determined to occupy extensive extensions of the abyssal plains. The total number of nodules in the Pacific Ocean was estimated to reach 1660 billion tons (Mero 1965). Beginning in the 1970s, the United States and the Soviet Union—followed by the United Kingdom, France, Germany, Japan, India and China—organized large-scale investigations of ferromanganese nodules focused on the delineation of nodule fields, the evaluation of the metallic resources that might be extracted from the nodules, and the need for preparatory work towards the future exploitation of nodules (Horn 1973; McKelvey et al. 1983), among others).

Manganese nodules are produced through different processes (Hein et al. 2013): (a) mineral precipitation from sea water, developing*hydrogenic nodules* on the ocean floor; (b) mineral precipitation from intrasedimentary fluids during sediment compaction and lithification, developing *diagenetic nodules* inside the sediments; and

(c) a combination of the two processes, developing *mixed nodules*at the sediment-water interface. The nodules show concentric shapes from a precipitation nucleus, such as a fragment of rock or the remains of living organisms. Their dimensions generally vary between 1 and 12 cm, with the most common values between 1 and 5 cm. While mainly made up of manganese and iron oxides and hydroxides, they can contain substantial and variable amounts of other metals such as nickel, copper, cobalt, lithium and molybdenum; and to a lesser extent, zinc, titanium, lead, REE, platinum and arsenic (Hein and Koschinsky 2013; Halbach et al. 1981). In general, the metallic components of these materials come from the magmatic activity of the ocean, from the contributions of chemical elements by means of continental waters and winds, and from chemical components contained in marine organisms, which are released when they die and decompose.

The highest abundance of nodules occurs in the abyssal basins on either side of the mid-ocean ridge, where sedimentation is low (Hein et al. 2013), or in areas of circumpolar currents (Fig. 4). The concentration of manganese nodules is lower in the Atlantic Ocean than in the Pacific and the Indian Oceans because of their higher sedimentation rate. In the Indian Ocean nodules are most abundant south of the equator and in the basins east and west of Ninetyeast Ridge. Some of the areas with the highest abundance of nodules are the central Indian basin, the southern and western Australian basins, and the Madagascar-Mozambique basin. Within the Pacific Ocean, the nodules are particularly abundant in the CCZ. The distribution of

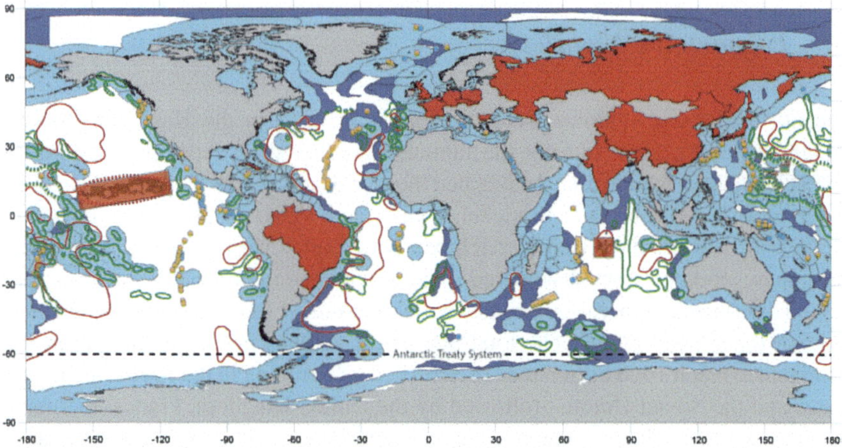


**Fig. 4** Map of global distribution of Exclusive Economic Zones (light blue), Extended Continental Shelf (purple) and the Area (white). Shown is the location of the three main marine mineral deposits: polymetallic nodules (red line); cobalt-rich ferromanganese crusts (green lines); polymetallic sulphides (active and inactive hydrothermal vents, in orange and blue circles, respectively) (Hein et al. 2013). The CCZ and the PCZ are represented by red and green dashed lines, respectively. The countries that have exploration contracts in the Area are indicated in red. The areas where the exploration contracts are located are also identified: polymetallic nodules (green areas); cobalt-rich ferromanganese crusts (yellow areas); polymetallic sulphides (red areas)

nodules is more irregular in the South Pacific, possibly due to its greater topographic diversity and the abundance of oceanic islands.

## *4.2 Cobalt-Rich Ferromanganese Crusts*

The first news about the existence of cobalt-rich ferromanganese crusts also comes from the HMS Challenger expedition. Yet they were not classified as a mineral aggregate (rather than nodules) until the study by Menard (1964), since their composition and origin are the same as those of nodules, but they present more cobalt and less iron and manganese. After 1970, systematic studies of ferromanganese crusts were conducted in the seamounts of the Pacific Ocean and, to a lesser extent, in the Atlantic and Indian oceans (Aplin 1985; De Carlo et al. 1987; Hein et al. 1987; Hein 1990, among others). Ferromanganese crusts are also hydrogenetic and diagenetic deposits of banded morphology arranged on various surfaces of the seabed.

The hydrogenetic development of ferromanganese crusts takes place with the precipitation of hydrated iron and manganese oxide colloids, which acquire traces of metals through surface sorption processes involving nickel, copper, chromium, titanium, platinum, molybdenum or arsenic (Hein et al. 2013). The growth rate of ferromanganese crusts is estimated between 1 and 10 mm per million years; the average thickness of the crusts is about 2.5 mm, but may reach 250 mm. The crusts tend to develop when sedimentation is null or very low, as occurs with manganese nodules.

Cobalt-rich ferromanganese crusts are located on seamounts, oceanic ridge slopes or summits, where the sedimentation rate is very low. Therefore, their spatial distribution depends on the presence of these morphological features of volcanic origin, whose development is linked to the formation of oceanic crust (Fig. 4). The mineral accumulations are generally found at depths between 400 and 4500 m, although those with the greatest thickness are located between 800 and 2500 m (Hein et al. 2009). Although the exact number of seamounts worldwide is not known, some authors estimate that there are more than 33,000 (Kitchingman 2004), about 57% of them in the Pacific. An area of special interest is the PCZ, in the western Pacific. It harbours the world´s oldest seamounts, developed during the Jurassic period, about 150 million years ago. The cobalt-rich ferromanganese crusts deposited on them have acquired significant thicknesses and high concentrations of REE (Hein et al. 2013), amounting to an estimated total of 7.5 billion tons of crust (Fig. 4). The presence of ferromanganese crusts has also been documented in the ridges of the polar oceans, but their distribution is largely unknown. Seamounts and ridges in the Atlantic and Indian Oceans have less ferromanganese crustal development than the Pacific because the number of sediment-free seamounts and ridges is lower (Hein et al. 2013).

### 4.3 Polymetallic Sulphides

The first evidence of hydrothermal activity in an expansion centre on the ocean floor was a temperature and salinity anomaly detected during a Swedish expedition aboard the research vessel S/S Albatross in its transit through the Red Sea in 1948 (Bruneau 1953). However, it was not until 1968–1969 that polymetallic sulphides were first recovered in the submarine Atlantis II Deep basin, also in the Red Sea (Degens and Ross 1969). In the 1970s, investigations were intensified in areas of hydrothermal activity where the presence of massive sulphide deposits was observed: the Atlantic Ridge, in an area called the Trans-Atlantic Geotraverse hydrothermal field (TAG) (Scott et al. 1974) and within the FAMOUS project framework (French-American Mid-Ocean Undersea Study) (Corliss et al. 1979); and the Pacific Ocean, in the vicinity of the Galápagos Ridge (Klinkhammer et al. 1977) and off the Mexico coast, within the CYAMEX (Cyana-MEXICO) project framework (Francheteau 1979). Since these early discoveries, hydrothermal deposits have been found along all segments of the world's oceanic spreading ridges. Hydrothermalism areas have been observed in other seafloor provinces, such as intraplate volcanic regions and back-arc basins, and are even found associated with volcanic ridges in subduction zones (Boschen et al. 2013; Scott 1985).

Marine polymetallic sulphide deposits are mineral deposits formed under hydrothermal conditions (<375 °C) caused by magmatic activity on the ocean floor (Cronan 2000). There are magmatic chambers in diverse marine geotectonic environments—mid-ocean ridges, back-arc ridges, island arcs, oceanic islands and seamounts (Herzig and Hannington 1995)—containing fluids at very high temperatures (approximately 1200 °C) that produce warming in nearby rocks by conductive and convective movement of the fluids they contain. This heating gives rise to a large number of water-rock reactions and transformations in the minerals that make up the rocks, generating metasomatic and metamorphic processes, and therefore the formation of new rocks and mineral deposits (Cronan 2000). The minerals are rich in metals such as iron, copper, zinc, lead, cobalt, nickel, gold and silver, and chemical elements such as barium and sulphur, among others (Scott 1985).

As mentioned previously, the distribution of the polymetallic sulphide deposits is associated with mid-ocean ridges (Fig. 4) (Herzig and Hannington 1995). Around the Pacific Ridge, they are located in the Galapagos area, in the East Pacific Ridge, and in the Salton Sea, Explorer and Juan de Fuca ridges; in the Atlantic Ridge, they are in the sectors of the Snake Pit, Broken Spur, Lucky Strike and TAG hydrothermal fields; in the Red Sea, they are near the Atlantis II Deep, Vema Deep, Gympsum and Kebritt Deep basins; and in the Indian Ocean, they are located in the Sonne inactive hydrothermal field. There are also deposits of polymetallic sulphides related to subduction zones in the Pacific island arcs and back-arc ridges, as for example, in the Fiji, Lau, Manus, Woodlark, Mariana and Okinawa islands, and in the Mediterranean Sea in the Palinuro seamount and in the Hellenic Volcanic Arc system (Boschen et al. 2013; Varnavasa 2020).

## 5 Exploration of the Mineral Resources of the Area

In the 1960s and 1970s, a series of consortia in Germany, the United States, Canada, Japan, France, Belgium, and Italy, among others, began exploratory activities of the seabed to learn about its mining potential and develop extraction technologies for polymetallic nodules in the CCZ in the central Pacific Ocean. With the establishment of the UNCLOS in 1982 and the ISA in 1994, the exploration activities of mineral resources in the Area began to be regulated. The year 2000 saw approval of the Regulations on Prospecting and Exploration of Polymetallic Nodules in the Area (ISBA/19/C/17), in 2010 the Regulations on Prospecting and Exploration of Polymetallic Sulphides in the Area (ISBA/16/A/12/Rev.1) were set forth, and in 2012 the Regulations on Prospecting and Exploration for Cobalt-rich Ferromanganese Crusts in the Area (ISBA/18/A/11). From 2001 to 2020, 17 countries and a consortium sponsor drew up exploration contracts for polymetallic nodules, ferromanganese crusts and polymetallic sulphides (Fig. 4): Belgium, Brazil, China, Cook Islands, France, Germany, India, Jamaica, Japan, Kiribati, Nauru, Poland, Republic of Korea, Russian Federation, Singapore, Tonga, United Kingdom of Great Britain and Northern Ireland, and the Interoceanmetal Joint Organization (Bulgaria, Cuba, Czech Republic, Poland, Russian Federation and Slovakia). The exploration zones are located in the Pacific Ocean, in the CCZ and in the Western Pacific Ocean; in the Indian Ocean, in its central part and in the central and south-western sectors of the Indian Ridge; and in the Atlantic Ocean, in the area of the Rio Grande Rise off the coast of Brazil and in the central part of the Mid-Atlantic Ridge (see Fig. 4). At present there are 31 exploration contracts: 17 contracts for polymetallic nodules at the CCZ and one for the Western Pacific Ocean; four contracts for polymetallic sulphides in the Indian Ocean and three in the Mid-Atlantic Ridge; and, finally, four contracts for ferromanganese crusts in the Western Pacific Ocean and one in the South Atlantic Ocean.

When requesting exploration zones, the maximum area contracted depends on the mineral resource involved. For polymetallic nodules, it is 150,000 km$^2$, which must be partially returned as the exploration progresses, finally being reduced by half (Regulation 25, ISBA/19/C/17). The maximum dimension in the case of polymetallic sulphides is 10,000 km$^2$, in blocks of 10 $\times$ 10 km with a maximum of 100 blocks, and part of the contract area must be returned as the execution of the contract progresses, so that after 10 years the area is 2500 km$^2$ (Regulation 27, ISBA/16/A/12/Rev.1). In the case of ferromanganese crusts, the request is made in a maximum of 150 blocks of 20 km$^2$, leaving an area of 1000 km$^2$ at the end of the exploration stage (Regulations 12 and 27, ISBA/18/A/11). The fee to be paid to obtain the exploration area is 500,000 USD or the equivalent in local currency in the case of polymetallic nodules and ferromanganese crusts (Regulations 19 and 21, ISBA/19/C/17 and ISBA/18/A/11). In the case of polymetallic sulphides, the fee could be 500,000 USD or an amount that depends on the extent of the exploration area (Regulation 21, ISBA/16/A/12/Rev.1). The exploration plans of an area cover a period of 15 years, although they can be extended for five more years (Regulation 26, ISBA/19/C/17; Regulation 28, ISBA/16/A/12/Rev.1 and ISBA/18/A/11).

The application for an exploration contract in the Area to the ISA must meet a series of requirements. The following entities may request approval of a work plan: (a) The Enterprise, acting on its own behalf or by virtue of a joint arrangement; and (b) State Parties, a State Enterprise or natural or juridical persons that possess the nationality of States or are effectively controlled by them or by their nationals, when sponsored by such States, or any group of the foregoing that meets the requirements (Regulation 9, ISBA/19/C/17, ISBA/16/A/12/Rev.1 and ISBA/18/A/11). The request for approval of a work plan for exploration will contain concrete and sufficient information to allow the Council to verify whether the applicant has the financial and technical capacity to carry out the work plan for the proposed exploration and to meet its financial obligations with the Authority (Regulation 12, ISBA/19/C/17; Regulation 13, ISBA/16/A/12/Rev.1 and ISBA/18/A/11). An annual report of the activities and results obtained must be sent to the Secretary of the Authority for its evaluation by the Legal and Technical Commission (advisory body of the ISA Council, LTC), which can make suggestions about the progress to the contractor or alert the Authority about non-compliance (Regulation 6, ISBA/19/C/17, ISBA/16/A/12/Rev.1 and ISBA/18/A/11). Of course, all the information provided to the Authority by the contractor is confidential, except for data and information that refer to the protection and preservation of the marine environment, in particular regarding environmental monitoring programs (Regulation 7, ISBA/19/C/17, ISBA/16/A/12/Rev.1 and ISBA/18/A/11).

In order to guarantee access to the seabed mineral resources for developing countries, the UNCLOS established the development of the Enterprise and the so-called reserved areas in exploration contracts. The Enterprise is an organ of the Authority established in Article 170 and in Annex IV of the UNCLOS. It is the entity through which developing countries may participate in the commercial exploitation of the mineral resources of the Area, although there are already developing countries that act as contractors (e.g. Brazil, Bulgaria, China, Cuba, Fiji, India, Nauru, Russia). At the moment, the creation of the Enterprise is in a very initial phase, since its development has important financial implications—the funds needed by the Authority amount to an estimated 345,000 USD per year. Even so, the LTC recommended in 2020 that the Council consider requesting the Assembly, subject to the availability of existing financial resources, that the Secretary General of the Authority appoint a person for the position of interim Director General of the Enterprise.

Furthermore, there are reserved areas, which are contributed by the contractors when they request exploration rights from the ISA (Regulation 16, ISBA/19/C/17). These areas are kept in a "site bank" reserved for access by developing countries or for the Enterprise (UNCLOS, Article 170, Annex IV and 1994 Agreement, Annex, Sect. 2). Therefore, any exploration request made must cover a total area large enough and entailing sufficient commercial value to allow for two mining operations. The proposed location need not be a single contiguous area. The applicant must divide the total area into two parts of equal estimated commercial value and provide data and information to corroborate the estimates. The LTC reviews the data and information provided by the applicant to verify that the two areas have equal potential. Based on its findings, the LTC makes a recommendation to the ISA Council as to what area should be allocated to the applicant and what should be kept as a reserved area. In the case of polymetallic sulphides and cobalt-rich ferromanganese crusts, a different system is applied. In light of the difficulty encountered by applicants in collecting sufficient data to identify two sites of equal estimated commercial value, the ISA Council gives applicants the option of contributing a reserved area or offering future participation in a joint venture with the Enterprise (Regulation 16, ISBA/16/A/12/Rev.1 and ISBA/18/A/11). At present, there is a total area of 888,218 km$^2$ available in the reserved site bank for polymetallic nodules, and 3000 km$^2$ for ferromanganese crusts.

## 6 Exploitation of Mineral Resources in the Area and the Most Important Challenges

In July 2016, the first working draft of the "Regulations and Terms of the Standard Contract on the Exploitation of Mineral Resources in the Area" was presented by the LTC to the ISA Council. Its purpose was to establish an effective regulatory regime to organize, control and manage—in an orderly, safe, efficient and rational way—the marine mineral resources in the Area, following solid principles of conservation, prevention, reduction and control of pollution and other dangers to the marine environment, including the coast, and avoiding interference with the ecological balance of the marine environment. Special care must be taken to protect against the harmful effects of activities in the Area in accordance with the best environmental practices, and a precautionary approach must be developed according to environmental regulations. The regulations also address the procedures to be followed when requesting approval of a work plan, and the requirements to be met for the concession of exploitation contracts, only to applicants duly qualified to carry out exploitation activities in the Area. Measures for the adoption and development of risk assessment and risk management are set forth, along with standards and systems to monitor and mitigate risks for health and the environment. Finally, operational performance should comply with the financial objectives of the UNCLOS and ensure a fair financial return to mankind for the resources. All these facets were deeply debated, and in July of 2019, the "Draft regulation on the exploitation of mineral resources in the Area" prepared by the LTC was presented to the Council for its consideration. This document contains 107 regulations, 10 annexes, four appendices and an addendum. There are still aspects of this regulation under development, for which reason its date of actual approval has yet to be determined.

Among the aspects that are still under discussion and development, the most relevant deserve mention in this section. The first would be the definition of the standards and guidelines that should be applied for a correct implementation of the draft regulations for the mineral resource exploitation in the Area. They would establish the obligations and recommendations that contractors must follow, covering aspects such as (i) development of Environmental Impact Assessments, the Environmental Impact Statement, and Environmental Monitoring and Management Plans; (ii) development and application of Environmental Management Systems; (iii) preparation and evaluation of a request and approval of a Work Plan for exploitation; (iv) preparation and implementation of emergency response and contingency plans; (v) the form and calculation of the Environmental Performance Guarantee; and (vi) safety management and the operability of mining support vessels.

Another issue under discussion, taking into account Article 150 (h) of the UNCLOS, which establishes that activities in the Area will be carried out in order to guarantee the protection of developing countries *"from adverse effects on their economies or on their export earnings resulting from a reduction in the price of an affected mineral, or in the volume of exports of that mineral, to the extent that such reduction is caused by activities in the Area…"* consists of a preliminary evaluation of the economic impact of polymetallic nodules from the Area on developing land-based producer States. These developing countries would be the ones that sustain their economy on the production of copper (Zambia, Democratic Republic of the Congo, Eritrea, Chile, Lao People's Democratic Republic, Mongolia and Peru), nickel (Madagascar and Zimbabwe), cobalt (Democratic Republic of the Congo), manganese (Gabon) or all four of these minerals (Mauritania, Namibia and Papua New Guinea). The "adverse effects" might cause, among other problems, a direct reduction in state revenues leading to fewer funds for development, an economic slowdown, increased unemployment, even social unrest and implications for political stability. In order to prevent all of this from occurring, the Authority should start establishing a compensation system or take other measures for economic adjustment, including cooperation with specialized agencies or international organizations. To this end, an economic assistance fund could be created by contractors, including the Enterprise, and voluntary contributions, in accordance with paragraph 1(a) of Sect. 7 of the 1994 Agreement. In any case, it will be necessary to conduct studies on trends and factors affecting supply, demand and the prices of materials from the area after deep-sea mining begins, bearing in mind the interests of importing countries and exporters, and in particular developing States.

The procedure to be followed for the equitable distribution of economic and non-economic benefits from deep-sea mining is also under discussion. The economic benefits cover aspects such as administrative expenses, funds allocated for the maintenance of the Enterprise, economic investments in favour of developing countries whose export earnings or whose economy suffer serious damage as a result of a drop in prices, or the exported volume of a mineral due to mining activity in the Area (UNCLOS, Article 151 (10)), reimbursement of the contribution of a Member State, creation of a fund for the sustainability of the seabed, and distribution among the State Parties based on equitable distribution criteria, taking into account the interests and needs of developing States, especially the least developed and the land-locked ones (UNCLOS, Article 82 (4)). Non-economic benefits include the development of training programs for developing countries, the establishment of research projects that favour the growth of scientific knowledge for the benefit of mankind, or activities aimed at environmental protection. The notion of profit sharing is based on the Aristotelian principle establishing that an asset must be distributed in proportion to the contribution (or claim) of each of the claimants. Presumably, the distribution of benefits should be progressive, to favour the poorest states. Distribution could be through cash disbursements to the States for uses most beneficial for their populations, or by backing projects aimed at improving living conditions in a specific region or country in a sustainable way, or else focusing on the mankind benefit as a whole rather than the benefit of individual States, for the mitigation of climate change, the promotion of scientific knowledge and new technologies, or the conservation of biodiversity and deep-water ecosystems.

Undoubtedly, mining operations will have substantial impact on the marine environment, especially nearby the mining area. Aspects considered in this sense include the technological development of machinery that would reduce environmental impact during exploitation, and measures for restoration and rehabilitation of the mining area once the activity ceases. The latter must be contemplated in the Closure Plan of the Exploitation Work Plan, as well as in the development of Regional Environmental Management Plans (REMPs) and the creation of Areas of Particular Environmental Interest (APEIs). The first REMP was established for the CCZ (the first area where exploration zones were requested), and it was adopted by the Council in 2012 (ISBA/18/C/22). It designated nine APEIs covering an area of 400 $\times$ 400 km, equivalent to approximately 25% of the exploration areas overall, which are protected from the future exploitation of mineral resources in the Area. In 2019, based on the information obtained from the Deep CCZ Biodiversity Synthesis Workshop in Friday Harbor (Washington, USA), the biodiversity of the CCZ was deemed to be high, though knowledge about it is still quite scarce. The lack of information can be attributed to: (i) the methods of analysis of the samples, not always comparable with each other; (ii) comprehensive biodiversity studies may not cover all possible species; (iii) benthic species have limited geographic distribution ranges; and (iv) the habitats of the zones rich in nodules are under-represented in the APEIs, and over-represented in the mining zones. Furthermore, the main drivers controlling biodiversity, community structure, and ecosystems throughout the CCZ were found to be closely related to particulate organic carbon fluxes, nodule abundance, and topography. Given this situation, new locations may be proposed for at least three APEIs in the CCZ, to improve representativeness and address any spatial gap in the current APEI network. In 2018 the Council moreover took note of a preliminary strategy to develop REMPs in priority regions where exploration activities are currently underway (ISBA/24/C/3): the Mid-Atlantic Ridge, the Indian Ocean triple junction ridge and nodule-bearing province, and the seamounts of the North-West Pacific and South Atlantic.

## 7 Final Remarks

Deep-sea mining is already a reality in some parts of the world: in the Gulf of Ulloa, in Baja California Sur, in the exclusive economic zone of Mexico, where the extraction of phosphate sands is carried out by the Odyssey Marine Exploration company, or in the exclusive economic zone of Papua New Guinea, where Deep Sea Mining Finance Limited is exploiting a polymetallic sulphide system for the extraction of copper, gold, zinc and silver. In the Area, the Regulation for the Exploitation of Mineral Resources is very close to being approved by the Member Countries of the Assembly of the International Seabed Authority, meaning that deep-sea mining can involve waters located beyond the jurisdiction of specific countries, conforming part of our mankind heritage. As stated in the text, several countries and companies have been exploring the seabed of the Area for more than 20 years in search of mineral reserves that will allow them to supply the growing demand by society, now and in the future. Since the 1970s, companies such as Ocean Mining Associates, The Ocean Management Inc., or Lockheed Ocean Minerals Company have been developing technologies for the extraction of minerals from the seabed; since the 1990s, contractor countries such as India, Japan, China and Korea have been using extractive machinery in shallow waters. The German Federal Institute for Geosciences and Natural Resources and Global Sea Mineral Resources plans to test a pre-prototype harvesting vehicle in the CCZ contract area in late 2020, and the Government of India will conduct extraction trials in its contract zone in the Indian Ocean in 2021. The panorama indicates that in a few years the exploitation of mineral resources in the Area, a significant part of one of the Global Commons, will begin, implying numerous challenges, not only economic and technological, but also social, political and environmental. The governments of all the countries involved should be prepared to face the great challenges that this new type of mining will pose worldwide.

## References

Aplin, A. C., & Cronan, D. S. (1985). Ferromanganese oxide deposits from the central pacific ocean. I. Encrustations from the Line Islands Archipelago. *Geochimica et Cosmochimica Acta, 48*(1), 427–436.

Boschen, R. E., Rowden, A. A., Clarka, M. R., & Gardner, J. P. A. (2013). Mining of deep-sea seafloor massive sulfides: A review of the deposits, their benthic communities, impacts from mining, regulatory frameworks and management strategies. *Ocean & Coastal Management, 84*, 54–67.

Bruneau, L., Jerlov, N. G., & Koczy, F. F. (1953). Physical and chemical methods. Reports of the Swedish Deep-Sea Expedition 3, Physics and Chemistry, Fasc. ii, Appendix XXIX-XXX.

Cathles, L. M. (2013). Future Rx: Optimism, preparation, acceptance of risk. In G. R. T. Jenkin, P. A. J. Lusty, I. McDonald, M. P. Smith, A. J. Boyce, & J. J. Wilkinson (Eds.), *Ore deposits in an evolving earth* (Vol. 393, pp. 303–324). Geological society. London: Special Publications.

Corliss, J. B., Dymond, J., Gordon, L. I., Edmond, J. M., von Herzen, R. P., Ballard, R. D., Green, K., Williams, D., Bainbridge, A., Crane, K., & van Andel, T. H. (1979). Submarine thermal springs on the Galápagos Rift. *Science, 203*, 1073–1083.

Cronan, D. S. (Ed.). (2000). *Handbook of marine mineral deposits* (pp. 1–424). CRC Marine Science Series 17. Boca Raton: CRC Press.
De Carlo, E. H., Pennywell, P. A., & Fraley, C. M. (1987). Geochemistry of ferromanganese deposits from the kiribati and travalu region of the West Central Pacific Ocean. *Marine Mining, 6*(3), 301–321.
Degens, E. T., & Ross, D. A. (1969). *Hot brines and heavy metals in the Red Sea. A Geochemical and Geophysical Account* (pp. 1–600). Berlin, Heidelberg: Springer-Verlag.
Francheteau, J., Needham, H. D., Chourkroune, P., & CYAMEX Scientific Team. (1979). Massive deep sea sulfide ore deposits discovered on the East Pacific Rise. *Nature, 277*, 523–528.
Glasby, G. P. (1979). Minerals from the sea. *Endeavour, 3*(2), 82–85.
Halbach, P., Scherhag, C., Hebisch, U., & Marchig, V. (1981). Geochemical and mineralogical control of different genetic types of deep sea nodules from the Pacific Ocean. *Mineralium Deposita, 16*, 59–84.
Hein, J. R., Conrad, T. A., & Dunham, R. E. (2009). Seamount characteristics and mine-site model applied to exploration- and mining-lease-block selection for cobalt-rich ferromanganese crusts. *Marine Georesources and Geotechnology, 27*, 160–176.
Hein, J. R., & Koschinsky, A. (2013). Deep-ocean ferromanganese crusts and nodules. In S. Scott (Ed.), *Treatise on geochemistry* (pp. 273–291). Amsterdam: Elsevier.
Hein, J. R., Mizell, K., Koschinsky, A., & Conrad, T. A. (2013). Deep-ocean mineral deposits as a source of critical metals for high- and green-technology applications: comparison with land-based resources. *Ore Geology Reviews, 51*, 1–14.
Hein, J. R., Morgenson, L. A., Ciague, D. A., & Koski, R. A. (1987). Cobalt-rich ferromanganese crusts from the exclusive economic zone of the United States and nodules from the Oceanic Pacific. *Earth Science Series, 6*, 753–771.
Hein, J. R., Schultz, M. S., & Kang, K. (1990). Insular and submarine ferromanganese mineralization of the Tonga-Lau Region. *Marine Mining, 9*, 305–354.
Herzig, P. M., & Hannington, M. D. (1995). Polymetallic massive sulfides at the modern seafloor. A review. *Ore Geology Reviews, 10*, 95–115.
Horn, D. R., Horn, B. M., & Delach, M. N. (1973). *Factors which control the distribution of ferromanganese nodules and proposed research vessels track North Pacific, Phase II Ferromanganese Program* (pp. 1–40). Washington DC: Tech Rept 8 Nat Sci Found-IDOE.
ISA, International Seabed Authority. (2010). *A geological model of polymetallic nodule deposits in the Clarion-Clipperton Fracture zone* (p. 211). Kingston, Jamaica: ISA Technical Study 6.
Kitchingman, A., & Lai, S. (2004). Inferences on potential seamount locations from midresolution bathymetric data. In T. Morato, & D. Pauly (Eds.), *Seamounts: Biodiversity and Fisheries* (Vol. 78, pp. 7–12). UBC Fisheries Centre Report.
Klinkhammer, G., Bender, M., & Weiss, R. F. (1977). Hydrothermal manganese in the galapagos rift. *Nature, 269*, 319–320.
Levin, L. A., Amon, D. J., & Lily, H. (2020). Challenges to the sustainability of deep-seabed mining. *Nature Sustainability*. https://doi.org/10.1038/s41893-020-0558-x.
Manheim, E. T. (1965). *Manganese-Iron accumulations in the shallow marine environment* (Vol. 3, pp. 217–276). University of Rhode Island, Occasional Publication of Narragansett Marine Laboratory.
Mayer, L., Jakobsson, M., Allen, G., Dorschel, B., Falconer, R., Ferrini, V., Lamarche, G., Snaith, H., & Weatherall, P. (2018). The nippon foundation-GEBCO seabed 2030 project: the quest to see the world's oceans completely mapped by 2030. *Geosciences, 8*(63). https://doi.org/10.3390/geosciences8020063.
McKelvey, V. E., Wright, N. A., & Bowen, R. W. (1983). Analysis of the World distribution of metal-rich sub-sea manganese nodules. *U.S. Geological Survey Circular, 886*, 1–55.
Menard, H. W. (1964). *The marine geology of the pacific* (pp. 1–271). New York: Mc Graw Hill
Mero, J. L. (1965). *The mineral resources of the sea. Elsevier oceanography Series 1* (pp. 1–312). Amsterdam, Netherlands: Elsevier Publishing Company.

Murray, J., & Renard, A. F. (1891). Deep-sea deposits (based on the specimens collected during the voyage of HMS Challenger in the years 1872 to 1876). *Report on the scientific results of the voyage of H.M.S. Challenger during the years 1873-76* (pp. 1–688). Endinburgh, United Kingdom: John Menzies and Co.

Price, J. G. (2010). The world is changing. *Society of Economic Geologists, Newsletter, 82*, 12–14.

Scott, M. R., Scott, R. B., Rona, P. R., Butler, L. W., & Nalwalk, A. J. (1974). Rapidly accumulating manganese deposits from the median valley of the Mid-Atlantic Ridge. *Geophysical Research Letters, 1*, 355–358.

Scott, S. D. (1985). Seafloor polymetallic sulfide deposits: modern and ancient. *Marine Mining, 5*, 191–212.

Sterk, R., & Stein, J. K. (2015). *Seabed mineral deposits: A review of current mineral resources and future developments* (pp. 1–27). Aberdeen, Scotland: Deep Sea Mining Summit, 9–10 February 2015.

USGS. (2012). Mineral commodity summaries 2012. *U.S. Geological Survey* (p. 198).

Varnavasa, S. P., & Papavasiliou, C. (2020). Submarine hydrothermal mineralization processes and insular mineralization in the Hellenic Volcanic Arc system: A review. *Ore Geology Reviews, 124*. https://doi.org/10.1016/j.oregeorev.2020.103541

**Adolfo Maestro-González** who holds a Ph.D. in Earth Sciences from the University of Zaragoza (Spain) since 1999, is currently a Research Scientist at the Geological and Mining Institute of Spain (IGME), where he is developing his research in Marine Geology. In addition to his research experience, he has been an Adjunct Professor in Geology in Environmental Sciences and Biology in the Faculty of Science in the Autonomous University of Madrid from 2003. He has participated in twenty-four oceanographic cruises in the Iberian and Antarctica continental margins and adjacent abyssal plains, and in fifty research projects, being Project leader/team coordinator of eleven, funded by the Spanish National Plan for Scientific and Technical Research and Innovation, the European Framework Programme for Research and Innovation, and IGME. He has also authored a total of 450 scientific contributions and co-directed Doctoral and Master Theses in Marine Geology. Moreover, he was member of the Subcommittee for the Delimitation of the Continental Shelf of the Inter-ministerial Commission on International Maritime Policy for the Extension of the Spanish Continental Shelf of the Ministry of Foreign Affairs in 2003, and he has been the team coordinator for the IGME of the Spanish Exclusive Economic Zone Working Group from 2003 to present, a member of the Marine Geology Expert Group of the EuroGeoSurveys from 2010 to 2019, a member of the Spanish Delegation at the Council and Assembly of the International Seabed Authority from 2016 to present, and an elected member of the Legal and Technical Commission of the International Seabed Authority from 2017 to 2021.

# Outer Space and the Future of Humanity

**Federico Yaniz**

**Abstract** Space, also known as outer space, has become an essential element for the development of Humanity. Indeed, the peaceful use of space for all kinds of activities provides many new possibilities for human progress. 63 years have passed since the first artificial satellite of our planet, *Sputnik,* was put in orbit on October 14, 1957, and in that time great progress has been made in the conquest of space. Nevertheless, Yuri Gagarin was not in orbit until April 12, 1961. Eight years later, on July 20, 1969, Apollo 11 expedition landed on the Moon. Since then, the number of artifacts that populate space has been rapidly increased and space junk multiplied. A new stage in the conquest of space began when *Salyut 1* space station was put in orbit on April 19, 1971. But there are many other subjects worthwhile to consider when speaking about outer space and the future of Humanity, among them the new race to explore the Moon and beyond, outer space and defense, and nations and space. This paper pretends to help a better appreciation of the importance that outer space has and will have for a peaceful and progressive future of Humanity. Furthermore, it is possible to find in this essay some of the most important initiatives that international organizations and some nations are implementing concerning outer space.

**Keywords** Outer space · European union · NATO · Moon · Humanity · Defense · Flight · Deep space · Capsule · NASA · Policy · Exploration · Operational domain

---

In: Security: the Global Commons and Beyond, Edited by J. Martin Ramirez, and Bartolomé Bauzá-Abril. © 2021 Springer International. Submitted: August 29, 2020; Accepted: September 14, 2020.

---

F. Yaniz (✉)
Federico Yaniz is Vicepresident of Eurodefense-Spain, Apartado 50359, 28080 Madrid, Spain
e-mail: federo101@hotmail.com



J. M. Ramírez and B. Bauzá-Abril (eds.), *Security in the Global Commons and Beyond*, Advanced Sciences and Technologies for Security Applications,
https://doi.org/10.1007/978-3-030-67973-6_5

## 1 Foreword

It is usually understood by outer space or simply space, the regions of the universe outside the atmospheres of the different celestial bodies. Without going into a detailed analysis of the concept of outer space, it seems appropriate to point out that outer space is not completely empty of matter but contains a low density of particles, mainly hydrogen, and electromagnetic radiation. Outer space is supposed to occupy virtually the entire volume of the universe and is now known to contain most of the existing matter on it. Matter that it is formed by electromagnetic radiation, cosmic particles, massless neutrinos, and other forms of matter not well known such as dark matter and dark energy. In fact, in the universe each of these components contributes to the total matter. According to some estimates in the Encyclopedia Britannica online (2005), the components of that matter are in the following proportion: cold condensed matter (0.03%), stellar matter (0.5%), neutrinos (massless particles, 0.3%), dark matter (25%) and dark energy (75%). The physical nature of these last two components is not well known.

There is no well-defined border between the Earth's atmosphere and outer space as the density of the atmosphere decreases as the altitude increases. However, the FAI[1] has established the 100-kilometer (62 miles) altitude, the Karman line, as a practical working boundary between atmosphere and space. During atmospheric re-entry, the altitude of 120 km marks the limit where atmospheric resistance becomes noticeable. The definition of "astronaut" and the criteria for determining who has achieved human spaceflight vary. According to FAI, (FAI 2009), the word astronaut may apply both to crew members and to scientific personnel aboard the spacecraft playing an active part in the mission during the flight. Space. flight is flight into or through outer space. Any flight over 100 km (62 mi) of altitude is consider a spaceflight. Nevertheless, in the United States of America, professional, military, and commercial astronauts who travel above an altitude of 50 miles (80 km) are eligible to be awarded astronaut wings. The ideas expressed above help us to perceive the complexity and extent of the study of outer space. In this essay significant attention is going to be paid to issues related to the exploration of outer space and the space defense.

It is indisputable that outer space has become in recent years an essential element for further development of Humanity. Indeed, the peaceful use of space for activities of all kinds provides new possibilities for human progress. Since the first artificial satellite, *Sputnik,* was put in orbit on October 14, 1957, progress has been made incessantly in the conquest of space, but the first steps were slow. Yuri Gagarin was not in orbit until April 12, 1961. Eight years later, on July 20, 1969, two astronauts—Commander Neil Armstrong and the pilot of the Lunar module Buzz Aldrin—formed the American crew that landed the Apollo Lunar module Eagle on the Moon. Six hours later, Neil Armstrong was the first man that walked on the Moon accomplishing one of the oldest dreams of human civilizations.

---

[1]Fédération Aéronautique International (FAI) (In English World Aeronautical Federation). The FAI is the world governing body for air sports. The FAI also stewards definitions regarding human spaceflight (FAI 2009).

Since then, the number of artifacts that populate space has been rapidly increasing and space junk multiplied. A new stage in the conquest of space began when the *Salyut 1*[2] space station was put in space on April 19, 1971. According to Zarya.info (2020) since the launching of /*Salyut 1*, 9 Soviet space stations have orbited Earth.

Yang Liwei, China's first man in space, was aboard the *Shenzhou V* (also known as *Shenzhou 5)* spacecraft launched on October 15, 2003. *Tiangong 1* was China's prototype un-crewed space station launched by a *Long March 2F/G* rocket. *Tiangong 1* orbited the Earth from September 29, 2011 till April 2, 2018, serving as laboratory and experimental testbed. The space station was visited by a series of *Shenzhou* spacecraft during its two-year operational lifetime. The crewed *Shenzhou* 9 mission docked in June 2012. With the *Tiangong* program, China aims to place a larger, modular station into orbit by 2023.

However, the most successful space station so far has been the International Space Station (ISS).[3] On the web page of the European Space Agency, (ESA 2020), we can read that the ISS is orbiting the Earth since 20 November 1998 and that international crews and visitors have continuously occupied it since 2000.

Space exploration will continue and even increase in the coming years and at the same time outer space is becoming, even more that now, a key element in international security. Furthermore, other major countries will create soon their own space agencies and commands. As a matter of fact, compared to the situation during the Cold War the number and quality of outer space actors has significantly increased. At the same time. We are also witness of the appearance in space of some private actors.

On July 30, 2020, at 4:50 a.m., EDT, NASA launched on a rocket Atlas V-541, the Mars 2020 Perseverance[4] rover that will seek signs of ancient life and collect rock and soil samples for possible return to the Earth. Furthermore, on August 2, 2020, SpaceX's Demo-2 mission crew splashed down in the Gulf of Mexico with two NASA astronauts on board, after returning from the International Space Station (ISS),[5] NASA (2020).

---

[2]*Salyut* (in Russian: Salute) was the generic name for the first series of space stations of the Soviet Union, launched with the Proton rocket. Between 1971 and 1982, 9 *Salyut* stations, of two different types, were launched. Six of them were manned by cosmonauts aboard. The Salyut program laid the groundwork for the development and operation of the next-generation modular *Mir* (Peace or World) space station.

[3]Since the ISS was habitable, researchers began using it to study the impact of microgravity and other space effects on several aspects of our daily lives. This unique scientific platform continues to enable researchers from all over the world to put their talents to work on innovative experiments that could not be done anywhere else.

[4]Facts about Mars 2020: Mission Name: Mars 2020: Rover Name: Perseverance. Main Job: The Perseverance rover will seek signs of ancient life and collect rock and soil samples for possible return to Earth. Launched: July 30, 2020; Launch Location: Cape Canaveral Air Force Station, Florida; Landing: Feb. 18, 2021; Landing Site: Jezero Crater, Mars. See: https://mars.nasa.gov/mars2020/.

[5]For the first time in history, NASA astronauts, Bob Behnken and Dug Hurley, splashed down safely in the Gulf of Mexico in a commercially built and operated American crewed spacecraft, returning from the International Space Station (ISS) to complete a test flight that marks a new era in human spaceflight.

## 2 Background

In today's changing environment, the whole of society must be involved in space exploration that it is indispensable for the future of Humanity. The Air and Space Forces are the spearhead of defense in the aerospace arena. To fulfill its mission, they must be well organized, composed of highly qualified personnel, and have the necessary capabilities. Even excluding a militarization of outer space, operations will impact stabilization operations and even deterrence. Our Defense establishment must assure our citizens, institutions, and businesses of the peaceful use of space. In this context, the Air and Space Force must assume its natural role, within the framework of joint action, in missions and operations to and from outer space.

The Treaty on Principles Governing the Activities of States in the Exploration and Use of Outer Space, including the Moon and other Celestial Bodies (UN 1967) entered into force in 1967. It was preceded by several resolutions by the UN General Assembly and years of discussion in the UN Committee on the Peaceful Use of Space. Till July 2017, 107 states have ratified the Outer Space Treaty, including almost every country that is involved in space activities.

The Outer Space Treaty remains to this day a key document of international law fostering the peaceful use of space and securing arms control in space. However, it seems that the United States of America, the United Kingdom, and the Russian Federation, the countries depositary of the treaty, are not paying too much attention to it. Other conventions such as the Environmental Modification Convention (ENMOD)[6] of 1977 and the Moon Agreement of 1979, (Moon 1979), also contain provisions on arms control in space. However, these agreements do not outlaw the militarization of space.

## 3 Return to the Moon

There are clear signs that attention to outer space is increasing both in international organizations such as NATO and the EU and in the world's most advanced nations. More than 50 years have passed since Neil Armstrong stepped on the Moon. In this half-century, China, India, Israel, the European Union (EU), and Japan, as well as the USA and Russia, have launched missions for the exploration of our satellite. The People's Republic of China's interest in space exploration is somehow recent and therefore observers were surprised by the landing of the *Chang'e-4* probe on the hidden face of the Moon on January 3, 2019. As has been mentioned, on October 15, 2003, China launched its first *taikonaut*, the Chinese version of American astronauts and Russian cosmonauts. China is currently confident in developing its deep space explorations in the new version of the Long March space rocket series.

[6]Formally Convention on the Prohibition of Military or Any Other Hostile Use of Environmental Modification Techniques.

The USA won the first space race half a century ago. Indeed, on July 16, 1969, the huge, 363-feet tall Saturn V rocket launches on the Apollo 11 mission from Kennedy Space Center, at 9:32 a.m. EDT. Onboard the Apollo 11 spacecraft are astronauts Neil A. Armstrong, commander; Michael Collins, command module pilot; and Edwin E. Aldrin Jr., lunar module pilot. After traveling 240,000 miles, Apollo 11 entered a lunar orbit on July 19. The next day, at 1:46 p.m., the lunar module Eagle, manned by Armstrong and Aldrin, separated from the command module, where Collins remained. The Eagle began its descent to the lunar surface, and at 4:17 p.m. the craft touched down on the southwestern edge of the Sea of Tranquility. Armstrong descended from the lunar module Eagle and put his left foot on the moon, 19 min later Aldrin followed. That mission is regarded as one of humanity's stellar moments as Armstrong expressed in his famous sentence: "A small step for a man, a great leap for Humanity." In December 1972, Apollo 17's Challenger lunar module landed on the Moon and its commander, astronaut Gene Cernan, is till now the last man to walk on the lunar surface. From December 1968 till December 1972 nine crews of astronauts walked on the Moon.

After "too many years" of doubt, in the USA there is renewed interest in outer space. One clear sign of it, is that in December of 2017, President Trump signed Space Policy Directive-1, in which the president directed NASA "to lead an innovative and sustainable program of exploration with commercial and international partners to enable human expansion across the solar system and to bring back to Earth new knowledge and opportunities." Following that bold call of Mr. Trump, in September 2018, NASA submitted to Congress a plan to revitalize and add direction to NASA's enduring purpose. The National Space Exploration Campaign calls for human and robotic exploration missions to expand the frontiers of human experience and scientific discovery of the natural phenomena of Earth, the Moon, and the cosmos. In this campaign, NASA is planning to return to Moon and then going to Mars. The construction of the NASA's Space Launch System (SLS) and of Starliner,[7] reusable crew capsules, will provide the foundation for exploration beyond Earth's orbit. The use of Starliner and the participation of private companies such as SpaceX[8] and Blue Origin[9] are going to change the future of space travel. Furthermore, a refurbished NASA has a plan for yearly Moon flights through 2030. Another sign of the renewal of the interest in space in the USA, is the restoration of the Space Command as a unified combatant command. The announcement was made on August 29, 2019 at an event presided over by President Trump in the White House Garden.

---

[7]The Boeing CST-100 Starliner (Crew Space Transportation-100) is a reusable crew capsule manufactured by Boeing as its participation in NASA's Commercial Crew Development (CCDev) program. Its primary purpose is to transport crew to the International Space Station (ISS) and to private space stations such as the proposed Bigelow Aerospace Commercial Space Station.

[8]SpaceX designs, manufactures, and launches advanced rockets and spacecraft. The company was founded in 2002 to revolutionize space technology, with the goal of enabling people to live on other planets.

[9]Blue Origin is a privately own aerospace company founded by Jeff Bezos in 2000 with idea to enable a future where millions of people are working in space to benefit the Earth.

The first flight of NASA's Space Launch System rocket and the new spacecraft Orion[10] will carry astronauts into deep space, and then return them home safely to Earth. On July 20, 2020, the 50th anniversary of the Apollo 11 moon landing, NASA confirmed that work on the Orion crew vehicle is complete. The reusable capsule is designed to carry up to six astronauts and is meant to offer "accommodation" for carrying humans to the Moon and other worlds. The crew capsule was scheduled to be launched in 2020, but the mission is now expected to fly for the first time in 2021. The first mission is going to be used to test the new spacecraft systems flying together for the first time, without crew, and the second flight will take astronauts on a flight test around the Moon.

The third flight of SLS and Orion will carry the first woman and the next man to the Moon in 2024. Together, Orion, SLS, and the Lunar Orbiting Platform Gateway, (LOP-G) represent the core of NASA's sustainable infrastructure for human exploration. The Lunar Orbiting Platform Gateway will enable crew expeditions down to the Moon surface, facilitating the exploration of new locations across the Moon. Gateway is also designed to operate autonomously as a deep space science outpost even without crew. Over time, the Lunar Orbiting Gateway will become a way station for the development of refueling depots, servicing platforms, and a facility for processing samples from the Moon and other bodies in support of science and commerce.

The SLS and Orion are critical to NASA's exploration plans at the Moon and beyond. The SLS is the world's most powerful rocket for sending humans on missions to deep space. Orion has built-in technologies that enable the crew and spacecraft to explore far into the solar system and it is specifically designed to keep humans alive hundreds of thousands of miles from home, where getting back to Earth takes days rather than hours.

## 4 Outer Space and NATO

NATO is the most successful defensive alliance in history. After more than 70 years, peace has been maintained in Europe and the end of the Cold War was achieved without armed confrontation. Furthermore, many of the countries that were members of the Warsaw Pact are now highly active members of the Atlantic Alliance. Given the current strategic situation, NATO must be alert to the multi-directional risks that characterize today's world and to those that may appear in the future. Traditional risks have been coupled with those involving terrorism, the proliferation of weapons of mass destruction, disruptive new technologies, failed states, and religious and political extremism. To the mentioned risks, we must add the others arising from

[10]NASA's Orion spacecraft is built to take humans farther than they have ever gone before. Orion will serve as the exploration vehicle that will carry the crew to space, provide emergency abort capability, sustain the crew during the space travel, and provide safe re-entry from deep space return velocities.

possible attacks on the storage, processing and transmission systems of data that work almost always in cyberspace. This circumstance has made cyber an operational domain to be considered in the comprehensive approach that any modern defensive organization and advanced nations need to have. Other emerging and disruptive technologies were considered by NATO Heads of State and Government at their meeting in London last December 2019, such as Big Data, Artificial Intelligence, robotics, space, and biotechnology.

This meeting (December 4, 2019 at the Grove Hotel, Hertfordshire), was initially presented as a summit celebrating the 70th anniversary of the Washington Treaty. However, it was downgraded to one session of the North Atlantic Council. The agenda was designed to avoid clashes between the US and its European allies. Space was formally acknowledged as a warfighting domain for the Alliance, following up on the 2016 pronouncement of cyber as a warfare domain. Besides, a new action plan was agreed to step up NATO's efforts in the fight against terrorism. NATO's leaders also agreed new security standards for telecommunications infrastructure, including 5G. In the London Declaration issued by the Heads of State and Government participating in the meeting, it can be read:

> 6. To stay secure, we must look to the future together. We are addressing the breadth and scale of new technologies to maintain our technological edge, while preserving our values and norms. We will continue to increase the resilience of our societies, as well as of our critical infrastructure and our energy security. NATO and Allies, within their respective authority, are committed to ensuring the security of our communications, including 5G, recognizing the need to rely on secure and resilient systems. We have declared space an operational domain for NATO, recognizing its importance in keeping us safe and tackling security challenges, while upholding international law. We are increasing our tools to respond to cyberattacks, and strengthening our ability to prepare for, deter, and defend against hybrid tactics that seek to undermine our security and societies. We are stepping up NATO's role in human security."
>
> NATO London Declaration, 4 December 2019

The London Declaration was the latest NATO statement in 2019 related to defense and space but, before it, NATO was already concerned about space and its defense. That is a clear sign of the importance that the space is taking and that, to avoid a war in space, it is a must to get ready to guarantee all nations free access and use of it.

## 5 NATO Space Policy

Space has facilitated and facilitates NATO's performance of numerous tasks, functions, missions, and operations both in peace and, if necessary, at war. Some of these functions are essential and could not be properly executed without space support, such as situational awareness and early warning, where the rapid identification of forces that may threaten allied borders is essential to deter or counter aggression. Similarly, space is essential for command, control, and communications, as well as for the deployment and monitoring of one's own forces. On the other hand, artificial satellites can detect missile launches and provide information on what other actors are doing on land, at sea, in the air, and in space. In any case, the use of space has a great impact on everyday life including communications, agriculture, weather forecasts, and broadcasting radio and television.

Since the Brussels Summit (July 2018), NATO's attention to space has been increasing dramatically. Paragraph 19 of the Declaration issued on July 11 after that meeting, states that:

> In the air domain, we have agreed a Joint Air Power Strategy, which is a key enabler for NATO's peacetime Air Policing and Ballistic Missile Defense missions. It will strengthen our Integrated Air and Missile Defense, and guide our aerospace capabilities to operate together jointly, more swiftly, and effectively in peacetime, crisis, and conflict. We also face new threats from cruise missiles and the proliferation of related technology as well as from new challenges, such as unmanned aerial vehicles, and will monitor developments that could affect Alliance security. Recognizing that space is a highly dynamic and rapidly evolving area, which is essential to a coherent Alliance deterrence and defense posture, we have agreed to develop an overarching NATO Space Policy.
>
> NATO Brussels Summit, 11 July 2018

A year later, on June 27, 2019, allied Defense Ministers approved the new Allied Space Policy: "(PO (2019) 0279 (INV)), NATO Overarching Space Policy", (NATO 2019). This document is the guide to the Alliance's activity in space, to take advantage of the opportunities it offers, and to respond to the challenges it presents. In a press conference following the meeting, Mr. Stoltenberg (2019) said:

> (…) it was not about militarizing space … We can play an important role as a forum for sharing information, increasing interoperability, and ensuring that our missions and operations can ask for the space support they need.
>
> Stoltenberg, 27 June 2019

Five months later, NATO Secretary General (Stoltenberg 2019) following the meeting of the North Atlantic Council at the level of Foreign Ministers on the 20th November 2019 said:

> Today, ministers took important decisions for NATO's continuing adaptation. We have agreed that space should be a new operational domain for NATO—alongside air, land, sea and cyber. Space is part of our daily life here on Earth. It can be used for peaceful purposes. But it can also be used aggressively. Satellites can be jammed, hacked or weaponized. Anti-satellite weapons could cripple communications and other services our societies rely on, such as air travel, weather forecast or banking.
>
> Space is also essential to the Alliance's deterrence and defense. Including the ability to navigate, to gather intelligence, and to detect missile launches. Around 2000 satellites currently orbit the Earth. And around half of them are owned by NATO countries. NATO has no intention to put weapons in space. We are a defensive Alliance.
>
> And our approach will remain fully in line with international law.
>
> But making space an operational domain will help us ensure that all aspects are considered to ensure the success of our missions. For instance, this can allow NATO planners to make requests for Allies to provide capabilities and services—such as hours of satellite communications or data for imagery.
>
> Stoltenberg, 20 November 2019

Although no further details about the NATO Overarching Space Policy emerged at the London meeting in December 2019, space was declared as an operational domain. This allows space to be used for military operations during times of war. However, NATO does not own or operate its own space systems that will remain under national control for the foreseeable future. Space support is provided by national resources of allies or by commercial services distributed by NATO agencies. Therefore, a coordination function is required to ensure that spatial support is continuous for the Alliance.

This support is provided through the Space Support Coordination (SpSC) feature that is structured into SpSC elements (SpSCE), located on some allied commands. On May 18, 2018, was signed the document "MC0670 Policy on Space Support in NATO Operations" which is the guide for organizing space support in the Alliance. A year later, as mentioned, NATO's new space policy was published. The SpSC plays a key role in allied tasks and operations and is part of the current operations divisions of various NATO commands. The role of SpSCE is defined in chapter five in the Allied Joint Publication 3.3 (AJP 3.3).5, NATO (2016). AJP 3.3 still requires more strategic guidance and currently speaks only to minor space-related subjects while other strategic documents are under development or still missing. To achieve the level of guidance that currently exists in major domains like Air, Land, Sea, and Cyber, Space will require advocacy at the highest levels within NATO.

The 64th Annual session of the NATO Parliamentary Assembly 2018 (NPA 2018) met in Halifax, Canada, from November 16-19, 2018. The parliamentarians approved Resolution 449 on "Opportunities and Challenges in a changing space arena". In the Resolution, the Assembly urges member governments and parliaments of the North Atlantic Alliance:

a. to work to ensure that space remains an arena of global cooperation despite its importance to national military and intelligence establishments.
b. to make a priority of establishing commonly shared rules and norms to provide more effective governance of the global commons in space, particularly as those commons grow more crowded with state and non-state actors.
c. to strengthen rules and norms that aim to minimize the problem of debris in orbits in which vital satellite systems are operating, including sharp restrictions on testing, and deploying anti-satellite weapons systems.
d. to deepen collaboration with private companies to ensure that their satellites are protected from any cyberattack.
e. to develop more effective fora engaging major players in space with the goal of fostering meaningful dialogue and decision making on space policy.
f. to encourage NATO to develop a focused space policy, interoperability and capability sharing across the Alliance, not because space will be the next frontier of conflict, but because NATO capabilities are increasingly dependent upon space-based assets.

The Resolution is an excellence guidance for the future approach of NATO to the use of space as an operational domain.

## 6 The EU and Space

When considering the EU's space capabilities, it is fair to recognize that the Union possesses world class capabilities in space, such as the Copernicus[11] and Galileo[12] systems, as well as a highly competitive industry. We can also consider that Europe's skills-base in the space sector is also a capability. Moreover, work is ongoing on various projects, such as Governmental Satellite Communications (GovSatCom) and two projects under the PESCO[13] framework: participating member states are developing an EU Radio Navigation Solution (EURAS) and a European Military Space Surveillance Awareness Network (EU-SSA-N). Nevertheless, most experts seem to agree that the EU requires greater investments in space capabilities and critical infrastructure protection.

The Conclusions adopted by the Council of the EU at its meeting on May 28, 2019, on "Space as an enabler"[14] (EU Council 2019), reflect the importance that the EU attaches to everything related to outer space. Other key documents of the EU related to space are: the Convention establishing a European Space Agency of May 30, 1975 as well as the Framework Agreement between the European Community and the European Space Agency (ESA 2020) which entered into force in May 2004 and was subsequently renewed. This framework agreement calls for regular joint and concomitant meetings of the Council of the European Union and the ESA Council at the ministerial level, known as the Space Council.

The above mentioned EU Council Conclusions, adopted by the Council at its meeting n May 28, 2019, EU Council (2019) underline the role of space as an enabler in achieving social, and economic benefits, expanding the boundaries of knowledge and supporting decision-makers and formulating policies in developing, implement and monitor sectoral policies. In addition, space contributes to the implementation of the 2030 Agenda and its objectives in sustainable development, industry, transport, maritime sector, agriculture, cultural heritage, rural development, forestry and fisheries, digitalization, and security and defense. Other Conclusions recognize that Europe needs to maintain safe, autonomous, reliable, cost-effective, and affordable access to space. In addition, the strategic importance of independent access to space and of contributing to the innovative and competitive spirit of the European space sector that reinforces Europe's role at the global level is reiterated.

---

[11]Copernicus, previously known as GMES (Global Monitoring for Environment and Security), is the European program for the establishment of a European capacity for Earth Observation.

[12]Galileo is Europe's Global Navigation Satellite System (GNSS), providing improved positioning and timing information with significant positive implications for many European services and users.

[13]PESCO is a framework and process to deepen defense cooperation between those EU Member States who are capable and willing to do so. PESCO was Introduced by the Lisbon Treaty (article 42.6, 46 and Protocol 10). 25 EU Member States have joined PESCO and subscribed to more binding commitments to invest, plan, develop and operate defense capabilities more together, within the Union framework.

[14]The Conclusions include the European Union documents on space starting with Articles 4 and 189 of the Treaty on the Functioning of the EU, which establish EU competence in this area.

The European External Action Service (EEAS) is starting a new effort to promote the need for sustainable space operations. Carine Claeys, Special Envoy for Space and Head of the EEAS Space Task Force, during a panel discussion at "Euroconsult's World Satellite Business Week"[15] that took place in Paris in September 2019, said:

> "The safety, security and sustainability of Outer Space (3SOS) public diplomacy (of the EEAS) initiative, will promote "ethical conduct" in space amid concerns about orbital debris.
>
> Claeys, Carine, September 2019

The Safety, Security, and Sustainability of Outer Space (3SOS) effort is triggered by the belief that low Earth orbits are becoming increasingly crowded with satellites and debris, a situation that will be aggravated by the deployment of mega constellations of satellites. Claeys (2019) called for some degree of space traffic management to avoid collisions, like placing transponders on satellites to better locate and identify them. That effort could include sharing of space situational awareness data and an "obligation" for satellites to deorbit themselves at the end of their lives.

Initially, 3SOS will focus on discussions with industry, space agencies, and think tanks, to build a common understanding of the issue and potential solutions. That would build on existing efforts, like the 21 space sustainability guidelines approved by the United Nations' Committee on the Peaceful Uses of Outer Space, UN COPUOS (2019) in June 2019. That effort does not include now imposing new regulations on satellite operators based in EU nations, out of concerns that such rules could put those companies at a competitive disadvantage. There is consensus among experts that the only way to preserve fair competition good behavior, and common understanding must be applied at the world level. Today, the avoidance process between two operational satellites is largely manual and ad hoc and will no longer be practical as the number of alerts rises with the increase in spaceflight. ESA is proposing an automated risk estimation and mitigation initiative as part of its space safety activities. This will provide and demonstrate the types of technology needed to automate the collision avoidance process, allowing machine generated, coordinated, and conflict-free decisions to speed up the entire process to protect vital space infrastructure in the future.

## 7 Nations and Space

Not only multinational organizations are concerned about their role in outer space but also the most advanced nations. See below some recent development related to space in four countries.

[15] Governmental Satellite Communications (GovSatCom) has been defined as one of the four capability development programs by the European Council in December 2013. The mandate was given to prepare the next generation of satellite communication (2025 timeframe).

## 7.1 France

French President Emmanuel Macron addressing military personnel a day before the Bastille Day parade of 2019, announced a new development in the organization of the Armed Forces: the creation of a space service. Space will not be a stand-alone service. It will be the Air Force that will "eventually" assume this responsibility, becoming the Air and Space Service. In his words, the President thus endorsed the "new military space doctrine" presented by his minister Florence Parly a few weeks earlier. This will "enable France to defend space and from the space." The new command has two objectives: to "strengthen our knowledge of space activity" and "to better protect our satellites, including actively." He considers a necessity to be present in the "new zones of confrontation" that have become the cyber and the exo-atmospheric or out of the atmosphere. And the French president to promise new "indispensable" investments. France has a 2019–2025 military spending plan that allocates 3.6 billion euros ($4 billion) to defense in space. As a matter of fact, France's declared interest in boosting its military readiness in space follows increased spending and interest in the area by the United States, China, and Russia.

## 7.2 Japan

On 18 May 2020, Japan launched its new space defense unit to monitor and counter threats to the country's satellites. The Space Operations Squadron, part of Japan's Air Self-defense Force, starts with 20 members and is expected to grow to about 100 members once the unit is fully operational in 2023. The role of the unit is mainly to monitor and protect Japanese satellites from enemy attacks or space debris. It will also conduct satellite-based navigation and communications for other units in the field. The launch of the new unit comes amid growing Japanese concern that China and Russia are seeking ways to interfere, disable or destroy satellites. The formation of the unit, which is set to be based at the JASDF's Fuchu Air Base in western Tokyo comes after the Ministry of Défense (MoD) secured JPY50.6 billion (USD460 million) from the Japanese Cabinet in December 2019 for space-related defense activities and programs, including the establishment of the space squadron.

## 7.3 Spain

Three national strategies on aerospace, civil protection, and cybersecurity have been launched recently by Spain. At the approval of the National Aerospace Security Strategy (2019) in a meeting of the National Security Council of Spain on April 12, 2019, Prime Minister Pedro Sánchez highlighted the importance of aerospace security, "because they define Spain's position on the governance of two key spaces for our security: air space and outer space".

Few countries have a security strategy that focuses on the control of outer space and fewer still have similar documents that join, in a single strategy, the analysis of security contingencies in both air space, and outer space. Both air space and outer space, which are open and without visible borders, connect the world and allow for the free movement of people, goods, services, information, and ideas. Their military, economic, industrial, and communication implications explain why the development of this National Aerospace Security Strategy presents such a key step. The strategy contains the main threats in this field: armed conflicts, terrorist actions, espionage, cyber threats, the proliferation of weapons of mass destruction, and the growing use of unmanned aircraft for illegal purposes. It also defines the measures to combat, reduce, and neutralize these threats.

## *7.4 United States of America*

A recent significant sign of renewed U.S.A. interest in outer space has been the restoration of Space Command as a unified combatant command. The announcement was made on August 29, 2019, at an event presided over by Donald Trump in the White House garden. On 14 October 2019, the NATO Military Committee's meeting was dedicated to space with a briefing by General John Raymond, Commander of the newly re-established US Space Command. General Raymond provided a briefing on the ongoing activities of the re-established Command. The Deputy Chairman of NATO Military Committee, US Lieutenant General Scott Kindsvater (2019) started the meeting by introducing NATO's approach to space, highlighting NATO's newly agreed space policy:

> In June 2019, Defense Ministers agreed NATO's first-ever space policy. They recognized that space is part of our daily lives, and while it can be used for peaceful purposes, it can also be used for aggression. Satellites can be hacked, jammed, or weaponized. Anti-satellite weapons could cripple communications. It is therefore important that we are vigilant and resilient – also in space.
>
> General Kindsvater, Deputy Chairman NATO MC, 14 October 2019

The USA have had a Space Command from 1985 until 2002 when it was dissolved. The command was re-established in August 2019 and will focus on the protection of US space assets and strengthen the military's posture in space. General Raymond (2019) explained that:

> Space has become a vital domain that is critical to the nation's security and economy and is no longer a benign environment. Though this command we will get better space intelligence by working more closely with foreign allies, with the US intelligence community and with commercial companies. Our goal is to deter conflict, but we need to be ready if deterrence fails.
>
> General Raymond, Commander US Space Command, 14 October 2019

Lieutenant General Kindsvater, concluded the session adding that NATO doesn't want to militarize space, but to play an important role as a forum to share information, to increase interoperability, and to ensure that NATO missions and operations can call and get the support they need, also in space.

## 8 Final Remarks

Recent developments related to the exploration and use of outer space, stress the importance of outer space can play in the future of Humanity. Outer space can be an enabler, (EU Council 2019), for social and economic benefits, for expanding the frontiers of knowledge, in particular in science, technology and applications, and for supporting decision and policy makers in developing, implementing and monitoring some sectoral policies, inter alia energy, public health, environment, climate change, industry, transport, maritime, agriculture, cultural heritage, rural development, forestry, and fishery, digitalization, security, and defense. It is also important to stress that space significantly contributes and will contribute to achieve the 17 Sustainable Development Goals and 169 targets of the 2030 Agenda of the United Nations, UN (2015). Space also plays an essential in global diplomacy and in inspiring and motivating the next generations.

The role of the outer space is already particularly important for the development of Humanity and it may be soon more accessible than ever. New launch vehicles will lower the cost of space access and outer space will be more congested and competitive. The expanded competition is increasing the fears of conflict out there.

NATO has made clear that the declaration of space as an operational domain "it is not about militarization of space" (Stoltenberg 2019) but "Space is part of our daily life here on Earth. It can be used for peaceful purposes. But it can also be used aggressively. Satellites can be jammed, hacked or weaponized. Anti-satellite weapons could cripple communications and other services our societies rely on, such as air travel, weather forecast or banking." (Stoltenberg 2019), For that reason, the implementation of Resolution 449 of the NATO Parliamentary Assembly 2018, (NPA 2018), will help to take advantage of the opportunities and to answer the challenges in a changing outer space arena.

Finally, having in consideration the technological advances and some gaps in the Outer Space Treaty, it will be very fruitful to revise and update the Treaty. Some international associations and organizations have elaborated proposals on how armed conflict in space can be prevented by a rigorous arms control regime. Always having in mind, the right of self-defense, also in the outer space.

## References

Claeys, C. (2019). *Euroconsult's world satellite business week*, Sept 2019. http://www.spaceagenda.com/events/detail/2019-09-10_euroconsult-world-satellite-business-week.
ESA. (2020). *Science and exploration*. https://www.esa.int/Science_Exploration.
EU Council. (2019). *Council of the EU conclusions on "Space as an enabler"*. http://data.consilium.europa.eu/doc/document/ST-9248-2019-INIT/en/pdf.
Encyclopedia Britannica online. (2005). https://www.britannica.com/science/dark-matter.
FAI. (2009). *FAI Sporting code section 8—Astronautics*. https://www.fai.org/sites/default/files/documents/sporting_code_section_8_edition_2009.pdf.
Kindsvater, S. (2019). *NATO military committee's meeting*, 14 October 2019. https://www.nato.int/cps/en/natohq/news_169643.htm.
Moon. (1979). *Agreement governing the activities of states on the moon and other celestial bodies*. http://www.unoosa.org/oosa/en/ourwork/spacelaw/treaties/intromoon-agreement.html.
NASA. (2020). Release 20-078, August 2, 2020. https://www.nasa.gov/press-release/nasa-astronauts-safely-splash-down-after-first-commercial-crew-flight-to-space-station.
NATO. (2016). *AJP 3.3. Allied joint doctrine for air and space operations*, actual version dated April 2016. https://standards.globalspec.com/std/10006249/AJP-3.3.
NATO. (2019a). *PO (2019)0279 (INV)) NATO overarching space policy*. https://www.japcc.org/space-support-in-nato-operations.
NPA. (2018). *64th NATO parliamentary assembly (2018)*, 16–19 November 2018, https://www.nato-pa.int/node/18611.
Raymond, J. (2019). *NATO military committee's meeting*, 14 October 2019. https://www.nato.int/cps/en/natohq/news_169643.htm.
Spanish National Aerospace Security Strategy. (2019). www.dsn.gov.es/file/3184.
Stoltenberg, J. (2019b). *Press conference after a meeting of the North Atlantic council at the level of foreign ministers on the 20th November 2019*. https://www.nato.int/cps/fr/natohq/opinions_171022.htm.
Stoltenberg, J. (2019a). *Press conference after the meeting of the NAC at the level of ministers of Defense*, 27 June 2019. https://www.nato.int/cps/en/natohq/opinions_167245.htm.
UN. (2015). *Transforming our world: The 2030 Agenda for Sustainable development*. https://sustainabledevelopment.un.org/content/documents/21252030%20Agenda%20for%20Sustainable%20Development%20web.pdf.
UN. (1967). *Treaty on principles governing the activities of states in the exploration and use of outer space*. http://www.unoosa.org/oosa/en/ourwork/spacelaw/treaties/introouterspacetreaty.html.
UN COUPOS. (2019). *United Nations' committee on the peaceful uses of outer space*. http://www.unoosa.org/oosa/en/ourwork/copuos/index.html.
Zarya.info. (2020). *Soviet, Russian and international space flight*. http://www.zarya.info/Diaries/StationsDOS/Salyut1.php.

**Federico Yaniz** joined the Air Force Academy and in 1986 he graduated as Staff Officer and was assigned to the Air Force Staff. In 1991, After receiving his diploma as Joint Staff officer in 1991, he got a planning position at the Joint Staff of Armed Forces. In the summer of 1993, he joined the International Military Staff at NATO Headquarters. After being promoted to General in 1997, he was appointed Chief of the Second Division of the Joint Staff of the Armed Forces. In June 2001, he was elected Assistant Director of the International Military Staff for Cooperation and Regional Security. During those four years he was highly active in implementing NATO initiatives Partnership for Peace and the NATO's Mediterranean Dialog. In 2006, he was appointed Director of the *Museo de Aeronáutica y Astronáutica*.

General Yaniz has a Doctor degree in *Ciencias de la Empresa*, a Master in Statistics plus other diplomas and qualifications. He obtained a degree in Journalism in 1973 and is an experienced journalist. He is the author of six books, has collaborated in many others and has written more than 300 articles related with Strategy, Aeronautics, Economics and History. Doctor Yaniz belongs to several nonprofit associations and he is vice-president of *Eurodefense-España* and member of the Board of the Atlantic Council of Spain. He has a monthly section on the Air Force magazine on NATO affairs and the Common Security and Defense Policy (CSDP) of the European Unión. Dr. Yaniz is highly active on strategic issues and he has made many presentations and has given many lectures on European defense matters, NATO affairs and Aviation history. Since May 2019, he is a member of the Academy of Military Arts and Sciences (ACAMI).

# Arms Control in Outer Space: A Diplomatic Alternative to Star Wars

**Paul Meyer**

**Abstract** Outer space enjoys a special status under the 1967 *Outer Space Treaty* as a realm "beyond national appropriation or claim of sovereignty", a "global commons" in which exploration and use should be "for the benefit and in the interests of all countries". This foundational treaty has allowed for half a century of ever expanding peaceful activity in space, free from man-made threats. Ironically, just as satellite launches are increasing exponentially to deliver a vast spectrum of services to humanity, we are witnessing a revival of confrontational approaches on the part of leading powers, one of which has formally designated outer space as a "war-fighting domain" in which military superiority over rivals is sought. There are diplomatic alternatives to the bellicose postures being adopted by some states. For cooperative security options to prevail however will require strong advocacy by concerned states and other stakeholders. If they fail to act their own interests and those of global security and well-being will be put in jeopardy.

**Keywords** Outer space treaty · Space arms control · Space security · Space diplomacy · UN · ASAT

## 1 Introduction

Outer space is an environment that has long captured the imagination of humanity. While many had dreamt of accessing it, it was only in 1957 that our "space age" was initiated with the launch into orbit of *Sputnik 1* by the Soviet Union. The United States (US) and the Soviet Union (USSR) -the two contending superpowers of the day- were soon engaged in a broad competition to send satellites and eventually crewed space

In: Security and the Global Commons, Edited by J. Martin Ramirez, and Bartolomé Bauzá-Abril. © 2021 Springer International. Submitted: October, 22, 2020; Accepted: November, 2, 2020.

P. Meyer (✉)
School for International Studies, Simon Fraser University, 7200-515 West Hastings Street, Vancouver, BC V6B 5K3, Canada
e-mail: pmeyer@sfu.ca



J. M. Ramírez and B. Bauzá-Abril (eds.), *Security in the Global Commons and Beyond*, Advanced Sciences and Technologies for Security Applications,
https://doi.org/10.1007/978-3-030-67973-6_6

craft into orbit. The moon landing of 1969 was a historic achievement that people everywhere took pride in. These initial years of space activity manifested a spirit of scientific enquiry and international cooperation even if the military potential of outer space was being explored in parallel by the two leading space-faring nations.

Other states however were also showing interest in outer space and despite their adversarial relationship, both the US and the USSR found it expedient to develop a legal framework for the exploration and use of outer space. Building on a series of United Nations (UN) General Assembly resolutions setting out principles for space activity adopted in the early 1960s, a treaty was negotiated and concluded in 1967 that provided a multilaterally agreed basis for interacting with outer space.

## 2 The *Outer Space Treaty* Regime

The *Outer Space Treaty* is one of the great achievements of multilateral diplomacy that deserves more appreciation than it receives. With 110 states parties it is a widely supported treaty that has established a benign and cooperative legal regime for the exploration and use of outer space that has provided massive benefits to the international community. The treaty affords outer space the special status of a 'global commons' ("the province of all mankind" in the language of the treaty) which cannot be subject "to national appropriation by claim of sovereignty, by means of use or occupation or by any other means" (OOSA 1967). The treaty recognizes the "common interest in exploration and use of outer space for peaceful purposes" and prescribes that states parties shall carry out their activities in outer space "for the benefit and in the interests of all countries".

The treaty's intent to promote peaceful uses of outer space is manifested in several ways. State parties are adjoined to carry out space activities "in the interest of maintaining international peace and security and promoting international cooperation and understanding". Article IV of the treaty prohibits placing nuclear weapons or other weapons of mass destruction in outer space and specifies that the Moon and celestial bodies should be used "exclusively for peaceful purposes", and that on them "military bases, fortifications, weapons testing, or military manoeuvres shall be forbidden". Pro-active consultations are stipulated in the event that any planned activity in outer space might result in "harmful interference" with the activity of another state party.

International cooperation is a refrain that runs throughout the treaty. Astronauts are to be treated as "envoys of mankind" and there is a clear obligation for states parties to share the results of their explorations with the UN Secretary General (for dissemination to the member states) as well as with the international scientific community. Cooperative measures such as the observation of space launches and visits to space-related installations are to be offered to the representatives of other states parties on the basis of equality and reciprocity. The treaty speaks to "the better angels of our nature" and reflects to some degree the general excitement and eagerness for international scientific cooperation that transcended the ideological divisions of the Cold War era.

The *Outer Space Treaty* was quickly followed over the next few years by four other supplementary treaties on *Rescue* (1968), *Liability* (1972), *Registration* (1976) and the *Moon Agreement* (1984), which together comprise the five core UN treaties governing outer space.

Although this cooperative framework was vital for the exploration and use of outer space, several states were also developing military capabilities for space that were pressing against the "peaceful purposes" orientation of the *Outer Space Treaty*. This trend in state practice was accommodated within the confines of the treaty by affirming that military uses of space could be characterized as peaceful uses as long as they were "non-aggressive" in nature. Given the limited numbers of space-faring nations at the time, this interpretation can be seen as a concession to the military pursuit of space-based capabilities in order to maintain an inclusive and cooperatively oriented legal regime to govern most of the activity in outer space.

## 3 External Events and the Evolution of Policy

The relatively benign situation with respect to outer space began to change in the early 1980s with the advent of military space programs that envisioned the placement of missile platforms in orbit. The most prominent of these was President Reagan's Strategic Defense Initiative (SDI) announced in 1983 and almost immediately tagged as the "Star Wars" initiative. Reagan's vision of a space-based ballistic missile defence system that would act as a shield for the American homeland generated much criticism, for reasons of costs, doubtful effectiveness and contravening the principle of mutual vulnerability that had underpinned the "strategic stability" relationship between the nuclear superpowers.

Disquiet over emerging technological advances that might give significant military advantage to an adversary power had led the Soviet Union in 1981 to introduce a new item on "The Prevention of an Arms Race in Outer Space (PAROS)" to the agenda of the UN General Assembly. The Soviet Union presented as well a draft treaty prohibiting the placement of weapons in outer space. The addition to the General Assembly's agenda and a subsequent direction to the Conference on Disarmament (CD) to negotiate an international agreement on PAROS was supported by UN member states which didn't want to see the terrestrial arms race between the two superpowers be extended into outer space.

Subsequent action by the CD which placed PAROS on its own agenda in 1982 and established in 1985 an Ad Hoc Committee to work on the issue was never able to overcome differences between the Western and Eastern camps (with the West wanting to focus on an agreement banning anti-satellite weapons (ASAT) whereas the Eastern camp preferred a more comprehensive agreement to preserve the peaceful status of outer space). Not only was the scope of the potential agreement in contention throughout, the West also wanted to keep the mandate of the Ad Hoc Committee on PAROS, one of *discussion* rather than *negotiation*. The Ad Hoc Committee continued to meet until 1994 when it fell victim to a wider dispute over a Programme of Work which has kept the CD in gridlock ever since. The difficulties experienced in these early efforts at developing a PAROS-relevant accord foreshadowed what was to come later (Meyer 2011).

Despite the disagreements and limited output of the CD, the declaratory policy of the international community regarding PAROS found clear and regular expression through an annual resolution on the subject adopted by the UN General Assembly since 1981, with Egypt and Sri Lanka as the traditional sponsors. This resolution clearly sets out the key objectives of the member states as regards outer space security. It asserts that "further measures should be examined in the search for effective and verifiable bilateral and multilateral agreements in order to prevent an arms race in outer space, including the weaponization of outer space". Reaffirming "the importance and urgency" of preventing such an arms race, which would represent a grave threat to international peace and security the resolution notes "that the legal regime applicable to outer space by itself does not guarantee the prevention of an arms race in outer space, ... [and] that there is a need to consolidate and reinforce that regime and enhance its effectiveness..." (UNGA 2019).

The General Assembly's PAROS resolution receives near universal support from states each year. At the UNGA session in 2019 it was adopted by a vote of 183 "yes", 2 "no" (US and Israel) and no abstentions. In 2018, signalling a hardening of its position the US shifted to a "no" vote after a decade of only registering an abstention on the resolution (USUN 2018). While the dissent of the leading space power detracts from the authority of the PAROS resolution its consistent strong support over the decades suggests that at least at the level of declaratory policy the international community wants to see further action on PAROS and the weaponization of space and considers the current legal regime of the Outer Space Treaty not sufficient to ensure this goal.

## 4 The Deteriorating Strategic Outlook

Although the demise of SDI had removed the immediate threat of weapons in space, the abrogation of the Anti-Ballistic Missile (ABM) Treaty by the Bush Administration in 2002 eliminated the legal prohibition on space-based ABM systems contained within it. The long-latent threat of a renewal of the ASAT testing that had been practiced by the two superpowers in the 1980s was manifested in 2007 with the surprise ASAT test by China at an altitude that resulted in considerable enduring space debris. The US demonstrated its ASAT capability in the destruction of one of its own satellites the next year, although at a much lower altitude that minimized debris. In 2019, India followed suit with a similar ASAT test employing a direct ascent missile. The spectre of destructive ASAT tests exacerbating the already worrisome problem of space debris in Low Earth Orbit (LEO) brought attention to the lack of real progress in realizing the goals of the PAROS resolution, despite the apparent near universal support for these aims.

The 2019 Indian ASAT test reflects a growing trend among the leading space-faring powers to develop militarily significant counter space capabilities. In addition to the direct ascent missile "kinetic-kill" ASATs employed in the Chinese, American and Indian tests, other counter space capabilities include co-orbital systems, lasers and other directed energy systems, electronic warfare and cyber operations. Investments in research and development of these non-debris generating systems reflect the general concern over contributing to the existing debris problem, but not to the extent of abandoning physically destructive systems altogether. In its comprehensive open-source assessment, the US NGO *Secure World Foundation*, concludes: "The evidence shows significant research and development of a broad range of kinetic (i.e. destructive) and non-kinetic counter space capabilities in multiple countries. However, only non-kinetic capabilities are actively being used in current military operations." The assessment however also asserts that "Today there are increased incentives for development, and potential use, of offensive counter space capabilities." (Weeden 2019).

The break down in the US-Russian strategic relationship became acute in the aftermath of the Ukrainian intervention and Crimea annexation in 2014. Normal strategic and military- to- military dialogues were suspended and the US in its public pronouncements became increasingly critical of Russian and Chinese space activities. This trend has been particularly salient under the Trump Administration which adopted a declaratory policy that characterizes outer space as a "war-fighting domain" in which the US military is to seek "dominance". The *National Space Strategy (NSS)* released in March 2018, was the first such official US strategy to employ this characterization of outer space. President Trump's subsequent decision to establish a "Space Force" as a separate, branch of the armed forces was in keeping with this new, more explicitly militarized vision of space. In its initial doctrinal statement, the Space Force has declared that "Humankind has changed, and our potential adversaries have significantly increased the likelihood of warfare in the space domain". The Space Force goes on to assert that "Just like warfare in any other domains, space war foresees a violent clash of opposing wills". (US Space Force 2020).

## 5 Diplomatic Efforts to Date

The repeated calls for renewed work at the CD and the development of additional measures to reinforce the legal regime for space, contained in the PAROS resolution have not translated into significant action. As is often the case in multilateral diplomacy, it seems to take dramatic external developments to spur the initiation of diplomatic proposals for space security.

It is not a coincidence that the principal diplomatic proposals on space security originated around the 2007–2008 timeframe that witnessed the revival of ASAT testing by major space powers. Although none of these proposals have been realized, it is important to review them in order to appreciate the nature of the opposition to them and what might be feasible in the future. The four specific proposals to be examined are: (i) the Sino-Russian draft treaty on *The Prevention of the Placement of Weapons in Outer Space, the Threat or Use of Force against Space Objects (PPWT)* first tabled at the CD in 2008 with a revised version in 2014; (ii) the EU initiated *International Code of Conduct on Outer Space Activities (ICoC)* first issued in 2008; (iii) Canadian proposals for space security confidence-building measures and "pledges" presented at the CD in 2007 and 2009; and (iv) two UN Group of Governmental Experts (GGE), the first to consider Transparency and Confidence Building Measures (TCBMs) which operated in 2012–2013 and the second to examine possible legal elements of a PAROS agreement, which ran from 2018 to 2019. The first GGE managed to produce a consensus report whereas the second GGE concluded in 2019 without being able to issue a report.

(a) *Prevention of placement of weapons in outer space treaty (PPWT)*

The only major proposal for a legally binding agreement for space security is the Sino-Russian draft treaty on the "Prevention of Placement of Weapons in Outer Space and of the threat or use of force against outer space objects" (PPWT). The PPWT was formally tabled at the CD in 2008, although its antecedents there date back to 2002 as a Sino-Russian response to the US withdrawal from the ABM Treaty. After some preliminary responses China and Russia submitted a revised version of the proposed treaty in June 2014 (CD 2008, 2014). Its sponsors have repeatedly said that they would welcome further discussion of the draft text, but given the lack of an agreed program of work at the CD and the absence of a consensus to re-establish an Ad Hoc Committee on its PAROS agenda item, there has been no subsidiary body at the CD to pursue official work on this proposal. For their part and despite frequent references to their proposal in statements on space security, China and Russia have been unwilling to take the draft treaty outside the CD for consideration. As a result, the PPWT remains in a form of suspended animation with diminishing prospects for the initiation of any official work on it in this forum as the CD has been unable to negotiate any new agreement since the conclusion of the Comprehensive Test Ban Treaty of 1996.

Since the tabling of the PPWT, the chief official action undertaken at the CD has been a critical analysis of the draft treaty submitted by the United States and a rebuttal of that criticism offered by China and Russia (CD 2008, 2009). The US criticism focused on the lack of verification provisions in the PPWT and its inadequate scope given its failure to cover terrestrial anti-satellite weapons (ASATs). The rebuttal argued that it is not feasible at this stage to verify a wider weapons ban, but only a prohibition on placement of space weapons and the use of force against space objects, although it foresaw the possibility of elaborating verification measures in the future. With regard to terrestrial ASATs, the Sino-Russian rebuttal asserted that the treaty's ban on the use of force against space objects would preclude the use of such weapons and should therefore eliminate the incentive to develop and deploy them. The Sino-Russian paper also hints at the major problem posed by missile defences with their inherent anti-satellite capability that would arise if an effort was made to cover terrestrial based ASATs in a treaty.

The impasse over the PPWT also reflects an underlying and on-going debate regarding the acceptability of legally binding arms control accords in the present geopolitical context. While the US continues to state that it is not opposed to space arms control agreements in principle it appears to be so in practice, having made no proposal of its own or endorsed any other. Recently, the State Department has issued a policy statement on the subject of outer space arms control, authored by Assistant Secretary of State Christopher A. Ford that describes space arms control as an "insoluble problem". Ford argues that a variety of factors, including problems in defining a "space weapon" and the lack of adequate verification capabilities preclude engaging in genuine arms control. He is particularly hostile to the PPWT, stating that its "...defects are thus simultaneously structural, insoluble and apparently intentional. This draft treaty is therefore not 'arms control' worthy of the name, and the world deserves better." (Ford 2020). In keeping with long-standing US positions, Ford offers no proposals of his own for 'worthy' arms control, although expressing openness towards possible TCBMs and suggesting that agreeing on norms governing proximity operations in space might be a place to start.

China and Russia in continuing to champion the PPWT as the route to follow reflect their longstanding preference for legally binding instruments when addressing international security matters. While Russia and China have acknowledged a potential role of TCBMs as a complement to legally binding agreements on space security, they are no substitutes for such agreements. As the experience with the 2018–2019 GGE will show, efforts to find alternative means to promote legally binding instruments have not succeeded and unless there is some means of bridging this gap in positions amongst leading space powers, it will be difficult to make progress on space security via the elaboration of new legally binding multilateral agreements.

(b) *The EU-International code of conduct for outer space activities*

This EU proposal, initially put forward in 2008 consisted of a set of voluntary measures, some re-packaged, some newly minted, which represented an effort (in the words of the preamble) "to safeguard the continued peaceful and sustainable use of outer space for current and future generations" (EU 2014).

Due in part to the complex intra-EU negotiations that gave rise to the initiative as well as several personnel changes in the European External Action Service, the diplomatic management of the consultation process with other concerned states proved to be lengthy and problem plagued. While the tempo and extent of consultations were increased in the 2013–2014 timeframe, the attitude of several non-European spacefaring states towards the EU's handling of the initiative had cooled significantly, although the idea of an international code of conduct as such was supported in principle.

Despite the signals of dissatisfaction on the part of several states, the EU decided that the draft ICoC was ready for a last round of multilateral negotiations to finalize and adopt the text. This meeting, convened in New York, July 27–31, 2015, however failed to produce the desired outcome. In particular, the states of the BRICS grouping (Brazil, Russia, India, China and South Africa) expressed major dissent. The BRICS issued a joint statement stipulating that "the elaboration of such an instrument should be held in the format of inclusive and consensus-based multilateral negotiations within the framework of the UN, based on a proper and unequivocal mandate, without specific deadlines and taking into account the interests of all States" (BRICS 2015).

Although the EU voiced its disappointment that this attempt to finalize the text of the ICoC had proven impossible after so much preparation, they did not seek a new UN-mandate for an open-ended negotiation process at the UN General Assembly, despite the fact that the Chair's summary of the July meeting recommended that course of action. While the ICoC had some promising content (e.g. provision for institutional support and biennial meetings of states) for the time being the ICoC remains in a diplomatic limbo with no state willing to champion it.

(c) *Canadian proposals on the Non-weaponization of Outer Space*

Canada has traditionally been diplomatically active in pursuit of the goal of the non-weaponization of outer space. In his address to the UN General Assembly in 2004, Prime Minister Paul Martin stated: "What a tragedy it would be if space became one big weapons arsenal and the scene of a new arms race. In 1967, the United Nations agreed that weapons of mass destruction must not be based in space. The time has come to extend this ban to all weapons." (Canada 2004).

Canada followed up on this political direction with specific proposals on outer space security in working papers submitted to the CD in 2007 and 2009. In the earlier paper, Canada proposed that: (i) states make better use of the confidence building measures contained in existing accords such as the Outer Space Treaty and the Hague Code of Conduct; (ii) a moratorium on ASAT tests be agreed and (iii) space situational awareness be conducted through a multilateral monitoring centre. In the 2009 paper, Canada suggested that states unilaterally commit to specific security "pledges"; namely, a pledge not to place weapons in outer space, not to engage in destructive ASAT testing and not to use a satellite as a weapon. (Canada 2007, 2009). These ideas were pitched as a middle ground between a legally binding agreement like the PPWT on the one hand and the "security-lite" character of the voluntary measures contained in the EU code on the other. Although these ideas were in keeping with Canada's usual effort at "bridge building" amongst contending positions, they received little traction at the UN and Canada failed to vigorously promote them. In 2020 Canada has reiterated, in statements to the CD and the UN General Assembly, its earlier suggestion advocating the negotiation of a ban on destructive ASAT tests (Canada 2020).

(d) *The UN groups of governmental experts (GGE) 2013 and 2019*

The UN General Assembly occasionally has recourse to the GGE mechanism that allows for an emerging armaments problem to be studied by a small, but representative, group of states. It normally entails 15–20 government nominated experts meeting for a few weeks over a two-year term and producing a consensus report at the end if they can all agree on one. Space security has been the subject of two such GGEs, one in the 2012–2013 period looking at Transparency and Confidence Building Measures (TCBMs) and another in the 2018–2019 timeframe that considered possible legal elements of a PAROS agreement. The consensus report on

TCBMs issued in 2013 generated a set of recommendations that could contribute to confidence building amongst states (UNGA 2013). These recommended measures included information exchange on national policies, notification of space activities, visits to space launch sites and a variety of consultative mechanisms. However, by the time the GGE report was presented to the CD and the General Assembly the geopolitical climate had worsened and there was little take-up of the GGE's recommendations. The 2018–2019 GGE appeared to have made good progress initially and there was an expectation that it would also be able to produce a substantive report, but at the eleventh-hour agreement was not forthcoming as the US representative on the group denied consensus. This rejection seemed motivated by a general antipathy towards legally binding measures, rather than opposition to any particular element of the report the group had prepared.

## 6 Possible Diplomatic Options for the Future

The previous section provided a brief history of what diplomatic proposals for space security have been previously tried and have failed to come to fruition. This section will consider some possible options for the future which may have better success. The four options suggested are: (i) an Optional Protocol to the *Outer Space Treaty* that will extend the ban on WMD to all forms of weaponry; (ii) a ban on destructive ASATs (and/or ASAT testing) that create debris in space; (iii) a revival of negotiations on an International Code of Conduct for Outer Space Activities via a multilateral process under a UN General Assembly mandate; and (iv) an agreement on one or more TCBMs that would help restore a degree of confidence amongst space-faring nations.

These options are not mutually exclusive, and work could progress on one or more in parallel if there was a willingness on the part of states to engage. Each of these options will be assessed in turn.

(a) *Optional protocol to the outer space treaty*

This proposal would entail the negotiation of an Optional Protocol to the *Outer Space Treaty* that would extend that treaty's prohibition on placing WMD into space to include all forms of weapons. An Optional Protocol is a legally binding instrument that supplements an existing treaty. One of the benefits of an Optional Protocol is that it does not require any modification or amendment of the underlying treaty. As there could well be concern amongst states parties to any opening up of the *Outer Space Treaty,* having a supplement to it in keeping with its broad goal of preserving space for "peaceful purposes" should appeal to states who favour a legally binding versus politically binding status for any new measure concerning space security.

Signing on to such an Optional Protocol would also be a concrete way of implementing the long-standing call of the PAROS resolution to prevent the weaponization of space by concluding "further measures". The simple focus of the Optional Protocol should also make its negotiation relatively easy via a multilateral process authorized by a General Assembly resolution or through an ad hoc diplomatic conference.

Among the objections that might be raised to this option is that it would not be possible to agree on a definition of a "space weapon" given the inherent "dual-use" nature of items in orbit which makes every screwdriver a potential weapon. Arms control has had to contend with many similar "dual-use" situations in the development of prohibition treaties (the Chemical Weapons Convention is but one example) and hasn't been prevented from making progress.

Definitional problems can also be exaggerated by those who are not keen on new arms control agreements being concluded with respect to specific weapons or militarized realms. Suffice it to recall that "nuclear weapons" are never defined in the text of the (Nuclear) Non-proliferation Treaty (NPT) which is the cornerstone of the global nuclear non-proliferation and disarmament regime. It could also raise issues if major space powers declined to adopt the envisaged Optional Protocol. We have seen however in other areas of multilateral disarmament that even states which do not formally sign on to widely supported prohibition agreements are often influenced by the norms these agreements create (think of the Ottawa Convention banning anti-personnel landmines, the Cluster Munitions ban and the Arms Trade Treaty).

(b) *A ban on destructive ASATs*

A hearty perennial in discussion of possible space arms control is a ban on ASATs that create debris. Variations of this proposal have been raised since the late 1970s with both states and non-governmental organizations expressing support. With the resumption of debris creating ASAT tests coupled with the upsurge of satellites being launched the appeal of a measure to preclude adding more enduring debris into this mix would seem self-evident. Formulated as a ban on testing it should be readily verifiable given the improvements in monitoring technologies. More ambitious would be a prohibition on the development, possession or use of ASATs which would entail challenging verification issues but could have strong normative value. While an initial focus on debris creating ASATs would be logical given the risk such debris poses for space operations, eventually this might be extended to all forms of ASATs, such as those that disrupt or disable the functioning of a space object through the employment of other physical principles (e.g. lasers, directed energy, cyber and electronic means).

Of course, some space powers who have invested in the development of "kinetic-kill" ASATs might oppose the initiation of negotiations on a ban on destructive ASATs, although given their own self-interest in keeping orbits free of excessive debris they might well consider such a prohibition a useful step. This might be particularly true of a space power that had non-debris causing counter-space capabilities. The corollary of this situation is that a space power that only possessed debris causing ASAT capabilities, might refuse to negotiate this weapons system away if their adversaries maintained ASATs of a non-debris causing nature. Still given the universal benefit of not adding to the already problematic debris problem, especially in low-earth orbit where the majority of active and planned satellites are located, a ban on debris-causing ASAT testing would seem to represent a "low-hanging fruit" for near term space arms control.

(c) *Revival of an international code of conduct under UN auspices*

Building on the work undertaken by the EU to develop an International Code of Conduct for Outer Space Activities (ICoC), it would be relatively straight forward to seek to initiate a multilateral negotiation under UN auspices. Such a negotiation could be authorized with a UN General Assembly resolution (decided on through a majority vote). The draft text left on the table at the end of the 2015 meeting could provide an initial basis for a resumed negotiation but could be modified during the course of the process, which would be (unlike the EU managed process) open to all UN member states. The development of an ICoC should appeal to those states which favour politically over legally binding measures for space security and could help provide a common "floor" at least for what is referred to as "responsible state behaviour" in this crucial if fragile environment. As noted earlier it might also permit agreement on establishing a regular institutional dialogue amongst states on issues of space security, a mechanism which the *Outer Space Treaty* as an early multilateral accord failed to provide for, again there could be concerns if leading space powers did not engage in renewed negotiation of an ICoC or declined to embrace an agreed outcome. Some states might also be concerned that the launch of such a multilateral negotiation could be drawn out or detract attention from developing other more constraining measures. There is also the risk that a multilateral negotiation with consensus-decision making might yield a package of steps so diluted as to be insignificant in light of the challenges contemporary space security must contend with.

(d) *Agree on one or more TCBMs*

At the lower end of the diplomatic spectrum of ambition for space security would be agreement on one or more TCBMs either through a multilateral process or as a product of a more restrictive negotiation amongst space-faring nations. After a series of disquieting moves that exacerbate rivalry amongst leading space powers and increase threat perceptions (and associated rhetoric) it would contribute to re-establishing a modicum of confidence and cooperation if TCBMs could be embraced. These measures could be subsumed in a wider multilateral negotiation of an ICoC if one was initiated or conducted as a standalone negotiation. Possible measures could draw from the existing menu of recommendations from the 2013 GGE report or focus on new measures. Noteworthy, in Christopher Ford's critique of space arms control he indicates a willingness to consider TCBMs and mentions agreement on rules to govern proximity operations of space craft as one candidate for discussion (Ford 2020). He also draws parallels with the on-going UN deliberations on "norms of responsible state behaviour in cyberspace" in suggesting that similar "norms" might be fashioned for state conduct in outer space. One might even consider a measure prohibiting cyberattacks against space objects or their related ground stations and the communication links between these.

TCBMs as politically binding measures also have the advantage of being less time consuming to negotiate and are not as binding on states subscribing to them (although this political status is a deficiency in the eyes of states preferring legally binding accords). As with the other diplomatic options discussed, there is a risk that some major space powers may not engage in such an effort although these states may come under considerable peer pressure to do so given that all states have supported TCBMs as potentially constructive additions to maintaining international peace and security in outer space.

## 7 Conclusions

Those concerned with the future of outer space activity are currently experiencing the paradox that at the very time that exploitation of outer space is growing exponentially and global society is increasingly dependent on the uninterrupted provision of space-enabled services, the international community is confronted with a troubling mix of great power rivalry and overt threats of space warfare. In a recent commentary, a senior space expert notes that "China, Russia and the US are now openly and unapologetically testing weapons enabling technologies and accusing each other of becoming the first to weaponize space". Remarking on the absence of serious endeavours "to find diplomatic ways to avoid a war in space", she calls for "frank discussions by the international community on the question of whether the world has now crossed the Rubicon into an uncontrolled arms race in outer space" (Hitchens 2020).

If this depiction of a world on the brink of a devastating arms race is to be countered, it will require a much higher level of engagement on the part of concerned space actors in the pursuit of constructive space security options based on diplomacy rather than weaponization. In particular, governmental and non-governmental stakeholders will need to become more active and vocal on behalf of preserving outer space for peaceful purposes. The *Outer Space Treaty* has given the international community a solid foundation for ensuring that the use of outer space is in furtherance of peaceful purposes and global well-being. The treaty is not self-executing however and the time is overdue for concerned and capable "middle powers" in concert with other stakeholders to wake up to the existing dangers to this "global commons" and engage constructively to prevent an arms race (and worse) in outer space.

## References

BRICS. (2015). BRICS joint statement regarding the principles of elaboration of international instruments on outer space activities, New York July 27, 2015. www.reachingcriticalwill.org.

Canada. (2004). Address by Prime Minister Paul Martin to the UN general assembly, September, 22, 2004 www.reachingcriticalwill.org.

Canada. (2007). Canadian working papers CD/1815 (20 February 2007).
Canada. (2009). CD/1865 (5 June 2009) www.unog.ch/disarmament.
Canada. (2020). Statement to the conference on disarmament, January 21, 2020 and statement to the first committee of the UN general assembly October 14, 2020 www.reachingcriticalwill.org.
Conference on Disarmament. (2008). *2014 treaty on the prevention on the placement of weapons in outer space and the threat or use of force against space objects*—CD/ 1839, 29 February 2008, CD/1985, 12 June 2014 www.unog.ch/disarmament.
Conference on Disarmament. (2008). US paper CD/1847 of 26 August 2008.
Conference on Disarmament. (2009). China-Russia paper CD 1872 of 18 August 2009 www.unog.ch/disarmament.
EU. (31 March, 2014). *Draft international code of conduct for outer space activities*. Available at www.eeas.europa.eu/non-proliferation-and-disarmament/pdf/space_code_conduct_draft_vers_31-march-2014_en.pdf.
Ford, C. A. (July, 2020). *Arms control and outer space: History and prospects*, State Department. www.state.gov.
Hitchens. (October 6, 2020). *UNIDIR and space security: Going boldly to promote a safer future*. www.unidir.org.
Meyer, P. (April 2011). *The CD and PAROS: A short history*, UNIDIR Resources www.unidir.org.
OOSA. (1967). *Treaty on principles governing the activities of states in the exploration and use of outer space, including the moon and other celestial bodies*, Entered into Force October 10, 1967. https://www.unoosa.org/oosa/en/ourwork/spacelaw/treaties/introouterspacetreaty.html.
UNGA. (July 23, 2013). Report of the group of governmental experts on transparency and confidence building measures in outer space activities, A/68/189*. www.un.org/disarmament.
UNGA. (December 12, 2019). *Prevention of an arms race in outer space*, UN general assembly resolution www.undocs.org/en/a/res/74/32.
US Space Force 2020—Spacepower-Doctrine for Space Forces July 2020 www.spaceforce.mil.
USUN. (November 6, 2018). "Explanation of vote on resolution L.3 'Prevention of an arms race in outer space", Cynthia Plath, US Deputy permanent representative to the conference on disarmament. www.reachingcriticalwill.org.
Weeden, B., & Samson, V. (2019). *Global counterspace capabilities: An open source assessment* (pp. 6–2). Secure World Foundation. www.swfound.org.

**Paul Meyer** is a former Canadian career diplomat who served as Ambassador and Permanent Representative to the UN and the Conference on Disarmament in Geneva (2003–2007). Since 2011 he has been an Adjunct Professor of International Studies and a Fellow in International Security at Simon Fraser University in Vancouver. He teaches a seminar on diplomacy and his research interests include outer space security, international cyber security and nuclear arms control and disarmament. He is the current chair of the Canadian Pugwash Group.

# The Outer Space as a New Theater of Operations; Some Ethical-Legal Considerations

**Juan Cayón and Saloomeh Yousefian**

**Abstract** The advance of non-state actors in outer space and the unilateral declarations and events of the leading space powers reveal an undeniable change in outer space's political and strategic *status quo*. This phenomenon should lead to changes in the standard configuration that the International Community has been giving until now to outer space as a *global common*. This contribution analyzes the mentioned legal regime and main recent milestones that lead to thinking about its manifest disuse to point out a series of ethical considerations. These considerations are fundamentally based on classical authors who are recognized fully valid, from whose attribution, a global rethinking of the great powers' spatial policies and strategies would have to be derived, benefitting humanity's security as a whole.

**Keywords** Global commons · Ethics · War law · Outer space · Operational domain · Defense

## 1 Introduction

Recent times have seen how the various powers with space capabilities and military doctrine confront a new operational space, the outer space in which regular military operations will foreseeably take place in the not too distant future. Conceived to

In: Security and the Global Commons, Edited by J. Martin Ramirez, and Bartolomé Bauzá-Abril.
© 2021 Springer International. Submitted: August, 29, 2020; Accepted: November, 29, 2020.

J. Cayón (✉)
Nebrija University, Madrid, Spain
e-mail: jcayon@nebrija.es

S. Yousefian
International Development Department, Nebrija University, Madrid, Spain

J. Cayón
C/LOS, Morales 12, 28411 Moralzarzal, Madrid, Spain

S. Yousefian
Avda. Valladolid 55, 2 interior 2, 28008 Madrid, Spain

 
J. M. Ramírez and B. Bauzá-Abril (eds.), *Security in the Global Commons and Beyond*,
Advanced Sciences and Technologies for Security Applications,
https://doi.org/10.1007/978-3-030-67973-6_7

date as a *global common* (Ostrom 1990) or Outer Space as a global common (like Cyberspace or High Seas), its new consideration raises a series of tensions, challenges, and defiance's both of an ethical, legal, and purely operational nature. This article gives birth to a series of works already in execution or planned by the research group on the Security and Risk and Conflict Management Department of Nebrija University (Spain). Therefore, the present work does not intend to exhaust but to point out some lines of innovative advance in the future, in the military doctrine of the Armed Forces, which will also require a clarification of the validity of International Agreements and the establishment of doctrine about the Outer Space.

## 2 Development

### *2.1 Some Conceptual Precisions*

**Global Common**: we define them as spaces not subject to the jurisdiction of one single state. Due to their characteristics, the global commons are the object of regular use and generally subject to different international treaties, as they are considered the common heritage of all humanity. Strictly speaking, they are the high seas and the seabed beneath them, the airspace, the outer space including the celestial bodies, and Antarctica, with some reserves. However, cyberspace has been commonly added to the list above (Añanos 2014).

**Outer Space**: space of international interest, located beyond the airspace whose exploration and use, including the Moon and other celestial bodies, is subject to a legal regime founded on the principles of freedom and equal service, non-national appropriation, denuclearization, and demilitarization, peaceful use, international cooperation, and mutual assistance.

**Outer Space Treaty**: a short form of referring to the treaty on the principles that should govern States' activities in exploring and using outer space, including the Moon and other celestial bodies.

### *2.2 Global Commons and Security*

Since the emergence of the Nation-States, and even before, Security and Defense used to follow a typical pattern that went through attacking or defending themselves from the other Nation States, generally the neighboring ones. Only the growth of historical empires brought the theater of operations to remote places, which also had geographical proximity to what was already dominated. Therefore, without notable exceptions, the conflict was always linked to the territory and domain of waters. The territorial proximity between the contending States or Nations was then an invariable constant, practically, until the two major wars of the twentieth century. From that moment, recent in historical terms, when the war started to spread to distant territories, often even on different continents, the contending states no longer necessarily had a border limit.

It is precisely at that historical moment, after the Second World War when the nations' concert began to address the issue of those spaces in which no State or government had jurisdiction, mainly non-jurisdictional seas or international waters. It happened first from the League of Nations and later from the then-novel United Nations. The formal search for universal peace required ending territorial disputes, setting borders, and declaring common spaces not subject to national jurisdiction. Moreover, this was followed by international Law, incorporating commonly accepted legal regimes to non-jurisdictional seas and, incidentally, to the only continent not yet exclusively inherited by any State, Antarctica. Some controversies had arisen concerning the areas of influence or economic use, including territorial claims. Argentina and Chile, precisely the two states bordering the continent, reasonably settled, or at least parked, after December 1, 1959, when the twelve countries that had carried out scientific activities in and around Antarctica during the 1957–1958 International Geophysical Year (IGY), signed the Antarctic Treaty in Washington. The treaty entered into force in 1961 and was approved by many nations. Regarding the field of security and defense, it is remarkable that Article 1 of the mentioned Treaty specifically states the following:

1. The use of Antarctica will be exclusively for peaceful purposes. All military nature measures, e.g., the establishment of military bases and fortifications, carrying out military exercises, and testing all kinds of weapons, are banned.
2. This Treaty shall not prevent the use of military personnel or equipment for scientific research or any other peaceful purpose.

It should make clear ab initio the international community's sentiment in this regard, searching for permanent peace and, therefore, no extension of war conflicts to global commons.

Already in the 60 s of the last century, a new area came into play which men access through their own technical and scientific advances: the outer space, which in the opinion of the nations should not be inherited by any power as it belongs, let us put it this way, to humanity. Later on, we will refer more extensively to its legal regulation and the growing reversion, at least apparent, of the international consensus on it. For now, it suffices to emphasize that, like Antarctica, nations so far agree that it should be a peaceful space without weapons, not susceptible to appropriation or heritage by any power.

By the end of the 90 s of the last century, a new global common of possible controversies began to spread as cyberspace. It is worth mentioning that International Law still does not have a legal solution for that. There is an absolute consensus in understanding that it is also, on this occasion, a global and shared space. Even the absence of international treaties on the matter augurs, and this is how it is today in practice, an incredibly active theater of operations linked to the security and defense sector.

Finally, in the XXI century, the complexity of postmodernity has come to make all the classic manuals obsolete, or at least, to require their adaptation to the new operating environments through the inclusion of new concepts, such as hybrid warfare, advanced frontier, comprehensive protection of critical infrastructures or cyber defense. Today, in practice, all conflicts are global. Terrorism has become international; pandemics devastate us all equally without understanding borders; international interference is constant; the use of fake news and social networks intervene in foreign policy, and even mere criminals integrate into transnational gangs or groups. Globalization, typical of postmodernity, has spread to the security and defense sectors and global commons with remarkable intensity.

In the operational sphere, the absence of norms generates enormous legal uncertainty. These legal issues are usually solved with the courage and decision of the Military by risking their guarantees and human rights. In an environment like the one we describe, the first to use the acronym VUCA (*Volatility*, *Uncertainty*, *Complexity*, and *Ambiguity*) were precisely the U.S. military at the end of the last century. Furthermore, the difficulty lies because it is complex to establish reasonably safe engagement rules. If we realize this "liquid," the volatile, uncertain, complex, and ambiguous environment is perfectly coincident in the operational sphere with postmodernity as a whole. We find it not only in working environments but also in politics or the Law as a total. Postmodernity manifests a contradictory phenomenon to the observer's eyes. For example, they appeal to environmental protection frequently while they promote unsustainable consumerism. They combine solidarity with the deprived of racism increase. They defend animal rights where the value of human life plummets or betray politicians' moral integrity; meanwhile, the accredited corruption elevates more than ever.

## 2.3 Outer Space and Its Regulation

Back in the first years of the Cold War, the former Union of Soviet Socialist Republics launches the Sputnik into orbit on October 4, 1975. Afterward, the space-age leads to a dispute between the powers to overcome the opposite in development and technology. Space-age finishes with the Cold War in 1989. At the same time, the Berlin Wall falls, and the Soviet Union collapses. However, it was not exclusively a race to gain international prestige, not dissuade the contrary by exhibiting their capacities. The domain of outer space was novel and provided undoubted tactical and strategic advantages. For this reason, they immediately sought military operational exploits that, until then, were mainly limited to obtaining intelligence through satellites, which, unlike the observation flights, were then undetectable and consequently could not be shot down, as well as the use of these for telecommunications.

In contempt of the increasing use of outer space and the legal challenges of a new world, the powers began to negotiate and address the question of how to treat this new frontier. This area would culminate ten years later, in 1967, with the first treaty on the spatial subject, to which we will refer in more detail in the next section. It is then, in the 70 s of the last century, when the new "space law" begins to develop with great impetus among internationalists, making its way with force like all young and vigorous academic disciplines due to practical necessity. The late 1960s and 1970s were the golden age of the new space law. However, at the beginning of the 1980s, the discipline was somehow stagnant in lethargy, most likely due to the absence of significant space race advances. The Cold War was declining. Space competition was already clearly dominated by the United States with its shuttle missions. There was a general submission, at least formal, to international treaties that equilibrate the balance between the contending powers.

This branch of Law has remained unfinished, and, as we will see shortly, the facts seem to indicate that it is even in disuse, at least given the current approach of the space powers. Although it would be essential respect the international treaties and achieve a greater degree of ratification by the authorities and reach agreements, perhaps within the United Nations, on some topics that not meticulously but merely expository, we quote:

(a) Those related to the use of wealth and raw materials are located in space or other heavenly bodies, not only by the States but also by commercial companies and other non-state actors that now find deregulated.
(b) Those related to debris damage the third parties and the environment, caused by or on the occasion of launching objects into outer space, mainly when these affect not only States and their territorial integrity, but also people or other environments, like the high seas or skies.
(c) The implications for safe use of outer space, that is, the use of it in peace, specifying whether peaceful use implies total demilitarization or exclusively absence of aggression, as well as a regulatory expansion of the prohibition of space weapons.
(d) The implications on matters of the applicable jurisdiction, starting with determining where the airspace ends, and the outer space begins, or the legal regime applicable to multinational stations, discoveries, or inventions made in space or the birth of people.
(e) Juridification of the status that extraterrestrial life would have, its necessary regulation, and the norms that will govern its conservation, exploitation, or importation to earth.

However, without thinking prospectively but rather from a historical perspective, there is already a primary legislative body in the field of International Law, as we anticipated, that regulates some essential aspects of the outer space environment. We will not dedicate this contribution to analyzing it in detail since the texts are easily accessible and therefore, a simple enumeration of said existing necessary legislation is sufficient:

I. Treaty on the principles that should govern the activities of States in the exploration and use of outer space, including the Moon and other celestial bodies of 1967. It has been signed and ratified by 109 States, to which we must add another 20 that have signed it but have not approved it yet.

II. Agreement on the rescue and return of astronauts and the restitution of objects launched into outer space of 1968.
III. 1972 Convention on International Liability for Damage Caused by Space Objects.
IV. 1975 Convention on Registration of Objects Launched into Outer Space.
V. The agreement of the state activities on the Moon and other celestial bodies of 1979 was signed and ratified by only 17 States. They add four more nations who signed it but have not yet approved it. It is noteworthy that among all of them, none of the more prominent space-fare nations figures.

From all the previous normative texts, we can extract a series of essential principles which may be of interest to know briefly, also interpreted in coherence with other statements without coercive legal value related to the consideration of the outer space as a global common good. Thus, the main thing, in our opinion, is to highlight the following principles or considerations:

- Global interest: The exploration and use of outer space must be done for all States' benefit and welfare, as they concern all humanity.
- Non-appropriation: The space or celestial bodies are not a viable object of national appropriation by claiming sovereignty, use, or occupation, or in any other way. They are a global common good.
- Compliance with International Law: the Charter of United Nations will carry out all activities in outer space under international Law and in the interest of maintaining international peace and security, promoting cooperation and mutual understanding.
- Peaceful space without weapons of mass destruction: There is a ban on placing nuclear weapons or weapons of mass destruction in orbit, in outer space, or on the celestial bodies. This norm implies, or at least that is how we understand it, the exclusively peaceful use of space, being forbidden to establish military installations or fortifications, carry out tests of any weapons or carry out military maneuvers.
- Consideration of astronauts as "Ambassadors of Humanity": in the sense of representing the entire humanity in its quest to advance technically and scientifically, also dominating outer space.
- Universal early warning: Obligation of space powers to report and disseminate observed phenomena that may pose a danger to humanity, astronauts or ships, devices, or safe space traffic.
- Liability for damages caused: which today affects the States that launch or promote the launch, as well as the States from which it is launched, always for the damage caused to another State Party and its people, both in the space itself. Extraterrestrial as in the airspace or the earth itself.
- Safe cooperation and mutual assistance, considering that in the global common good, the principles of solidarity and support in case of need prevail.
- Information and transparency: All space powers should report transparently on the nature, progress, location, and results of the exploration and use of outer space for peaceful purposes.

- Accessibility: All stations, facilities, equipment, and vehicles located on the Moon and other celestial bodies will be accessible to all States based on reciprocity.

As we can see, they are a series of basic principles, elementary perhaps, that will need more specificity and development, maybe even institutional, within international organizations. And so far, the current regulation of outer space that, without a doubt, is surpassed by the facts.

## 2.4 *The Timelines of Outer Space as a Theater of Operations*

The militarization of outer space is a growing fact, which is superimposed on its already classic use in the twentieth century to obtain intelligence and the foreseeable use.

It is still difficult to define, and the intellectual, political, and university debates prove it, how the configuration of international politics will be in this twenty-first century. Postmodernity is a mutually contradictory phenomenon and an unclear panorama. Traditional and emerging powers play different roles, with still unclear results. In the field that concerns us, we can only see unilateral statements and reports so far. For example, on February 11, 2019, the North American Defense Intelligence Agency (DIA) published a fascinating report.[1] It focused attention on the challenges that the United States faces against the operational military capacity with effects in other powers' space field. We take the following summary from the official press release.[2]

In particular, the report notes that:

- Chinese and Russian military doctrines indicate they view space as crucial to modern warfare and counter-space capabilities as a means to reduce U.S. and allied military effectiveness.
- Both countries have developed robust and capable space services, including space-based intelligence, surveillance, and reconnaissance.
- China and Russia are making improvements to existing systems, including space launch vehicles and satellite navigation constellations.
- These capabilities provide their militaries with the ability to command and control their forces worldwide with enhanced situational awareness, enabling them to monitor, track, and target U.S. and allied forces.
- Chinese and Russian space surveillance networks can search, track, and characterize satellites in all earth orbits. This capability supports both space operations and counter-space systems.

---

[1]You can find the complete report in: https://www/dia.mil/Military-Power-Publications/.

[2]Cfr. https://www.dia.mil/News/Articles/Article-View/Article/1754150/defense-intelligence-agency-releases-report-on-challenges-to-us-security-in-spa/.

- Both states are developing jamming and cyberspace capabilities, directed energy weapons, on-orbit capabilities and ground-based antisatellite missiles that can achieve a range of reversible to non-reversible effects.

As can be seen in the transcribed text, with terminology and specific meaning of a new Cold War, severe threats to the United States' security by other space powers are justified and detailed, precisely within outer space. There is no doubt that the Popular Republic of China, the Russian Federation, and also the United States of America itself has, for some time, been directing their military strategy towards the use of cyberspace and outer space[3] as operational domains for defense. The creation of specially dedicated army corps and proven operations in different cases evidence in the cyber field. Strategic innovations, public statements, and even the creation of special forces for that purpose augur it in outer space. Although the difference is essential between one area and the other, since in the first, humanity lacks international legislation, in the second, it seems that the existing legislation remains or will remain shortly, surpassed by the facts.

Regarding outer space as an operational domain, we recommend an informative summary, the one made by Paulauskas (2020) in the *Nato Review*. The evolution of NATO thinking about space is narrated in an authentic way, which ironically, as the author quotes, goes from a typical concern (referring to the assigned office space) to one of its relevant strategic needs. There is no doubt that our society's technological dependence finds one of its pillars in outer space, which has seen its use increased exponentially in the last twenty years. Particularly in the military field, in deployed operations throughout the world, satellites are essential not only for obtaining intelligence but also for maintaining communications and conducting operations. Both refer to the precise positioning, observation, weather forecast, early warning of enemy movements, or even if God forbids the launching of intercontinental ballistic missiles. With a long but rapid evolution (García Servet and Rubio Bravo 2020), all this has led to the meeting of Heads of State and Government of NATO members on December 4, 2019, declaring outer space as the fifth operational domain together with land, sea, air, and cyberspace.

Furthermore, it is also worth finally bringing up the most express recent declaration that things are changing. The univocal criterion of powers considering outer space as a common good of all humanity may already be a matter of the past. Unfortunately, as in so many other things in life, it seems that economic interests are above the word given or the concord between nations. On April 6, 2020, the President of the United

[3]The United States Space Force was created on December 20, 2019, just a few months after the DIA report. Its mission was organizing, training, and equipping space forces to protect American and allied interests in space. Its aim was also to provide space capabilities to the joint force, including the development of professionals, the acquisition of military space systems, the maturation of military doctrine for the space domain, and space forces' organization. It is highly recommended to visit their website found at the link: https://www.spaceforce.mil/.

States signed the executive order *encouraging international support for the recovery and use of space resources*[4] which clearly states that

> Americans should have the right to participate in the exploitation, recovery and commercial use of resources in outer space following applicable Law.[5] Outer space is a legally and physically unique domain of human activity, and the United States does not regard it as a global common good.

Moreover, to finish making the U.S. position clear, he adds in the second section that

> (...) the United States is not a party to the Moon Agreement. Also, it does not consider the agreement as an effective or necessary instrument to guide national States regarding the promotion of commercial participation in long-term exploration, scientific discovery, and the use of the Moon, Mars, or other celestial bodies. Consequently, the Secretary of State will oppose any attempt by any other State or international organization to consider the said agreement as a reflection or expression of customary international law.[6]

Given the preceding, we think there can be no rational doubt regarding the change in outer space's legal status in the commercial and military sphere, which deserves the task of deepening its legal assessment effect and its profound implications ethical.

## 2.5 *Some Ethical Considerations*

As we can see in the references of Valladolid Controversy back in 1550–1551,[7] the Indians of the New World have souls and, consequently, we should treat them as persons and children of God (Dumont 2009). In the same way and under the penalty provided by Law in case of non-compliance, we face an epochal moment when outer space is concerned. An open, free, intellectually well-founded debate and far from the usual hypocrisies is required to legally regulate this new frontier of humanity in nations' concert.

---

[4]Access to full text and the attached sheet on the White House page by following the link below: https://www.whitehouse.gov/presidential-actions/executive-order-encouraging-international-support-recovery-use-space-resources/.

[5]The underlining highlights that, although the need to the applicable law is recognized, this sentence is contrary to what is internationally agreed and ratified by the same international actor under another presidency.

[6]This highlights that The United States of North America will be part of the Moon Agreement and oppose considering that it is part of international custom and a source of law in this area is well known.

[7]The Valladolid controversy was a famous debate that took place in 1550 and 1551 at the Colegio de San Gregorio (Valladolid), within the so-called controversy of the natives (Native Americans or Indians), and that faced two antagonistic ways of conceiving the conquest of America. The thesis of the defenders of the Indians represented by Bartolomé de las Casas, and those of Juan Ginés de Sepúlveda, who defended the right and the convenience of the dominion of the Spaniards over the indigenous people, whom he also conceives as naturally inferior, were confronted.

It does not seem sensible to allow or encourage an arms race in outer space. A space conflict in the vicinity of the earth will undoubtedly bring a massive amount of uncontrolled space debris that will eventually fall to the earth, not without, probably, first damaging satellites of potential contenders, but also third States. In addition to the environmental consequences of a conflict in outer space, which are equally difficult to assess due to the more than possible alteration of the space environment and the planet itself, the possibility of causing collateral damage is intuitively high. We are contrary to the utopian vision of a world without war. However, the implications of a space war, such as a nuclear war, or both simultaneously, are so important that it seems prudent to analyze the issue from the prism provided by legal ethics.

From the most remote history to the present day, men have fought with each other; and also since ancient times, they have sought justifications to do so through what comes to be called *Ius ad Bellum*, that is, the right (thus, with a capital letter) to war. Aware of the atrocities that can go hand in hand with an armed conflict, almost at the same time, the doctrine of the so-called *Ius in Bello*, that is, the legal regulation of the material aspects of the conflict while it is taking place, has dealt with since ancient times. The Spirit of trying to lessen the war's damage by confining it to the combatants as much as possible. In conclusion, it is worth mentioning that the legal regulation of the contestants' behavior and mainly of the winners called *Ius post-Bellum*, has also been abundantly dealt with by the doctrine.

Without pretending to be a historical study, we will go to this core part of our contribution to history to take back from it the classics and their doctrine, perhaps much more applicable to our days than we are in a position to commonly accept. Moreover, if we look back and analyze the armed conflicts between nations, the number of dead, disabled and wounded, destroyed families, displaced civilian personnel, the outlook is chilling. If we look at the newspaper or television, we verify that, although time has passed since those first wars from classical authors, human nature does not escape from war, no matter how much our age claims to be more civilized or peaceful (Contreras 2020). Therefore, the armed conflict is a constant of humanity, never having existed and, predictably, never existing in the future, despite the idealistic approaches to use, a world in complete peace and harmony. Ever since, in the biblical texts, the man leaves paradise because of his sin of pride, rebelling against his Creator. Consistent with this ambitious nature, some have always wanted to impose themselves on others and, if necessary, have used force to achieve their intentions. New forms of conflict hitherto unknown or at least not generalized in the current postmodernity leave the West with some perplexity and much concern because its dominance is questioned, probably, as never before. Traditionally and beyond internal conflicts, wars broke out between nations for territory or religion. The legitimate powers decreed and formally declared that regular armies (or irregular forces but integrated into regular cadres) participated. They used similar tactics and strategies. They identified clear fronts, and the technology used was generally comparable between the sides, notwithstanding, of course, the technological advances used by the contenders, the technological factor being precisely one of those that most affected the chances of victory. Currently, on the other hand, as many studies show in recent decades, in most of the living conflicts on the planet, we find wars started by unconsolidated political leaders, without a formal declaration, frequently with the active participation of irregular combatants. Using tactics and strategies that are very different from the classic ones, without concrete or determined fronts and in any case, flexible, almost liquid, and as regards the substance of the matter that we are dealing with here, with a very disparate use of technology.

Hereafter, we try to describe the analysis of *Ius ad Bellum*, *Ius in Bello*, and *Ius post-Bellum* in the context of a hypothetical space war, where we must develop our reflections. For obvious reasons of time and space, this communication will focus on the first of them, the Right to War. However, we trust that in future contributions, we will also address the no less exciting questions relating to the Law of space warfare and the still today new post-war Law to aid in repairing the damage caused.

Since immemorial time, the implications and interactions between war, morality, and Law have been the subject of attention by the doctrine.[8] Nevertheless, in the great Catholic authors, we find the most classical foundation of the *Ius ad* Bellum, already from the earliest times of Christianity with Saint Augustine, later in the monumental contribution of Saint Thomas Aquinas, and, finally, in the so-called School of Salamanca. In our opinion, it is only worth to remember them with the Thomist order established in Summa Theologica II-II, *quaestio* 40 when considering whether there is any lawful war, but with an eye on outer space as a potential setting. Thus, we bring with Saint Thomas the Augustinian bases. One of Hipona quotes the evangelist in the sermon *De Puero Centurionis (400 A.C.)*:

> If Christian doctrine inculcates all wars, the healthiest advice for those who ask for it according to the Gospel would be to abandon their weapons and completely stop being the militias.
>
> Nevertheless, to them, it was said (Lk 3, 14): "You shall not hurt anyone; Your stipend will suffice." "Those he ordered to be content with their pay; he did not forbid them to go to war."

Aquinas deduces the three conditions required for a war to be, namely, the authority of the prince who orders it, cause for it, and upright intention of the contenders, that is, intention aimed at promoting good or avoiding evil. Nothing in this approach differs in the space environment from any other since we are not speaking correctly of the operational domain but of the ultimate foundations of the decision to fight an enemy with force.

### 2.5.1 Legitimate Authority

Regarding the legitimacy of the authority that, according to Law, can exercise the right to war, Saint Augustine (1993) in book *II Against Manich* (391 A.C.) says:

> Whoever wields the sword without superior or legitimate authority that commands or grants it, does so to shed blood. Nevertheless, whoever uses the sword with the authority of the

[8]We recommend as a summarized compendium the interesting work developed by the Section of Philosophy of Law of the Royal Academy of Jurisprudence and Legislation entitled *War, Morality and Law, Actas*, Madrid, 1994 ISBN 84-87863-30-2.

> prince or the judge, if he is a private person, or by zeal for justice, as by the authority of God, if he is a public person, does not wield it himself, but they serve from what another has entrusted to him. That is why he does not incur punishment,

being clear, therefore, that:

> It is not the responsibility of the private person to declare war, because he can assert his right before a higher court; Furthermore, the private person does not have the competence to summon the community, which is necessary to wage war. Since the princes entrusted the care of the republic, it is up to them to defend the city's public good, kingdom, or province under their authority. In the same line, that they lawfully defend it with the material sword against internal disruptors, punishing evildoers, according to the words of the Apostle: to punish the wrongdoer" (Rom 13, 4), it is also incumbent on him to defend the public good with the sword of war against external enemies. That is why it is recommended to princes: "Deliver the poor and bring the helpless out of the hands of the sinner" (Ps 81, 41), and Saint Augustine, for his part, in the book *Against Faust.* it teaches: "The natural order, accommodated to the peace of mortals, postulates that the authority and deliberation to accept war belongs to the prince.

In light of these texts, what human authority has the legitimate power to unleash a space war in the vicinity of the planet, which would probably damage impossible or challenging repair to all humanity? We consider the question also for a global thermonuclear war. What human authority can legitimately order the disappearance of the known world that would occur after a nuclear attack and the sure and forceful response of the attacked power? There is no doubt that government art often requires the adoption of brutal, harsh, even unpopular measures. Sometimes the government decision requires the use of force.

For this reason, among other reasons, the government traditionally reserved itself for the best or a well-advised elite. For this reason, the western legal tradition differentiated between legality and legitimacy (Sepúlveda 1991). The question is, are our leaders their best in postmodern democracy? Furthermore, does anyone have the necessary legitimacy to unleash a war of this nature for any time and place? We leave the answers to the reader, stating that due to the nature and consequences of a nuclear war, like those of a space war in our planet's vicinity, there is no legitimate authority with the power to unleash them with justice.

### 2.5.2 Just Cause

As far as the just cause is concerned, Saint Augustine in the book *Quaest* (391–400 A.C.) said:

> Just wars are those that come with injuries; For example, if there has been a place to punish the people of the city that neglects to punish the outrage committed by their own or to restore what has been unjustly stolen.

This means that those who are attacked must deserve it for some reason of general or particular justice. In this sense, it seems evident that, in principle, defensive wars will always be legitimized regarding the just cause (although they may be illegitimate because they do not meet any other of the requirements that we have been analyzing). However, in classical doctrine, offensive warfare is also allowed in certain situations; for example, whenever legitimate rights are claimed over territories or goods and taking into account the elementary criteria of prudence and avoidance of damage more significant than the intended interests defended or guaranteed. At this point, we can only call attention to the difficulty of determining the just cause in a world that is already conceptually very distant from which existed at the time of the development of these theories. Since the dissolution of the traditional order, the end of the theocentric scheme standard, the disappearance of a complete conception of Law, including Natural Law and the requirement that positive law respect and specify in the practical order, like other challenging factors. However, we will ignore so as not to distract from the object of this communication.

In this sense, we should ask ourselves if the war in the new spatial domain can have a just cause, and for this, the simplest thing is to consider the assumption that we were facing an attack and the doubt, therefore, would be to use a spatial response. In the same way, as in nuclear matters, it seems that regardless of how reasonable it is to defend oneself, the proportion in the means used is a requirement of justice. Suppose the attack were in turn space since the damage will already be done. In that case, the junk resulting from the satellites' destruction in circulation and the environment's damage will be predictably caused. The absence of space response will only increase the risks and damage general to humanity. As in nuclear matters, whoever strikes first strikes twice, and the respondent only has to do so to destroy the enemy (and the entire humanity in the nuclear case). If, on the contrary, the attack was conventional, the spatial response would appear disproportionate, just as the nuclear response would be disproportionate.

Therefore, the truth is that in our opinion, it is only possible to affirm exhaustively that an attack space war can never be justified (as neither would a massive nuclear one). Simultaneously, a defensive space reaction could have the just cause requirement as long as it was not massive either, even at the risk of increasing the confrontation's effects on humanity.

### 2.5.3 Right Intention

Finally, the classical doctrine requires that the contenders' intention be correct; that is, an intention aimed at promoting good or avoiding evil. That is why Saint Augustine (1993) also writes in the book*De Verbis Domini* (391–400 A.C.):

> Among the true worshipers of God, the same wars are peaceful, since they are promoted not out of greed or cruelty, but out of a desire for peace, to restrain the wicked and favor the good guys.

Therefore, according to the classics, it may happen that, the authority of the one declaring war being legitimate and the cause just, it nevertheless turns out to be illicit due to malicious intent. Saint Augustine (1993) writes about it in the book*Against Faust*:

> Indeed, the desire to harm, the cruelty to take revenge, the unrepentant and implacable spirit, the ferocity in the fight, the passion to dominate and other similar things, is, injustice, vituperable in wars.

As in the same case of the nuclear confrontation, we do not doubt that a global space war can never reflect the contenders' right intention. That of the attacker is conspicuous by its absence as it seeks to impose itself unilaterally by destroying enemy space targets, even at the risk of provoking their reaction and, even if it did not occur, causing irreparable damage to all humanity. Likewise, that of the hypothetical defender will never fulfill the requirement of the right intention because, by unleashing the global spatial reaction, we can not achieve any good except the complete annihilation of the enemy and humanity as a whole. We can not promote any good with this hypothetical total space conflict. We can not avoid any evil; on the contrary, we should assume a greater evil when globally using space media. On the other hand, in the case of specific spatial actions in response to other specific spatial actions, the damage suffered by humanity if it occurs makes it possible to think that it will be proportional to the deterrence achieved with the response.

Therefore, it is challenging to find the concurrence of the three classic conditions of the just war in a hypothetical space confrontation in the terms in which we are handling it today, that is, in the globe's environment and concerning the satellites of other powers. Thus, any military intervention in space will not only be violating international treaties to that effect, with the corresponding legal consequences.[9]

Moreover, it is that anticipating the conclusions, the arms race in space, or it is approached from the merely dissuasive point of view, as happened with the nuclear escalation during the cold war, or it lacks any sense, for the Law, of course, but also, for the most elementary ethics.

### 2.5.4 Some Additional Considerations from Postmodernity

In conclusion, according to traditional doctrine, those who wage just war also try to make peace. Hence, Saint Augustine writes in *Ad Bonifacium*:

> Peace is not sought to move war, but war is inferred to achieve peace. So be peaceful fighting, so that with victory you bring the usefulness of peace to those you fight.

Therefore, the classics and the doctrine that develops these approaches maintain that war preserves international order, understanding, of course, as a universal common good. Although it has come to be called the new international order, our opinion represents nothing more than a mere accumulation of commercial and political interests of rugged origins. In Vitoria's terminology, the achievement and maintenance of a just peace, the *Totus Orbis* (De Vitoria 1964) should not flee from

[9]It is worth mentioning that the 1967 treaty lays the main foundations of Space Law and could well be understood as an international custom that has been peacefully respected for more than 50 years, regardless of its incorporation or not into national law by way of ratification. With this interpretation, any action of this nature would be considered illegal.

armed violence. That meets the requirements mentioned earlier in its execution. No matter how much in the spatial sphere, it seems highly unlikely that those conditions necessary to be considered a just war are present.

Very different are the current approaches, which long ago abandoned the thought of the classics. Due to modernities' irruption in doctrine and legal-political philosophy, all the bases and mental schemes exposed to now through the classics' mouth are denigrated and obsolete. Modern logic deliberately sets aside natural Law and the natural order of things to replace the classical references with a new idealistic philosophical universe. All reference to God disappears and is confused by legality and legitimacy (Legaz Lacambra 1958). Outside the positive Law dictated by the democratic ruler, neither is the legitimacy for the individual or the nations. In this way, the divine legislator is replaced by the human, as God leaves his central place in philosophical developments to give it to modern man, the new Creator of the whole as a whole.

Modernity incurs the paradoxes that reach the paroxysm in postmodernity. As we see these days, under the external form of laws, we observe the most significant crimes and rights limitations. After demolishing the already decaying remnants of old Christianity, the philosophical foundations of the Protestant Reformation and the French Revolution lay the foundations of the modern state where power and authority will reside through national sovereignty. Therefore, states start to reference and interact with each other based on international legality emanating from artificial supranational entities, in a new logic that emerges after the brutal disasters associated with the two world wars of the twentieth century. It is still interesting to see how the paradigm of modernity, the totalitarian European states that collide in the Second Great War, are defeated by an alliance between another totalitarian state. Together with the supposed Western democracies, immediately exploding the so-called cold war in the one that each side captures for its ranks an endless number of satellites that operate remotely in the international environment from the new cultural metropolises.

After the fall of one of the blocks due to its inefficiency, we entered fully into postmodernity full of confusion and chaos. Following the foundations laid in the previous period, the United Nations Organization grants legitimacy for war. Especially its Security Council, in which, as it is known, the victorious powers of the Second World War are a permanent part and have the right of veto. Given that postmodern legality and legitimacy are linked to such a subjectively organized international organization, nowadays, the only war that meets the condition of being approved by the security council will be formally just regardless of its status. It could be an offensive or defensive character of the authority that proclaims it, the justice of the cause alleged by the parties or the combatants' right or evil intention.

However, a practical problem facing this postmodern world is that the agreement between the dominant powers and the veto's right is not always possible, which leaves a margin for action to undertake armed actions. Of doubtful legality/legitimacy according to this postmodern scheme to which we have briefly referred. The protection and coverage of the international community are bought and sold in a system that, at times, seemed to become unipolar. The examples in the Middle East and

North Africa are clear regarding what we affirm, being led by the member powers of said Security Council: Libya, Iraq, Syria.

It was precisely at the dawn of the historical twenty-first century when the sign of the times changed, although its last consequences are not clear yet. Naturally, we refer to September 11, 2001, and the irruption in the international area. A series of different conceptual movements and performances have been seen. A series of offensive and defensive capabilities that are not inconsiderable can also deploy our actions anywhere globally, an enemy of the liquid, vaporous, and unpredictable postmodern system. At least it is how Western public opinion perceives it. Only time will perhaps allow us to know the insides of Al Quaeda or Daesh, as well as those that will surely succeed them, their origin and financing, more than likely associated with some of the allies that allegedly fight them.

Nevertheless, the truth is that in the face of the said enemy, United Nations resolutions are becoming less and less effective, since they are spread over frontier territories and act thanks to supporting and against very different enemies, sometimes coincident and other divergent. In this chaos, real pandemonium, the remote-controlled international coalitions, or the states that aspire to recover the greatness of other times, act freely in the field of war, keeping, yes, the forms under an apparent pseudo-international legitimacy of fact or Law. In-depth analysis of this bleak panorama's legal, philosophical terms is beyond this contribution's scope, but our intuitive approach is pointed out in these short lines.

Furthermore, suppose we refer to space, increasing privatization, and the "democratization" of the ability to put satellites in orbit. It could be an extension of terrorism in space, either through cyber-attacks or the control of our satellites acquired in the market. With the critical nuance that we have written about the powers, how much more must be preached about criminal and terrorist organizations or failed states.

## 3 Conclusions

- Contrary to the international treaties on outer space, the great powers and commercial companies are already viewing outer space as a potential theater of both commercial and purely military operations.
- On an economic level, the privatization of outer space resources is as dangerous as their heritage by one or more States.
- The concert of nations is doing nothing to prevent it, and even though all humanity is concerned, there is no international public debate on this issue.
- Outer space starts from the advantage of having governing regulations, no matter how outdated or generic they are, unlike cyberspace and its conflicts. However, the actors take advantage of a gap or loophole in the Law, which needs to be regulated.

- An extensive interpretation of the 1967 treaty would be appropriate for world peace to consider it a commonly accepted international custom to increase international pressure against space powers with the military capacity to deploy, freeze or limit their capacity and, progressively, destroy the existing one.
- Nevertheless, the unilateral declarations and decisions of the different powers leave such regulations on paper, in the face of international silence, without any pronouncement from supranational organizations or States.
- The consequences of considering space as a new theater of military operations predictably will lead to a new dissuasive race that will hopefully remain there.
- A space conflict will have consequences for humanity that are difficult to assume, especially for non-involved third States that will see their security compromised and their very survival.
- It is reasonable to think that if the conflict in outer space occurs, it will pit great powers against each other. Since today only they have military space capacity and on a specific or limited and non-global basis (otherwise, it would probably lead to the disappearance of life on the planet).
- In case of an escalated conflict in space, even if it does not bring up the end of humanity, it will be limited to space. Therefore, we will probably be in a war with apocalyptic dimensions, especially if the nuclear factor also comes into play.
- Given the particular legal uncertainty, we could apply the same concepts and rules of *Ius ad Bellum*, *Ius in Bello*, and *Ius postbellum* to outer space. In that sense, it maintains the conflict exclusively in an environment that does not belong or should not be able to belong territorially to any State.
- For this reason, from the Right to War, it can be said that any ethical and moral military action in space for aggressive purposes and almost any action for defensive purposes must be condemned.

## References

Augustine. (1993). *Complete pieces of San Agustin. Volume XXXI. Anti-manichaean writings (2)*. Bilingual Edition. Madrid: Library of Christian Authors.

Añanos, M. C. (2014). La idea de los bienes comunes en el Sistema internacional: ¿Renacimiento o Extinción? *UNISCI discussion papers*, No 34. https://revistas.ucm.es/index.php/UNIS/article/download/44838/42248.

Contreras, A. (2020). Guerra global, asimétrica e irregular agresores estatales en acción. *Sao Paolo and Al Qaeda Forum* (pp. 1–2).

De Vitoria, F. (1964). *Relecciones sobre los Indios y el derecho de guerra.* Mexico: Espasa Calpe, S.A.

Dumont, J. (2009). *El amanecer de los derechos del hombre. La controversia de Valladolid.* Madrid: Ediciones Encuentro.

García Servet, R., & Rubio Bravo, F. J. (2020). El espacio como dominio operacional en la OTAN. *Academy of military arts and sciences*, Spain. https://acami.es/wp-content/uploads/2020/06/espacio-dominio-operacional-OTAN-web.pdf.

Legaz Lacambra, L. (1958). Legalidad y legitimidad. *Revista de estudios políticos* (Vol. 101, pp. 5–24).

Ostrom, E. (1990). *Governing the commons. The evolution of institutions for collective action*. New York: Cambridge University Press.
Paulauskas, K. (2020). Space: NATO's latest frontier. *Nato Review*. https://www.nato.int/docu/review/articles/2020/03/13/space-natos-latest-frontier/index.html.
Sepúlveda, M. -S. C. (1991). *Legality and legitimacy: The theory of power* (p. 1991). Madrid: Actas.

**Juan Cayón** He is a Doctor of Law from the Pontificia Comillas University in Spain, obtaining the qualification of *cum Laude*. He also has a BA in Law and a MA in Legal Practice from the same university. He holds a Higher Diploma in French Language and Civilization from the Sorbonne University of Paris. He has been practicing Law since 1991 and is a member of the Illustrious Bar Association of Madrid since then. He is also a member of other Professional Associations of Jurists and Legal Advisors such as the General Secretary of International Association of Catholic Jurists, dependent on the Vatican Secretariat of State. He is a founding member and former Vice-President of the Association for the Study of University Law and the first President of the Ibero-American Network of University Law. He is the Vice President of the CICA International Foundation, Trustee of the Elías de Tejada Foundation, and Erasmo Pércopo and of the Speiro Foundation. Currently, he is the President of the Ibero-American Association of Catholic Culture. He is Fellow of the World Academy for Arts & Sciences and has been awarded on several occasions, such as the First-class distinguished Cross of San Raimundo de Peñafort awarded by the Ministry of Justice of Spain and the Great Cross of the Naval Merit of the Spanish Kingdom. He has published numerous chapters in dozens of books and thirty articles and reviews in specialized magazines. He has held different positions and one-person government bodies in different universities such as Vice-Rector for Institutional Relations, Vice-Rector for International Relations, General Secretary, and the Legal Cabinet's Chief Lawyer. Currently and since 2014, he is the Magnificent Rector of the Antonio de Nebrija University in Madrid.

**Saloomeh Yousefian** She is a Ph.D. Candidate in Linguistics at the Complutense University of Madrid. She holds a Master's Degree in Applied Linguistics from Nebrija University (Madrid, Spain) and two Bachelor Degrees in Chemistry and Hispanic Philology from the Free University of Tehran. She actually works as the Head of International Development Department at Nebrija University and teaches in the Masters in Spanish Teaching as a Foreign Language at the same university. She is specialized in the Degree of Assertiveness and Attenuation in the Academic Discourse. Apart from her work experience in Spain, she has worked during thirteen years at the Kish Institute of Iran, as the Director of Foreign Languages Center and has worked as a Spanish Philology Professor at the Allameh Tabatabai University in Tehran. She has a Certificate of Excellence, issued by the United Nations Organization on Drugs and Crime (UNODC), for her collaboration as an interpreter in the Plan for Drug Abuse Prevention, organized between Spain and Iran.

# Cyberspace: An Advantageous Terrain for War?

**Giorgio Spagnol**

**Abstract** Cyber is an operational domain of conflict joining sea and air as other domains in which conflict may occur. Cyber defence is part of collective defence. Most crises and conflicts today have a cyber dimension, so treating cyber as an operational domain will enable to better protect one's missions and operations. Cyber-security is a priority in the field of International Relations, as cyber espionage can harm any global economy and hacking attacks are the modern way of committing espionage. Countries are increasingly militarizing the cyberspace where there is an ongoing confrontation between states: such confrontation is a mirror image of the ongoing international tensions. On the subject of law, countries should develop internationally agreed definitions of key terminology in the cyberspace in order to determine what constitutes an act of cyber warfare. A further concept to be considered is cyber resilience. Organizations should understand the impact of a potential cyber-attack and the steps required to prevent, survive, and recover from such an attack. In short, the cyber world, rapidly growing and increasingly sophisticated, constitutes a new sphere and implies a new type of relationship in international relations which need a "cyber policy" space, the most recent and most important area of interest in the theoretical and practical field.

**Keywords** Cyberspace · Cybersecurity · Internet of things · Digital borders

---

In: Security and the Global Commons, Edited by J. Martin Ramirez, and Bartolomé Bauzá-Abril. © 2021 Springer International. Submitted: August, 24, 2020; Accepted: September, 18, 2020.

---

G. Spagnol (✉)
Force Readiness, NATO, Bruxelles, Belgium
e-mail: bassano1052@yahoo.it

 
J. M. Ramírez and B. Bauzá-Abril (eds.), *Security in the Global Commons and Beyond*, Advanced Sciences and Technologies for Security Applications,
https://doi.org/10.1007/978-3-030-67973-6_8

# 1 Foreword

The world has moved into a new and unsettling geopolitical phase. It is not just multipolar, but multi-conceptual. This creates new risks and uncertainties, rising military tensions and causing economic and commercial disruptions (Done 2012, Chap. 2, pp. 35–51).

Security is today highly dependent upon the ability to go through the global commons. Secure global commons facilitate the protection of national territory and interests and enable the transit of goods, people, communications and data, upon which every member of the international community depends.

Nations increasingly rely upon the commons in a globalized world where the security of one state is tightly linked to the security of all.

The fundamental interdependency of these domains transcends their unique attributes and creates specific opportunities to improve security. By examining the twenty-first century's challenges within the global commons side by side, it will be possible to take steps to counter these challenges by addressing the threats, strengthening governance, and promoting stability within the commons (Murphy 2010).

# 2 Cyberspace Challenges

Cyberspace challenges transcend geographic boundaries and are usually trans-regional. States possess resources to sustain sophisticated cyber campaigns to penetrate even well protected networks, manipulate software and data, and destroy data, computers, and systems.

Aggressive non-state actors like criminals and hacktivists pose lesser threats than states but can still damage military capabilities and critical infrastructure (U.S. Cyber Command 2018).

The cyber domain makes it possible to gather privileged information, disrupt industrial processes, and create havoc by targeting critical infrastructures. Cyberspace offers an unprecedented level of plausible deniability, as the real perpetrator of a cyberattack is always difficult to identify with certainty.

By 2025, with the development of the Internet of Things (IoT), the cyber domain will connect more than 75 billion devices, many of which will control key functions of our daily lives and most of our critical infrastructures (Rugge 2018).

## *2.1 The Last Shot of the Internet*

While the attacks of September 11 were physical, we are facing increasing threats from hostile adversaries in the realm of cyberspace as well. Internet has now replaced land borders with digital ones, making it possible to connect the entire world into one sphere.

Of primary concern is the threat of organized cyberattacks capable of causing debilitating disruption to a nation's critical infrastructures, economy, or national security (U.S. White House 2003, p. 5).

A cyberattack is a powerful means to a wide variety of ends, from propaganda to espionage, by using methods that can cause dysfunctions of computer operations, stealing personal information, phishing, and stealing passwords of the user.

A small team that is highly motivated and equipped with the right set of tools and access can achieve huge monetary amounts without a multi-million-dollar investment.

Former U.S. President Obama speaking about cybersecurity did maintain, "America's economic prosperity, national security, and our individual liberties depend on our commitment to securing cyberspace and maintaining an open, interoperable, secure, and reliable Internet. Our critical infrastructure continues to be at risk from threats in cyberspace, and our economy is harmed by the theft of our intellectual property. Although the threats are serious and they constantly evolve, I believe that if we address them effectively, we can ensure that the Internet remains an engine for economic growth and a platform for the free exchange of ideas" (U.S. White House 2014).

## 3 Cyberspace Implications

Cyberspace is managed by stakeholders from civil society, the private sector, and, to a lesser degree, by governments. The latter, however, are increasingly asserting their role in cyberspace, leading to a redistribution of power in which states are not only competing with other stakeholders, but also amongst each other (Klimburg 2018).

The idea of deterrence, one of the main strategic elements ensuring some stability during the Cold War, is not adaptable to the cyber arena. Due to the intrinsic characteristics of cyberspace, the classical perception of power has limited applicability in the digital domain.

Beside deterrence, both the domain of ambiguity and of anarchy as rules are still in the making and states cannot rely on well-known and shared practices used in the kinetic domain. Therefore, defining rules for state behaviours is an absolute priority, especially when it comes to the use of force and coercion in cyberspace.

Attempts at the international level have been made but they left important issues unresolved. The absence of clear norms may ultimately lead, in the context of renewed international tensions, to a rapid escalation with potential dramatic "real world" implications (Rugge 2018).

To assess challenges, vulnerabilities, and implications in the cyberspace game and to identify what states can lawfully perform in such an environment, we have a look at five cases: Estonia, Iran, Ukraine as victims; Russia and China as attackers.

### 3.1 Estonia

Estonia was one of the first countries to experience cyber-security attacks, an event that still shapes the country today. This cyber-attack occurred during two days of protests in the capital (Tallinn), carried out by ethnic Estonians: the reason of the protests was that the Bronze Soldier, a symbol of the liberation from Nazism, was being moved from the centre of Tallinn to the outskirts of the city, in a military cemetery. This decision was due to the fact that ethnic Estonians did not see Red Army soldiers as liberators, but as occupiers; therefore, the statue represented a symbol of oppression, rather than of liberation: it was a political decision. Nonetheless, it sparked outrage among Russian Estonians, mainly because of the spread of many fake news regarding this government decision, coming from Russian news: for example, the fact that the statue was being destroyed. Within this delicate context, cyber-attacks started, and they were mainly thought to come from the Russian government (although there was no official evidence of this). The consequences of these attacks were that cash machines and online banking services were sporadically out of action; government employees were unable to communicate with each other on email, and newspapers and broadcasters suddenly found out they could not deliver the news. The attack showed how easily a hostile state can exploit potential tensions within another society. But it has also helped make Estonia a cybersecurity hotshot today: the government decided to set up a voluntary Cyber Defence Unit, where IT experts are trained on a voluntary base, donating their free time to defending their country online by practising what to do if a major utility or vital service provider is brought down by a cyber-attack.

### 3.2 Iran

Stuxnet is a computer virus that in 2010 hit the data banks of power plants, traffic control systems and factories around the world. Among the capabilities of the virus, there was the ability to turn up the pressure inside nuclear reactors, or switch oil pipelines while telling the system operators that everything was normal. Stuxnet exploited security gaps that system creators are unaware of, which are known as zero-days. The details of a zero-day can be sold on the black market for as much as 100,000 dollars. The term "zero-day" may refer to the vulnerability itself, or an attack that has zero-days between the time the vulnerability is discovered and the first attack. Cyber-weapons are developed by hacking groups and cybercrime to exploit zero-days on high-value targets. The target of Stuxnet was the centrifuges that spin nuclear material in Iran's enrichment facilities. The Washington-based Institute for Science and International Security (ISIS) said the virus may have shut down 1000 centrifuges at Iran's main facility, Natanz. Later that year, the UN's nuclear watchdog said that Iran had suspended nuclear activity without explaining why. The Bushehr Iranian facility, which was still under construction, was also hit by the virus, and if turned out that it could have caused a national electricity blackout. The response from Iran was an open call for hackers to join the Iranian Revolutionary Guard. There is still uncertainty regarding who was behind Stuxnet. Some references to the Hebrew Bible in the code suggested the involvement of Israel. Others considered the US to be involved. However, it may be more important to ask who will redesign the virus: 9 months after its detection, it has been made available online for anyone to download, an open-source weapon that is ready to be used again by anyone.

### *3.3 Ukraine*

Ukraine was the victim of a Russian-suspected cyber-attack, the only one that caused a real-world blackout. The Russian group that is suspected of attacking Ukrainian electric utilities in 2015 (and 2016) was Sandworm; these attacks cut off power to hundreds of thousands of people. Russia has been at war with Ukraine since it invaded the Crimean Peninsula in 2014 with Putin. Since then, not only the attacks caused national blackouts, but also the destruction of hundreds of computers at media companies; the deletion or permanent encryption of terabytes of data held by government agencies; the paralysis of many infrastructures such as the railway ticketing system. Also, the recent NotPetya ransomware epidemic that disabled thousands of networks (in Ukraine as well as in the rest of the world) is thought to come from Sandworm. These examples point out that cybercrime is a tremendous threat to today's digital society.

### *3.4 Russia*

Besides Ukraine and Estonia, Russia is considered to have attacked the Democratic National Committee in the US in 2016. Russia's approach to cyberspace has been deeply shaped by its Soviet Union past, in particular from the information war fought—and lost—against the West.

In 1998 Russians wanted to discuss both cybersecurity and the limitations to destabilising online content. The West refused to have that discussion, on the ground, essentially, of its self-proclaimed moral superiority, arguing that it was not possible to negotiate about information's content. Ironically, twenty years later, the West is forced to discuss with Moscow about the threat of manipulated online content, which probably is, in itself, a score on the Russian side.

To achieve its goals, Russia appears to have successfully developed technological capabilities and a particular informal public–private partnership with the hacker community (Rugge 2018).

### *3.5 China*

Chinese authorities resorted to ITs in 1980 and were thus able to control communication through the "Great Firewall of China", isolating the domestic Internet community from the rest of the world.

In January 2010, China is attributed to have launched cyber-attacks against 34 U.S. companies, including military contractors. Another instance was the breach of Australia's Security Intelligence Organisation in 2013. Even though both the U.S. and Australia attributed the attacks to the Chinese state, no sanctions were applied against the country (Carment and Belo 2018).

## 4 NATO's Role in Cyberspace

Cyber threats to Alliance security are becoming more frequent, complex, destructive, and coercive. Most recently, in 2018, NATO agreed on how to integrate sovereign cyber effects, provided voluntarily by Allies, into Alliance operations and missions, as well as standing up the initial Cyberspace Operations Centre. But addressing the complex and evolving challenges of cyberspace cannot be achieved only through military means (Brent 2019).

Some Allies have signalled a new policy to attempt to reduce malicious cyber activity while continuing to explore how best to similarly engage in cyberspace, as even a below-the-threshold cyberattack can be highly damaging, disruptive, and destabilising.

To date, the United States and the Netherlands are the most forthcoming about the role that offensive cyber operations could play in military operations and strategy. Whether cyber as another domain of conflict prompts greater openness regarding offensive cyber operations from other nations, NATO provides a degree of legitimacy for such operations as a part of alliance strategy that has been absent in the past.

But, as long as offensive cyber operations are still met with near-zero retaliation and Western defences remain inadequate, the attractiveness of cyber offence will continue to grow. Each time Western political, economic, and societal values might appear paralysed, the Western model loses public appeal at home as well as squanders credibility on the global stage.

### *4.1 Cyber Defence Cooperation Between NATO and the EU*

NATO and the EU currently have 21 member countries in common. Senior officials from NATO and the European Union met at the Alliance's Headquarters in Brussels on 17 December 2019 for discussions on cyber defence.

Over the last years, NATO and the EU have intensified their engagement on cyber. They exchange real-time information between incident response teams, participate in each other's exercises, and work on training and research, networks, and initiatives to promote cyber stability between states. They also addressed ways to prevent, deter and respond to malicious cyber activities (NATO 2019).

A Technical Arrangement on Cyber Defence was concluded between the NATO Computer Incident Response Capability (NCIRC) and the Computer Emergency Response Team for the EU Institutions, providing a framework for exchanging information and sharing best practices between emergency response teams.

## 5 World Order in the Cyber Age

According to Henry Kissinger (2014), there has never been a true world order. For most of history, civilizations defined their concepts of order. China conceived of a global cultural hierarchy with the emperor at its pinnacle. In Europe, Rome imagined itself surrounded by barbarians; when Rome fragmented, European peoples refined a concept of an equilibrium of sovereign states and sought to export it across the world. Now that international affairs take place on a global basis and the previous historical concepts of world order are meeting, Kissinger considers the possibility of a current world order and a cyber balance of power as opposed to a traditional one.

Kissinger (2014) does maintain, "Our age is insistently, at times almost desperately, in pursuit of a concept of a world order. Are we facing a period in which forces beyond the restraints of any order determine the future? Is, after Westphalia, a Balance of Power (BoP) possible in the cyber age? Or, in other words, which are the conditions for a balance of power, and which are the differences between a traditional balance of power and a cyber balance of power? The balance of power is not a celebration of power but rather an attempt to limit its use. The greatest need of the contemporary international system is an agreed concept of order. In its absence, the awesome available power is unrestrained".

Consistently with the cyber age, the conflict has turned from physical into virtual. Already in 1998, Shapiro (1998) did maintain: "Cyberspace is an autonomous place. What happens "there" is in some way unconnected to what happens "here". The real significance of cyberspace is not in its being elsewhere but, quite the opposite, in its coming increasingly closer to us and becoming ever more powerful, ultimately assuming the ability to transform or even undermine the legal and political foundations of our society. Cyberspace is a locus of control. It is a filter through which we can do almost anything: learn, work, socialize, transact, participate in politics. It is an interface that allows us to control other things: the information we are exposed to, the people we socialize with, the resources of the physical world. Cyberspace derives from the term cybernetics, which is the science of communications and control theory, particularly the study of automatic control systems. It derives from the ancient Greek word *kubernetes*, which meant steersman."

In such a context, according to Sun (2014), "States are the principal actors in the international system, as they set the terms of the intercourse, monopolize the legitimate use of force within their territories, and generally conduct foreign policy in a single voice. Hence states are also considered to be unitary actors in the international system. This assumption is important because if non-state or transnational actors are powerful enough to challenge state actors, power configuration in the world may no longer be considered in terms of polarity but, instead, in terms of the number of layers of policy networks."

In the XIX century, England and in the XX century the US towered over the entire world: in today cyber age it is up to the IT best performers to have a decisive say.

## 6 Strategy in the Cyber Age

As in the past, with the discovery of America, the pivot of power moved from the Mediterranean to the Atlantic, now it is shifting to the Pacific. Meanwhile, the current multipolar international system has witnessed the weakening of the US in coincidence with the wide availability of cyber technology to everybody.

In the current cyber age, there are two predominant traditions for principles of war: the western view of Clausewitz and the eastern view of Sun Tzu. Clausewitz conceptualizes war using mass, objective, and manoeuvre among other principles in a state-on-state kinetic war for a political objective. Sun Tzu conceptualizes war focusing on the criticality of intelligence, deception to defeat the mind of the enemy, and knowing that relationships between things (that is the network, the very structure of the cyber world) matter most in the strategy of war.

Due to the "non-kinetic" aspect of cyber warfare, Sun Tzu success for cyber strategy is due to its "one size fits all" remarks. Clausewitz is far more sophisticated and reading it is not easy. It is probably why there are few studies on how his vision of war can shape the fighting model in cyberspace.

Clausewitz's approach is related to sovereign States and war is an act of force, a zero-sum game. On the contrary, for Sun Tzu the best general is the one who wins the war without fighting but by securing a firm strategic position: what China is achieving by building artificial islands in the Pacific.

### *6.1 Cyber Versus Nuclear Weapons*

The world is heading into a less rules-based order in which actors can achieve in cyberspace what would be too risky in any other space. While in the event of a nuclear attack there is some time available to react, a cyberattack is characterized by invisibility and rapidity without any previous notice.

While the nuclear system is symmetric, in the asymmetric cyber system the success of the stronger contestant is not granted.

Nuclear weapons do have the capacity for tremendous destruction, but nuclear explosions are infrequent. By contrast, cyberattacks are incredibly frequent, such as to be more harmful in aggregate.

Bottom line: while the cold war balance of power was dynamic, the balance of power in cyberspace prioritizes more defence than attack.

## 7 Responsibilities

Organisations like the UN, NATO, the EU and OSCE can achieve the establishment of legally binding rules, taking into account the fact that the subjects are not just the States, but also IT industries and individuals.

United Nations (UN) Governmental Group of Experts is currently the only platform that has united the U.S., Russia, and China with commonly accepted norms and suggestions. Since the scope of interests in cyberspace includes all groupings of society including governmental and federal entities, private and public sectors as well as common citizens on a national level, private supra-powers regulation beyond borders and being responsible for larger audiences, there is an urgent need to focus on cooperation and establishment of fundamental rights in cyberspace as well as the mechanism to establish security in this sphere Parzyan (2017).

International conventions and treaties do not envision cyberspace so far. Cyber legislation could be anyway seen as an addition to the existing portfolio of current international norms: but until this new legislation is available, we should expect continued turmoil even if, as of today, only a few cyber actions have crossed the red line.

## 8 Cyber Security

Law enforcement is not yet adapted to cybercrime because of the newness and skill-intensive nature of the same.

According to Menny Barzilay, a former Israeli intelligence officer, "we're living in a very interesting time, where companies are becoming unwilling pawns in cyber warfare" and "nobody can say where the responsibilities of a company may end and those of a nation might begin" (Regalado 2014). For this reason, collaboration between public and private entities is vital to effectively combat cyber espionage.

On the subject of law, countries should develop national cyber strategies: this should be the base for the creation of international frameworks for cooperation with internationally agreed definitions of key terminology in the cyberspace.

As for cyber resilience, it should be applicable for any institution to understand the impact of a potential cyberattack and prevent, survive, and recover from such an attack.

## 9 How to React

The solution to potential challenges from Russia and China is not a military one but a political and collective one based on baseline requirements for building resilience, strong state capacity, authority, and legitimacy.

In building resilience, the main role of the military is not to challenge Russian or Chinese influence with hybrid tactics but to envision a wider end state in which the application of non-violent techniques such as civil-military activities, social media operations, and public affairs are more effective than the direct use of force.

NATO must work more closely with the Organization for Security and Cooperation in Europe (OSCE) and the European Union (EU). The latter have both capacities that NATO does not, such as maintaining a position of impartiality in mediating ethnic conflict, economic and humanitarian political resources, inclusive and consensus-based decision-making, and a history of non-violent involvement in complex conflicts (Carment and Belo 2018).

As for OSCE, it is the largest regional security organization in the world (extending from Vladivostok to Vancouver) with 57 participating States from Iceland to the former Soviet republics of Central Asia and from Norway to Malta. The United States, Russia, and Canada also are participating States, as are the smaller European states of Andorra, the Holy See, and San Marino.

Simultaneous oversight measures mandated by the OSCE and the EU are essential to achieving a coordinated and inclusive response.

## 10 Further Considerations

Fundamentally, the balance of power is based on a compromise: it cannot satisfy every actor in the international system completely. It works best when it keeps one state from predominating and prescribing laws to the rest and prevent the aggrieved parties from seeking to overthrow the international order. It does not purport to avoid crises or even wars. Its goal is not aimed at reaching peace, but rather moderation and stability (Klimburg and Faesen 2018).

The lack of experience in resorting to cyber operations is hampering states to define new norms and develop new techniques for coercion.

If the victim is not allowed by law to react, an aggressor may proceed unpunished with his attacks. Cybersecurity should therefore establish consequences for malicious cyber actions by establishing the boundaries of permissible behaviour in cyberspace.

Any cyber opponent needs to be aware that hacking is not penalty-free: legal tools such as countermeasures, sanctions and indictments should therefore be identified and effectively enforced.

While involving also private actors in the process, the central role of the UN must be accepted and recognized worldwide. We need ideas that recognise the world as it is, conflictual and dominated by states.

## 11 Conclusion

Today's geopolitical situation involves a desire to solidify new norms of conduct. The solution to challenges is not a military one but a political and collective one.

If the international stability becomes volatile, the risk of escalations of the conflict in the conventional domain becomes increasingly concrete, and the international balance of power more and more difficult to assess.

Although it is very difficult to understand "what is going on" in cyberspace and to rely on a certain attribution of responsibility for cyberattacks, a lot of information is available, and a common understanding is developing about each international actor's motivations and behaviour (Rugge 2018).

Cyberattacks can pose a serious threat to national security as they inflame not only regular warfare but may also provoke irregular warfare with equal information access and anonymity. Moreover, what is lacking are common norms and definitions as well as specifically composed legislation for peaceful and collaborative regulations of problematic issues.

Cybersecurity is an urgent strategy, which must lead to cooperation, free and secure access to and sharing of information.

NATO must work closely with the European Union and OSCE to effectively extend security guarantees to its members.

As already stressed, identifying rules for state behaviours is an absolute priority, as the absence of clear norms may ultimately lead to potentially dangerous implications.

## References

Brent, L. (2019). *NATO's role in cyberspace.* NATO review. https://www.nato.int/docu/review/articles/2019/02/12/natos-role-in-cyberspace. Accessed 13 Aug 2020.

Carment, D., & Belo, D. (2018). *War's future: The risks and rewards of grey-zone conflict and hybrid warfare.* Canadian Global Affairs Institute. https://www.cgai.ca/wars_future_the_risks_and_rewards_of_grey_zone_conflict_and_hybrid_warfare. Accessed 13 Aug 2020.

Done, A. (2012). *Global trends: Facing up to a changing world.* London: Palgrave Macmillan.

Kissinger, H. (2014). *World order: Reflections on the character of nations and the course of history.* New York: Penguin Press.

Klimburg, A., & Faesen, L. (2018). *A balance of power in cyberspace.* The Hague Centre for strategic studies. https://www.jstor.org/stable/resrep19350. Accessed 13 Aug 2020.

Murphy, T. (2010). Security challenges in the 21st century global commons. *Yale Journal of International Affairs, 5*(2), 28–43.

NATO. (2019). *NATO, European Union experts review cyber defence cooperation.* December 17, 2019, https://www.nato.int/cps/en/natohq/news_172157.htm?selectedLocale=en. Accessed 13 Aug 2020.

Parzyan, A. (2017). Cyberspace—A manmade domain for wars. *21st Century, 1*, 42–57.

Regalado, A. (2014). *Spying is bad for business: Can we trust an Internet that's become a weapon of governments?* MIT Technology Review. March 18, 2014. https://cdn.technologyreview.com/s/525526/spying-is-bad-for-business/?set=525511. Accessed 13 Aug 2020.

Rugge, F. (Ed.). (2018a). *Confronting an "axis of cyber"? China, Iran, North Korea, Russia in Cyberspace.* Milano: Ledizioni LediPublishing.

Rugge, F. (2018b). *"Mind hacking": Information warfare in the cyber age*. Italian Institute for International Political Studies, No.319. https://www.ispionline.it/en/pubblicazione/mind-hacking-information-warfare-cyber-age-19414. Accessed 13 Aug 2020.
Shapiro, A. L. (1998). The disappearance of cyberspace and the rise of code. *8 Seton Hall Const. L.J., 703*, 715–723.
Sun, M. (2014). *Balance of power theory in today's international system*. E-International Relations, February 12, 2014. https://www.e-ir.info/2014/02/12/balance-of-power-theory-in-todays-international-system/. Accessed 13 Aug 2020.
U.S. Cyber Command. (2018). *Achieve and maintain cyberspace superiority: Command vision for U.S. Cyber Command*. https://www.cybercom.mil/Portals/56/Documents/USCYBERCOM%20Vision%20April%202018.pdf?ver=2018-06-14-152556-010. Accessed 13 Aug 2020.
U.S. White House. (2003). *The national strategy to secure cyberspace*. Department of Homeland Security. https://us-cert.cisa.gov/sites/default/files/publications/cyberspace_strategy.pdf. Accessed 13 Aug 2020.
U.S. White House. (2014). *Statement by the president on the cybersecurity framework*. Feb 12, 2014. https://obamawhitehouse.archives.gov/the-press-office/2014/02/12/statement-president-cybersecurity-framework. Accessed 13 Aug 2020.

**Major General (retired) Giorgio Spagnol** was posted from 1997 to 2000 to the Italian Embassy in Islamabad (Pakistan) as Defence, Army, Naval and Air Force Attaché. In 2001 he was appointed Deputy Commander of the SEEBRIG (Southern Eastern Europe Brigade) located in Plovdiv (Bulgaria). One year later, he attended the Centre des Hautes Etudes Militaires (CHEM) and the Institut des Hautes Etudes de Défense Nationale (IHEDN) in Paris (France). After commanding the Brigade, in 2004 he was appointed Italian Senior National Representative in the United States for Operations "Iraqi Freedom" (Iraq) and "Enduring Freedom" (Afghanistan). From 2005 to 2007 he was in Belgium as European Union Director of Operations (EUDO) responsible, among others, of Operation EUFOR ALTHEA in Bosnia-Herzegovina. From 2007 to 2009 he was in Turin as Director of the Post Conflict Operations Study Centre (PCOSC). And since then until 2012 he served at NATO, in Belgium, as Director Force Readiness.

He has a Master in Strategic Studies and a Master in International Relations. He is currently member of the: Institut Européen des Relations Internationales—IERI (Brussels—BE); International Institute of Humanitarian Law—IIHL (Sanremo—IT); and European Federalist Movement—EFM. He cooperates with: United Nations Interregional Crime and Justice Research Institute—UNICRI (Turin); United Nations System Staff College—UNSSC (Turin); Istituto per gli Studi di Politica Internazionale—ISPI (Milan); and Istituto Affari Internazionali—IAI (Rome).

# Cyberspace as a Global Common: Framing the Libyan War in RT, RTVE and La Sexta Television Videos

**José Manuel Moreno-Mercado, Óscar G. Luengo, and Javier García-Marín**

**Abstract** In recent years, scholars have been increasingly concerned by the attempted manipulation associated with false information in traditional mass media and the Internet (one of the emergent Global Commons). In fact, a new terminology has become popular, like the increasing use of the term "Fake News". These attempts of manipulation have been associated with state actors who might want to intervene in different political systems, such as the Russian, Iranian or Chinese. We propose the comparison of the coverage of traditional media outlets with those non-democratic State-Sponsored media. In particular, *RT* (Russia), *RTVE* and *La Sexta Television* (Spain), in their YouTube channels and websites. Since the beginning of this century, media and conflict research has brought five generic and recurring frames in every armed confrontation: *conflict*, *humanitarian consequences*, *responsibility*, *economy* and *morality*. However, the *security* frame has been very present in the news coverage of wars, especially since the beginning of the so-called war on terror that arose after the 9/11 attacks. Our hypothesis is formulated as follows: the frames portrayed by the non-democratic state-sponsored media are different to the traditional media. The one of the most important conflicts after the Arab Spring: the Libyan war.

**Keywords** Cyberspace · Framing · Security · Human drama · Media · Libya

In: Security in the Global Commons and Beyond, Edited by J. Martin Ramirez, and Bartolomé Bauzá-Abril. © 2021 Springer International. Submitted: September, 14, 2020; Accepted: October, 14, 2020.

J. M. Moreno-Mercado (✉) · Ó. G. Luengo · J. García-Marín
University of Granada, Granada, Spain
e-mail: jmmoreno95@correo.ugr.es

Ó. G. Luengo
e-mail: ogluengo@ugr.es

J. García-Marín
e-mail: jgmarin@ugr.es

 
J. M. Ramírez and B. Bauzá-Abril (eds.), *Security in the Global Commons and Beyond*, Advanced Sciences and Technologies for Security Applications, https://doi.org/10.1007/978-3-030-67973-6_9

## 1 Introduction

Scholars of international relations have continually underlined the growing intangible component of war. Cyberspace has become more of a battleground, explaining that there has been an explosion of research about misinformation or influence operations. This complex reality invites us to think that the role of new media and social networks are fundamental in understanding political and sociological processes. A characteristic example of this phenomenon is found in the study of Fernández-García and Salgado (2020), which shows how online anti-elite comments present similar results in Spain and Portugal, despite the different electoral success of populist parties in these two countries.

No one doubts that the use and exploitation of the Global Commons is a strategic element of significant importance to states. At the beginning of this millennium, Barry Posen (2003) noted that U.S. military hegemony came not only from the control of those Global Commons, but from its ability to deny access to outsiders. Examples include the Persian Gulf War (1991), the intervention in Somalia (1993) or the Libyan war (2011), among others. Within the spaces that International Law makes up as Global Commons, cyberspace is arguably the most volatile and influential element of all. On the one hand, because it is a totally virtual environment created by man in which private actors and non-state entities are fundamental. And, on the other hand, the consequences and effects of electronic warfare are considered to be on the same scale as those of conventional warfare. In addition, cyberwar is considerably more affordable than conventional warfare, depending primarily on human resources. Therefore, even countries with scarce resources can become formidable adversaries in cyberspace.

Specialized literature on how states use information technologies, and new media as public diplomacy are becoming increasingly abundant. In this sense, there is an important academic interest in the role of countries, such as Russia, Iran and China in the spread of fake news and disinformation processes. In the Russian case, some authors point out that the Kremlin sees cyberspace as a perfect way to weaken and undermine its strategic adversaries (De Pedro 2019). However, there are a few applied studies that analyze the anomaly behavior of the Russian media with an external presence.

However, it is not easy to demonstrate that the media with state bonds are controlled, in their newsrooms, by those same states (with the understanding that control is propaganda). After all, many democratic governments control some media outlets as public entities (the British *BBC* being one of the best examples). However, mass media has routines inherent to the journalistic profession. Therefore, a good way to show whether a media outlet is a propaganda agency, is to demonstrate that such journalistic routines do not exist in its coverage.

Thus, this research aims to compare the behavior of two official media, *RTVE*[1] (Spain) and *RT*[2] (Russia) and one private-owned, *La Sexta*[3] (Spain), on their respective websites and YouTube channels, when reporting an event of important strategic interest (the war in Libya) for the European Union (EU) and Russia. We understand that the two Spanish media, belonging to a democratic country, will be dominated, fundamentally, by journalistic routines and not by spurious interests. Through the analysis of two generic frames, *security* and *human drama*, we will attempt to answer the question of whether the Russian media exhibits similar behavior to traditional Spanish media. In short, to provide empirical evidence to the debate on Russia's role in disinformation to European audiences.

## 2 New Media, International Relations and Conflicts

The genesis of media-government studies lies in the socializing role of the media in democratic processes. This prominence of the media, including social media, relies on the freedom of expression. Beyond the comparative theoretical debate, relevant authors point out the importance of political communication as a tool of public diplomacy, both in times of war and peace. An illustrative example would be the case of the Israeli *Hasbara*. In the words of Jędrzejewska (2020): "even though Israel is trying to influence the foreign public opinion with facts it may not win in this battle of 'hearts and minds'" (p. 116). For this reason, the technological revolution is seen as a major challenge for the external projection of states.

The informational needs of the *information age*have led to the inclusion of new media in military reports and in the development of one's own strategic thinking. Torres-Soriano (2009) argues that any actor who wishes to influence the story must adapt to the rhythms and logics of the "media show" (p. 35). In other words, the impact on cyberspace has gone from being a residual element, to being considered a decisive political-military factor. Proof of this is the importance of the cyber world in the so-called *Gerasimov's Doctrine* (Gerasimov 2013) or the Chinese approach to information warfare[4] (Zhang et al. 2010).

However, the emergence of new discussions and concepts is not only applicable in the case of the foreign policy of states. Web 2.0 has made clear the potential of the decentralization and democratization of major social movements (Luengo and Fernández-García 2017). This explosion of cyberspace has reconfigured communication logic in both countries (Spain and Russia), with high and highly restrictive freedom rates. This statement is based on the importance of the Internet and social media in large mobilizations (in countries with very different degrees of freedom),

[1] Acronym of Radio Televisión Española.

[2] Previously called Russia Today.

[3] The Sixth, in Spanish language.

[4] *Xinxihua zhanzheng*.

such as the Velvet Revolution in Armenia (Atanesyan 2019), the Arab Spring (Benkirane 2012), the 15-M Movement in Spain (Toret 2013), or the Black Lives Matter Movement protests following the murder of George Floyd in the United States (Jones 2020), among others.

It is common among international relations scholars, to indicate the relevance of the Internet in the development of armed conflicts. The various papers mostly point to four fundamental elements. Firstly, the end of traditional media hegemony. Secondly, the cybernetic explosion of non-state actors in asymmetrical conflicts. Thirdly, the ease of mobilization of individuals and the strengthening of loyalties. And, fourthly, the low economic cost of influence operations.

There is an important literature that analyses the use of these information technologies but very few studies compare how traditional media have moved to the new cyber environment. Nevertheless, there is unanimity in stating that the armed conflicts of the future will be strongly influenced by the technological environment that facilitates the media dimension of the same (Torres-Soriano 2011).

YouTube's case is especially relevant in the conflicts. Research that has dealt with the *YouTube Wars*phenomenon can be classified into two distinct blocks. On the one hand, studies that analyze the website as a more digital platform in which different actors create, visualize and expand their own content (Crilley and Chatterje-Doody 2020; Makhortykh 2020). And, on the other hand, papers addressing the possibilities of platform as well as its advantages and weaknesses (Mirrless 2015; Trottier and Fuchs 2014). The latter block features very significant research such as Andén-Papadoupoulos (2009), showing how videos produced by U.S. soldiers served as a media counterweight to official information on the Iraq war.

In the authors' view, research developed provides novel data. YouTube's huge broadcast has been exploited by the Kremlin through its official *RT*channel (formerly called Russia Today) albeit with disparate effectiveness (Orttung and Nelson 2019). Although*RT*'s activities have been extensively studied, we observe a comparative literature deficit. The comparison between traditional European and emerging media, such as *RT*, is a field of research yet to be addressed (Moreno-Mercado and García-Marín 2020). On the other hand, most analyses that focus on RT and their coverage of armed conflict, focus on the cases of Syria and Ukraine (Dajani et al. 2019; Szostek and Hutchings 2015). Vladimir Putin's successive foreign policy speeches point to Russia's attempts to expand its areas of influence beyond Central Asia and post-Soviet space. For this reason, the authors consider the study of the media dimension of other conflicts, such as Libya's, as a significant scientific necessity. Especially given that Russia was one of the great aggrieved by the fall of dictator Muammar al-Gaddafi and has shown itself to be one of the most important international players in the Libyan conflict (Tekir 2020).

The UN mission in the Arabic country (UNSMIL[5]) estimated that, in April 2020, more than 893,000 people needed humanitarian aid. Official data on the number of deaths during battles between actors vary depending on the sources and stage of the conflict itself. Carlos Echevarría (2020), together with other analysts, narrows

[5]Acronym of United Nations Support Mission in Libya.

three distinct stages. First, the armed clashes that ended the*Arab Jamahiriya* with the assassination of Colonel Gaddafi in Sirte. Second, the civil conflict that followed the 2014 elections with the establishment of two governments, one in Tripoli and one in Al Baida (2014–2019). And, third, a final stage initiated with the offensive (later failed) of General Haftar to Tripoli with the subsequent intervention of Egypt and Turkey (2020-present).

Successive stages of war have led to extensive debates about the future of conflict, responsibility and the role that NATO, or the fight against terrorism must play. However, there is unanimity in calling the conflict a strongly internationalized confrontation. Megerisi (2020) argues that "the internationalization of the conflict poses a geostrategic nightmare for the United Nations (UN)'s efforts towards stabilization and has upped the stakes for Libya's civil war, posing an even greater threat to international security". Of course, Russia's role has not gone unnoticed from Western political and military spheres that point to the Kremlin's willingness to occupy a position of importance in MENA[6] region. U.S. diplomat Ethan Chorin (2017) noted that Libya is a distant target of Russian interests but at the same time represents a medium-term opportunity. In other words, Vladimir Putin's government sees in Libya an opportunity to present itself as a peacemaker of the region as well as a possible way to expand Russia's economic interests. Likewise, scholars, such as Dyner (2019) consider Russian support for Haftar to be part of an ambitious Russian diplomatic campaign (with military priorities) towards Africa.

## 3 Methodology

Along these lines, attempts have been made to show the connection between new media, international relations and armed conflicts. This study is based on the framing theory in order to provide an empirical vision that conjures these three areas of research. The framing aims to explain how some aspects and considerations stand out over others within a political debate (Bartholomé et al. 2017), which justifies its importance. On the basis that the conflict is one of the main guidelines of the news, and that conflict of ideas is the backbone of democracy, how information is exposed to the audience will undoubtedly determine certain judgments, assessments, decisions and behaviors that it makes. Comparing *RT*, *RTVE* and *La Sexta*'s YouTube channels when reporting on the war in Libya is a necessary contribution to studies on political communication, international relations and security and defense. Especially, because Libya is a key strategic enclave for a number of important international and regional actors, such as the EU, Turkey, Egypt or the United States (U.S.).

The use of frames as a methodological tool is well established in political communication studies. In essence, authors indicate that frames are devices which journalists use to explain reality in a way that is consistent with the cultural background of a given group. Thus, they also form part of journalistic routines. In a standard media

[6]Acronym of Middle East and North Africa.

environment, the frames used by the media change according to the information that is to be transmitted. Obviously, this does not prevent manipulation by the media themselves. But routines do not usually disappear. In our case, we should see how the media uses traditional frames to report on armed conflicts, alternating between the human drama and security frames, depending on the content of the information: the former to talk about victims and the latter to refer to the political consequences of the conflict. This should be stable in different societies, as long as there is no strong interference in the news making process.

The overall objective of the research is, thus, to compare the use of those two exclusionary frames (*security* and *human drama*) on the YouTube channels and websites of *RT*, *RTVE* and *La Sexta* media outlets, when reporting on the Libyan conflict (2014-present). The most recent papers point to an abnormal behavior of *RT*compared to traditional media (Moreno-Mercado and García-Marín 2020). To reinforce this idea, it has been decided to compare the use of *RT* frames with a traditional public medium (*RTVE*) and a private medium (*La Sexta*). In our view, it is a very pertinent way of entrenching the theoretical debate on the non-consideration of *RT* as a traditional means of communication.

As mentioned in the theoretical framework, the crisis in Libya began with protests against the Gaddafi regime in the context of the Arab Spring. However, this study takes as a reference the subsequent conflicts of the 2014 parliamentary elections. This dimensioning of the study period is due to two fundamental reasons. First, the intervention in Libya against Gaddafi's government in 2011 was unanimously supported by the countries that make up the UN Security Council. Second, the consolidation of two governments facing each other in 2014, led to polarization among international actors when positioning themselves in the civil war. In other words, a more internationalized period of war has been chosen with a more active role of non-State foreign actors.

The so-called Second Libyan Civil War, which actively pits into action the GNA[7] and the LNA,[8] has already been studied from a media point of view. Of course, research on this issue shows the agreement between the coverage of certain agencies, such as *Al-Jazeera* and *Al-Arabiya*, and the external agendas of states involved in the conflict, such as Qatar and Saudi Arabia (Adhikari and Slyvany 2020). However, this chapter is not intended to analyze media positioning, but to demonstrate the use of different journalistic routines in traditional media (through the disparate use of frames). Especially, in the case of*RT* as its information line is continuously questioned in European countries. Therefore, the following hypothesis is established:

H: The Russian media (*RT)* and the Spanish media (*RTVE* and *La Sexta*) diverge their respective frames when reporting on the conflict in Libya.

A conventional methodology, content analysis, has been followed to respond to the hypothesis. Following Krippendorff (1990), this technique is widely used in Political Communication studies, as it combines quantitative and qualitative elements. YouTube videos have been extracted from the media channels themselves in their

[7]Government of National Accord.

[8]Libyan National Army.

Spanish versions. Due to the absence of its own tags towards the Libyan topic, the content in the Spanish media has been extracted from the newscasts posted on the respective YouTube channels. The search for the news was made on the dates when important events of the conflict took place, such as *Operation Dignity* or ceasefire negotiations in Moscow. The justification for such selection is due to the impossibility of having a rapidly extracting database (such as *Lexis-Nexis*) and the Libyan conflict having less media attention in Spain than other wars, such as Syria. The study period is from 1 January 2018 to 25 August 2020 (N = 200). This period has been chosen with the intention of giving the most up-to-date view possible of the media dimension of the conflict. Likewise, it is important to note the difficulty of locating videos prior to 2018, since the content on the conflict is inscribed in other videos of a more generalist nature (especially in the case of *La Sexta*).

The search for frames has been carried out from the categories proposed by Entman (1993). As the case of study is an event typical of international politics, the frames have been codified from the definition of the problem. The first reading of our sample justifies the study of the two frames analyzed, since the Libyan conflict was not covered under a unique frame. These frames correspond to the classic frames present in -almost- all armed conflicts and have very specific dynamics:

(1) The *human drama* frame: the video-news story refers to the suffering of the Libyan population, aspects of the humanitarian situation, violent deaths of women and children, gender oppression on traditional aspects or refugee movements to Europe and other countries.
(2) The *security* frame: the video-news story refers to the instability of the region, jihadist activities, the role of international actors (USA, Russia, Turkey, etc.), battles or aspects of the securitization of the migration flows.

The coding has been carried out in an exclusive way (presence/absence). In other words, dichotomously. In addition, the codebook has included other technical aspects: video description, mention of official sources, presence/absence of experts, genre (news, reports, interviews or critics) and comparison with other conflicts.

## 4 Findings

The search and selection of the videos has had certain difficulties that must be noted. The contributions of Santín and Alvarez-Mazoncillo (2020) show the need for the Spanish press to adopt more effective strategies on their YouTube channels. It is true that the media analyzed are not part of the written press, but of the television field. However, only in the case of*RT* it has been possible to access the content quickly and directly through the YouTube platform's own search engine. In the cases of *RTVE* and *La Sexta* all videos have been extracted from their own web sites. In addition, *La Sexta*has audiovisual material available from 2018 only, which has certainly limited this research. This difficulty shows that the possibilities offered by the platform in the digital ecosystem are not properly exploited by traditional Spanish means. This gap is also evident in other areas, such as in the case of the Spanish political class (Ramírez-Gil and de Travesedo-Rojas 2020).

As for the frequency of coverage, it has remained more or less constant over the past two years. Figure 1 shows that the Libyan conflict is an international event of importance for the three media. Nevertheless, informational growths and decreases vary substantially depending on the medium. In the case of traditional Spanish media (*RTVE* and *La Sexta*), the moments of greater coverage coincide with serious humanitarian events. *La Sexta* concentrates its biggest production of videos in July 2018, a month where more than 1000 migrants were rescued in the Mediterranean in a single day. In addition, this period coincides with the Italian government's refusal to allow the arrival of boats full of immigrants. August 2019 is the most relevant month for the coverage of *RTVE*, a month which devoted great importance to the collaboration between the NGO-ship *Proactiva Open Arms* and National Maritime Rescue to rescue immigrants near Spanish waters. This data was expected due to the state character of *RTVE*. Finally, *RT*'s behavior differs from the previous two media. As can be seen, the growths coincide with newsworthy events for the three media, but the moments of greater dissemination differ. April 2019 is the most significant month for the Russian channel. In this period, Marshal Haftar's offensive to snatch Tripoli from the GNA (*Operation Dignity*) began. According to the experts cited by the *BBC*, the LNA offensive is considered one of the worst crises since the overthrow of Gaddafi (BBC 2019).

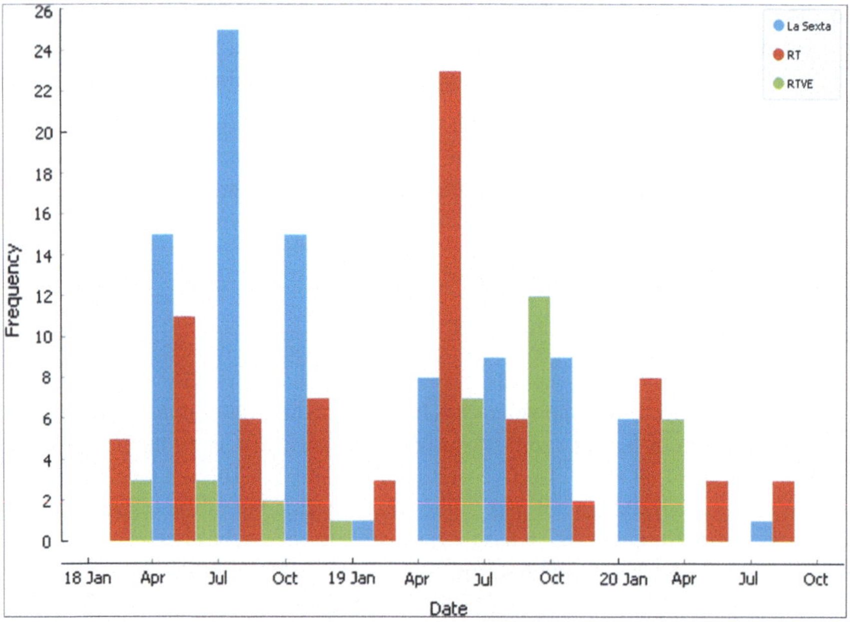


**Fig. 1** Number of videos per month and year (2018–2020). *Source* Own elaboration

**Table 1** Use of frames in Spanish and Russian media videos. *Source* Own elaboration

| | La Sexta (Spain) | | RTVE (Spain) | | RT (Russia) | |
|---|---|---|---|---|---|---|
| Security frame | 8 | 9% | 10 | 29.4% | 49 | 63.6% |
| Human drama frame | 81 | 91% | 24 | 70.6% | 28 | 36.4% |
| Total | 89 | 100% | 34 | 100% | 77 | 100% |

The frequency of publication of the videos and the timing of their publication are a good measure of how the media has framed the Libyan crisis. The content analysis used (with mutually exclusive frames) has left very significant and enlightening results for the hypothesis. Table 1 shows that *human drama* frame has been mostly used by both *RTVE* and *La Sexta*(70.6% and 91% respectively). As with the written press, humanitarian explanations play an important role in the media, although a process of securitization has been experienced in recent years (García-Marín and Calatrava-García 2018; Moreno-Mercado 2018). Since 2015, Spain has participated in the*EUNAVFORMED*[9] *Sophia* mission although the naval mission in the Mediterranean was temporarily cancelled in 2019[10] due to the lack of European consensus on landing of rescued migrants. Since the failed 2014 elections, and the subsequent fight against ISIS in Libya, several NGOs based in Spain have been responsible for giving voice and rescuing the thousands of people trying to reach Europe from the African country. The intense activity of these organizations and their spokespersons (in addition to the collaboration with the Spanish public administration) is continuously addressed by the Spanish media: "The Open Arms is still waiting for a safe harbor" (*RTVE*, 04/08/19), "Aquarius requests safe harbor to disembark 141 migrants" (*RTVE*, 12/08/18), "IOM warns of massive boat departure from Libya: 600 people in 48 h" (*La Sexta*, 22/11/19). In this sense, the position of the government of Matteo Salvini in blocking the arrival of ships at Italian ports is also highly relevant.

As mentioned earlier, *RT* results fall within the expected parameters. In the case of the Russian channel, the *security*frame clearly dominates media coverage (63.6%). The literature review analyzed points to the Putin government's interest in giving a way out of the Libyan conflict through support for a strong leader, such as Haftar, who unifies the various military factions operating in the country while combating groups related to ISIS and Al-Qaeda (Núñez-Villaverde 2020). However, the Russian position in the face of the conflict has been varying, given that Haftar had strong support from Washington at the beginning of the war and Turkey's strong commitment to its military support for the GNA: "Russia rejects U.S. accusations of making fake money in Libya" (*RT*, 31/05/20), "Trump yields to Egypt and Saudi Arabia to support Haftar" (*RT*, 13/05/19), "Accuse NATO of using weapons with depleted uranium in Libya", (*RT*, 14/07/18).

The flexibility of the selected methodology has made possible to operationalize other variables of importance to research. In this respect, the coding of the technical aspects of the videos are a good parameter to know the professional routines of the analyzed media. Figure 2 shows very clear differences between the media studied.

---

[9]Acronym of European Naval Force Mediterranean, Operation Sophia.

[10]Operation Sophia is developed by the Grappa Detachment of the Spanish Air Force.

Firstly, the quote to journalistic sources yields interesting results. The state-Spanish channel *RTVE* mentions the sources consulted in 70.60% of the videos produced while in the private-owned medium, *La Sexta*, this frequency is 84.30%. As shown in Table 1, the *human drama* frame is mostly used by these channels, resulting in a large use of organizations, such as *Proactiva Open Arms*, *Amnesty International* or the UN, as sources of information. Obtaining information from these organizations is clearly identifiable in the titles of some videos viewed: "UN warns of risk of humanitarian crisis in Libya", (*RTVE*, 13/04/19), "Doctors Without Borders accuses Libya of endangering the lives of migrants in a rescue", (*La Sexta*, 28/07/18). Important data is observed in the case of *RT*. The Russian channel only mentions its sources in 50.60% of the videos, a fact that can be interpreted as a challenge to the very credibility of the medium. True, the media's more than 1000 satellite networks allow it to be projected to an audience of millions of people (RT 2020). However, Yablokov (2015) argues: "Its capacity as a public diplomacy tool to advocate for the policies of the Russian state and the difficulties it faces in providing balanced news coverage its reputation among wider audiences" (p. 311).

Secondly, the use of experts to entrench/reinforce ideas has also left differences to be taken into account. As in the previous aspect, *RT* gets significantly lower results (19.50%) compared to *RTVE* (47.10%) and *La Sexta* (40.4%). Video titles also show noticeable qualitative differences. In the case of *RT*, the term "Expert" is commonly used while in Spanish media it is common to cite the name and organization of the specialist consulted. Furthermore, most experts consulted by *RT* come from the world of intelligence analysis dedicated to security, defense and geopolitics. In contrast, *RTVE* and *La Sexta* support, for the most part, their editorial line in NGO and activists operating in the Mediterranean and Libya: "Expert: EU mission in Libya will have no positive effect", (*RT*, 18/02/20), "Vicente Raimundo (Save the Children): "Minors

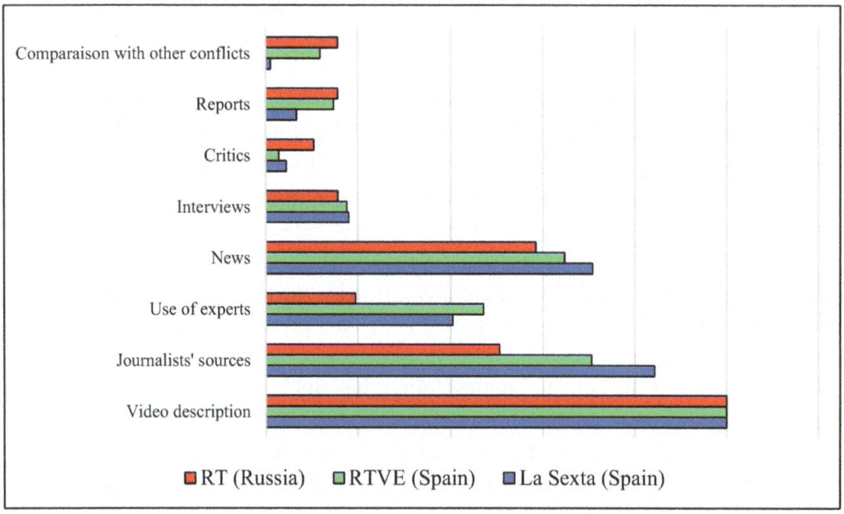


**Fig. 2** Technical aspects of the videos. *Source* Own elaboration

are fleeing war and famine situations. There are trafficking-victim girls" (*La Sexta*, 28/12/18).

Finally, the specific genre of the video shows how the "news" format predominates in all three media. The expected data, considering that most videos are framed within the newscasts of the channels. The Russian news channel is the medium that devotes the most to reviews and reports (10.4% and 15.6% respectively). The results are within the expected parameters, as the existing literature shows *RT*'s informative interest in showing alternative views to Western information. In this vein, Fig. 2 points out that *RT* is the most comparative medium between the Libyan crisis and other armed conflicts. Something logical considering *RT*'s extensive coverage of conflicts where Russia plays a decisive role, such as those in Syria or Ukraine. In this sense, a professional routine very marked by general criticism of the American and European position in the MENA region that is consistent with Yablokov's initial research (2015) which stands out: "U.S. military presence: million-dollar costs and thousands of dead, *RT*, 02/01/20", "Iraq, Libya, and now Syria: three interventions, three disasters, *RT*, 16/04/18".

Based on bibliographic review conducted, the following hypothesis was established: The Russian media (*RT)* and the Spanish media (*RTVE* and *La Sexta*) diverge their respective frames when reporting on the conflict in Libya. The establishment of dichotomous frames (*security* and *human drama)* has led to the conclusion that our hypothesis has been validated. The selection of a public medium (*RTVE*) and a private medium (*La Sexta*) has been very relevant as a measurement parameter for classifying the Russian channel. Our goal, therefore, was not to delve into the media point of view, but to demonstrate that *RT*'s behavior differs from what we might consider traditional means. The Spanish case is also ideal, since Spain perfectly meets the criteria of the Polarized Pluralism model. In our view, *RT*'s professional routines are more conditioned by the restrictive nature of the Russian political system itself (Economist 2020; Freedom House 2020) than his (state) property.

## 5 Conclusion

The explosion of the Internet, understood as a network of networks, has made cyberspace the predominant channel to inform in recent years. The possibilities it allows, the low production costs and the magnitude of potential audiences have consolidated it as the Global Common with more possibilities and challenges to explore. In the field of international relations, the latest research points to the need to acquire greater knowledge in disinformation, cybersecurity and cyberwarfare in the military sphere (González-Concha and Ramos-Castillo 2020). Consequently, this is an extremely important fact. The informational threats associated with soft power have effectively followed similar patterns to conventional military threats (Hatuel-Radoshitzky and Yarchi 2020), as shown by the *rally' round the flag* effect (Mueller 1973).

Following Sanagovich (2017), the economic disaster that led to the demise of the Soviet Union (USSR), along with foreign intervention, have led the Kremlin to have put in place great efforts to build sophisticated propaganda and counter-propaganda tools. In this sense,*RT*'s emergence into the international scene and its coverage of international events has captured the interest of academics and analysts. However, there is still little research applied that empirically demonstrates the irregular behavior of this type of media. Although there are already some studies that focus on *RT*'s interest in international policy events (López-Olano and Fenoll 2019; Moreno-Mercado 2019).

In addition to the confirmation of the hypothesis (validated), other conclusions have needed to be drawn. The search and selection of videos indicates the successful use which *RT* is making from platforms like YouTube. The vast majority of videos located on their web portal has links to the famous video platform. On the contrary, in the Spanish media the search has had more difficulties. On the one hand, because much of the media content had advertising spots (which may be unattractive to an audience seeking quick and concise information). And, on the other hand, because much of the information relating to the Libyan conflict, especially in the case of *RTVE*, was available in podcast format (intended for a more professionalized audience).

It is surprising that there are no videos about the pre-2018 conflict, particularly in the case of *La Sexta*. While it is true, the fact that the European Union has not had a single voice in the face of the Libyan conflict, we must not forget the importance of Libya for Spain. Firstly, because of the migratory flows since they only separated by 2489 km. And secondly, because successive Spanish governments have maintained close diplomatic relations with the previous Gaddafi government.

In short, this paper is intended to be an important contribution within the Media and Conflict Studies. The future over the media effects of conflict coverage appears to be unpredictable. Moreover, a larger process of media distribution through digital platforms, such as YouTube, will be critical to counteracting the possible influences of pro-Kremlin speeches. Speeches by a Russia that aspires to influence all possible scenarios, including in areas of distant influence, such as Libya. Especially, because while Spanish media coverage may be classified as very limited, opinion barometers indicate that a significant part of Spanish society is interested in international policy (Elcano 2020).

## References

Adhikari, P., & Slyvany, I. (2020). Libyan conflict in the eyes of Arab Media: A comparative study of how Al-Jazeera & Al-Arabiya news agencies represented the fighting groups in Libyan conflict and their claim to be the legitimate government.

Andén-Papadopoulos, K. (2009). U.S. soldiers imaging the Iraq War on YouTube. *Popular Communication, 7*(1), 17–27.

Atanesyan, A. V. (2019). The impact of social networks on protects activities (the case of Armenia). *Sotsiologicheskie Issledovaniya*, (3), 73–84.

BBC. (2019). Asedio a Trípoli: la cruenta ofensiva rebelde que ha sumido a Libia en su peor crisis desde la caída de Gadafi. *BBC News*.

Bartholomé, G., Lecheler, S., & de Vreese, C. (2017). Towards a tipology of conflict frames. Substantiveness and intervetionism in political conflict news. *Journalism Studies*, 1–23.

Benkirane, R. (2012). The alchemy of revolution: The role of social networks and new media in the Arab Spring. *GCPS Policy Paper, 7*(1).
Chorin, E. (2017). Rusia juega a la espera estratégica en Libia. *Monografías CIDOB*, 17–22.
Crilley, R., & Chatterje-Doody, P. N. (2020). Emotions and war on YouTube: Affective investments in RT's visual narratives of the conflict in Syria. *Cambridge Review of International Affairs*, 1–21.
Dajani, D., Gillespie, M., & Crilley, R. (2019). Differentiated visibilities: RT Arabic's narration of Russia's role in the Syrian war. *Media, War & Conflict*, 1–22.
De Pedro, N. (2019). Desinformación rusa contra la Unión Europea. In Torres-Soriano M (coord.) (ed) *#Desinformación. Poder y manipulación en la era digital* (pp. 29–42). Granada: Comares.
Dyner, A. M. (2019). *Russia's Libya Policy*. Poland: Polski Instytut Spraw Międzynarodowych.
Echevarría, C. (2020). Libia una guerra interminable. *Revista General De Marina, 278*, 909–918.
Economist. (2020). The inclusive Internet index 2020. *The Economist*.
Entman, R. M. (1993). Framing: Toward clarification of a fragtured paradigm. *Journal of Communication, 43*(4), 51–58.
Fernández-García, B., & Salgado, S. (2020). Populism by the people: An analysis of online comments in Portugal and Spain. *SMSociety'20: international conference on social media and society*, 210–219.
Freedom House. (2020). Nations in Transit 2020. Dropping the democratic facade, *Freedom House*.
García-Marín, J., & Calatrava-García, A. (2018). The use of supervised learning algorithms in political communication and media studies: Locating frames in the press. *Communication & Society, 31*(3), 175–188.
Gerasimov, V. (2013). El valor de la ciencia en la anticipación. *Военно-Промышленный Куреьр*, (8), 8–476.
González-Concha, L. Á., & Ramos-Castillo, G. A. (2020). *La asignatura de guerra cibernética y la formación académica especializada de los cadetes de comunicaciones de la Escuela Militar de Chorrillos Coronel Francisco Bolognesi 2019*. Perú: Comando de Educación y Doctrina del Ejército Escuela Militar de Chorillos.
Hatuel-Radoshitzky, M., & Yarchi, M. (2020). Rally' round the flag revised: External soft threats and media coverage. *Media, War & Conflict*, 1–21.
Instituto Elcano. (2020). 41ª Oleada BRIE, abril 2020. *Real Instituto Elcano*.
Jones, K. L. (2020). #BlackLivesMatter: An analysis of the movement as social drama. *Human & Society, 44*(1), 92–110.
Jędrzejewska, K. Z. (2020). Hasbara: Public diplomacy with Israeli characteristics. *Torun International Studies, 1*(13), 105–118.
Krippendorff, K. (1990). *Metodología de análisis de contenido*. Barcelona: Paidós.
Luengo, O., & Fernández-García, B. (2017). Political participation and new technologies of communication in Spain. *Przegląd Politologiczny*, (3), 21–31.
López-Olano, C., & Fenoll, V. (2019). Posverdad, o la narración del *procés* catalán desde el exterior: BBC, DW y RT. *El profesional de la información, 28*(3).
Makhortykh, M. (2020). Remediating the past: YouTube and second world war memory in Ukraine and Russia. *Memory Studies, 13*(2), 146–161.
Megerisi, T. (2020). Geostrategic dimensions of Libya's civil war. *Africa Security Briefs*, (37).
Mirrless, T. (2015). The Canadian Armed Forces "YouTube War": A cross-border military social media complex. *Global Media Journal: Canadian Edition, 8*(1).
Moreno-Mercado, J. M. (2019). La comunicación estratégica en RT: construcción de encuadres en los conflictos de Yemen y Ucrania. *Revista Política Y Estrategia*, (133), 97–117.
Moreno-Mercado, J. M. (2018). La cobertura mediática de los conflictos armados. El caso de Siria. *Revista de Paz y Conflictos, 11*(2), 115–142.
Moreno-Mercado, J. M., & García-Marín, J. (2020). Conflictos armados y cobertura mediática: aproximación al aprendizaje de máquina supervisado. *Convergencia: Revista de Ciencias Sociales, 27*, 1–26.
Mueller, J. E. (1973). *War, presidents and public opinion*. New York: Wiley.
Núñez-Villaverde, J. (2020). Libia sigue sin encontrar la salida. *Real Instituto Elcano, 5*.
Orttung, R. W., & Nelson, E. (2019). Russia today's strategy and effectiveness on YouTube. *Post-Soviet Affairs, 35*(2), 77–92.

Posen, B. (2003). Commands of the commons: The military foundation of U.S. hegemony. *International Security, 28*(1), 5–46.
RT (2020) Quienes somos. *RT*.
Ramírez-Gil, M., & de Travesedo-Rojas, R. G. (2020). Gestión política española en YouTube. Una asignatura pendiente. *Observatorio (OBS*), 14*(1).
Sanagovich, S. (2017). *Computational propaganda in Russia. The origins of digital misinformation.* Nueva York: New York University.
Santín, M., & Álvarez-Monzoncillo, J. M. (2020). YouTube en la prensa española: un modelo por definir. *El profesional de la información (EPI), 29*(1).
Szostek, J., & Hutchings, S. (2015). Dominant narratives in Russian political and media discourse during the Ukraine crisis. In S. McGlinchey, M. Karakoulaki, & R. Oprisko (Eds.), *Ukraine and Russia: People, politics, propaganda and perspectives* (pp. 183–196). Bristol: International Relations.
Tekir, G. (2020). Russian-Turkish involvement in the civil war in Libya. *Türkiye Rusya Araştırmaları Dergisi, 2*(3), 190–215.
Toret, J. (2013). Tecnopolítica: la potencia de las multitudes conectadas. El sistema red 15M, un nuevo paradigma de la política distribuida. *IN3 working paper series.*
Torres-Soriano, M. R. (2011). Guerras Youtube. El impacto de las nuevas tecnologías de la información en el tratamiento mediático de los conflictos armados. *Cuadernos De Estrategia*, (148), 129–157.
Torres-Soriano, M. R. (2009). Información y conflictos bélicos en la era de Internet. In J. J. Fernández-Rodríguez, J. Jordán-Enamorado, & D. Sansó-Rubert Pascual (Eds.), *Seguridad y defensa hoy: construyendo el future* (pp. 29–51). Madrid: Plaza y Valdés.
Trottier, D., & Fuchs, C. (2014). *Social media, politics and the state: Protests, revolutions, riots, crime and policing in the age of Facebook, Twitter and YouTube.* Routledge.
Yablokov, I. (2015). Conspiracy theories as a Russian public diplomacy tool: The case of Russia Today (RT). *Politics, 35*(3–4), 301–315.
Zhang, Y., Liu, S., & Xia, C. (2010). Lun xinxihua zhanzheng de zhanju kongzhi yishu. *Zhongguo Junshi Kexue, 2*, 24–31.

**José Manuel Moreno-Mercado** is Ph.D. Candidate in Department of Political Science at the University of Granada. Graduate in Political Science by University of Granada and Master's degree in Peace Culture, Conflicts, Education and Human Rights by Institute of Peace and Conflicts (IPAZ) and the same university. Also is author of several articles and collaborations on books about Media and Conflict Studies and has participated in numerous conferences.

**Óscar G. Luengo** is an Associate Professor of Political Science at the University of Granada. Chair of the Re-search Committee on Political Communication (RC22) of the International Association of Political Science (IPSA). Director of the Ibero-American School of Higher Studies in Local Government of the Ibero-American Union of Municipalists (UIM). Visiting researcher at the European University Institute (Florence, Italy), at the Johannes Gutenberg-Universitat (Mainz, Germany), and the Amsterdam School of Communications Research (Netherlands). Visiting professor at the University of California, Berkeley (USA) among other international universities.

**Javier García-Marín** is an Associate Professor in the Department of Political Science and Administration at the University of Granada. He holds a Ph.D. in Political Science, a degree in Contemporary History and a Master's degree in Economics and International Relations. He has been a visiting professor at the London School of Economics and Political Science, Glasgow Media Unit, the Amsterdam School for Communications Research, the Institut d'Etudes Politiques de Bordeaux and the University of Buenos Aires. He is a contributor to multiple international projects.

# Does Foreign Cyber Intervention in Electoral Processes Violate International Law?

**Sonia Boulos**

**Abstract** Foreign cyber interference in electoral processes is on the rise. While this phenomenon in is not new, cyber interference in particular has gained a considerable international attention, especially with the surge of allegations on a Russian interference in the 2016 United States (US) elections. However, the unanimous political condemnation of foreign interference in elections was not paralleled with a unanimous agreement on their legality under international law or lack of. This chapter analyzes the legality of remote cyber interference in foreign elections focusing on three central principles of international law: State sovereignty, the principle of non-intervention and the right to self-determination of peoples.

**Keywords** Cyber interference · Elections · Sovereignty · Non-intervention · Right to self-determinations

## 1 Introduction

Foreign interference in electoral processes through cyber means is on the rise. While election meddling is not new, the alleged Russian cyber meddling in the 2016 US elections marked a shift in political and legal debates on the legitimacy and legality of foreign interferences in electoral process (van der Staak and Wolf 2019).

The alleged Russian interference in the 2016 United States (US) election included: hacking into state and local boards of election with no evidence of votes being affected; the hacking of the Democratic National Committee servers and obtaining e-mails of senior Democratic officials such as John Podesta, and releasing the data via WikiLeaks and DC Leaks; spreading disinformation and "fake news" on social

In: Security in the Global Commons and Beyond, Edited by J. Martin Ramirez, and Bartolomé Bauzá-Abril. © 2021 Springer International. Submitted: September, 15, 2020; Accepted: October, 2, 2020.

S. Boulos (✉)
Nebrija University, Madrid, Spain
e-mail: sboulos@nebrija.es

 
J. M. Ramírez and B. Bauzá-Abril (eds.), *Security in the Global Commons and Beyond*, Advanced Sciences and Technologies for Security Applications,
https://doi.org/10.1007/978-3-030-67973-6_10

media; and spending more than two million dollars to purchase anti-Clinton and pro-Trump advertising on Twitter, Facebook, and Instagram. It is alleged that Russian trolls used social media to encourage approximately forty anti-Clinton protests and pro-Trump rallies in swing states. The aim of this complex influence campaign was not merely boosting the chances of Trump and denigrating Hilary Clinton, it also aimed at keeping certain voters from the polls and undermining public faith in the electoral system (Hollis 2018; Schmitt 2018).

Both the U.S. and the Soviet Union/Russian Federation (hereinafter Russia) have a long history of interference in foreign elections. In fact, they intervened in one out of nine of competitive national-level executive elections held between 1946 and 2000. A total of 117 partisan electoral interferences were conducted by the US. and the Russians, with the majority of the operations (69%) being conducted by the US (Levin 2019). Approximately 64% of these interventions were covert and were not known to the public before the elections. According to Levin (2019), such operations had significant effects on election results, often determining the identity of the winner.

One might ask what was so unique about the alleged Russian intervention in the US elections that triggered intensive political and legal debates? The answer to this question lies in the recognition that modern information and communication technologies have transformed foreign meddling in elections making it less costly. Cyberspace has enabled more States to exert influence on foreign election. It also made foreign meddling more effective, since it allows foreign States to influence directly large masses. According to van der Staak and Wolf (2019), more national elections currently rely on different combinations of traditional and technology-based procedures. This new reality creates certain vulnerabilities in relation to electronic voting. Also, voter registration databases and electoral management bodies are becoming more vulnerable to cyber-attacks. Other forms of cyber interference in foreign elections include: conducting cyberattacks against election-related infrastructure aimed at breaching the confidentiality, integrity and availability of election technology and data; engaging in disinformation campaigns and spreading fake news to undermine the credibility of the electoral process; conducting cyberattacks against electoral stakeholders such as parties, candidates, media and campaigns; and engaging in disinformation campaigns designed to shape the political debate on crucial issues (van der Staak and Wolf 2019: 13).

While foreign cyber interference in elections is universally condemned by States, there is debate on whether such methods of interference constitute a violation of international law. This chapter attempts to analyze the legality of cyber interference in foreign elections by referring to three central principles of international law: State sovereignty, the principle of non-intervention and the right to self-determination of peoples. The chapter will analyze the applicability of these principles to cyber operations targeting foreign electoral processes. The chapter is divided into three main parts: the first part addresses the principle of sovereignty and its application to cyber interference in foreign elections; the second part focuses on the principle of non-intervention, and the third part focuses on the right to self-determination.

The chapter suggests that cyber operations targeting foreign elections take advantage of the gray areas in international law. Only in exceptional and rare cases, such as the case of cyber-attacks that alter election results or cyber-attacks that prevent elections from taking place, international law is clearly violated. The chapter also suggests that compared to the principle of sovereignty and the principle of non-intervention, the right to self-determination offers the strongest legal framework for analyzing cyber meddling in foreign elections.

## 2 The Principle of Sovereignty

The principle of sovereignty refers to the supreme authority within a territory (Besson 2012). In the Island of Palmas arbitration case, sovereignty was defined as follows:

> Sovereignty in the relations between States signifies independence. Independence in regard to a portion of the globe is the right to exercise therein, to the exclusion of any other State, the functions of a State. (1928: 838)

Beyond representing supreme authority in a given territory, this definition highlights another important component of sovereignty, i.e. the independence and freedom of States (Besson 2012). Sovereignty encompasses two elements: territoriality and State functions (Schmitt 2018). One of the difficulties in relying on the concept of sovereignty to analyze the legality of foreign meddling in local elections is the lack of consensus on the legal status of Sovereignty. There is a dispute whether sovereignty constitutes a primary rule of international law. The Tallinn Manual 2 on the International Law Applicable to Cyber Operations (Tallinn Manual 2) states that sovereignty is a rule of international law (Schmitt 2017). Also the UN Group of Governmental Experts on Developments in the Field of Information and Telecommunications, which was composed of State representatives, concluded that:

> State sovereignty and international norms and principles that flow from sovereignty apply to the conduct by States of ICT [Information and communication technologies]-related activities and to their jurisdiction over ICT infrastructure within their territory. (UN 2015: para. 15)

It seems that some countries are retracing from their earlier position that views sovereignty as a primary rule of international law. For example, in an article coauthored by Colonel Gary Corn, the Staff Judge Advocate of U.S. Cyber Command, and Robert Taylor, a former senior attorney from the Department of Defense's Office of General Counsel, both argued that sovereignty is a principle but not a primary rule of international law (Corn and Taylor 2017).

Others view sovereignty as "a baseline principle of the Westphalian international" (Corn 2017). As such, sovereignty is protected by the prohibition on the use of force against other states or in the customary norm on non-intervention. However, it is not an enforceable rule in itself (Corn 2017). If sovereignty does not constitute a primary rule of international law, then Russian alleged interference in the US elections and other cases of election meddling cannot qualify as an internationally wrongful act. Some view sovereignty as both a primary rule of international law and a principle. This position was adopted unanimously by the Tallinn Manual 2 (Schmitt 2018).

Even if sovereignty constitutes a primary rule of international law, applying it to foreign cyber meddling in elections raises certain difficulties. In the Tallinn manual 2, the Group of International Experts, who convened for drafting the manual, generally agreed that a remotely conducted cyber operation, which causes physical damage to cyber infrastructure, constitutes a violation of sovereignty even when the damaged infrastructure is private (Schmitt 2017). Since foreign cyber meddling in election rarely produces physical damage to cyber infrastructure, this qualification provides little help in assessing the legality of such actions. Usually, States opt for lesser means to conduct their cyber operations, such as causing loss of functionality of election systems or loss of functionality of cyber infrastructure with a nexus to the election (such as the servers of a political party) (Schmitt 2018).

The Tallinn Manual 2, expanded the notion of damage to cover loss of functionality. The Group of International experts believed that rendering cyber infrastructures ineffective should be equated with physically damaging them. However, even on this point there were some disagreements. The Group of International Experts did not reach a consensus as to the precise meaning of loss of functionality. Some experts believed that a violation of sovereignty requires an irreversible loss of functionality, others opted for a lower threshold, mainly situations in which some physical repair is necessary (Schmitt 2017). However, remote cyber-attacks targeting elections rarely meet such thresholds.

The concept of sovereignty as "State function" seems more promising in tackling foreign cyber interference in electoral processes. While the concept of an "inherently governmental function" lacks clarity, some functions can easily be qualified or disqualified as an inherent governmental function. For example, commercial activities of States clearly do not fall under the category of inherently governmental functions. This is reflected, *inter alia*in carving out exceptions to the doctrine of foreign State immunity to exclude commercial activities from immunity (Kaczorowska-Ireland 2015). Conversely, law enforcement and defending the territorial integrity of the State constitute classical examples of inherently governmental functions (Schmitt 2018). Holding election too pertains to the core of the notion of "inherently governmental function" (Schmitt 2018). A violation of State sovereignty occurs when the actions of a foreign State constitute interference in or usurpation of the victim State's ability to perform inherently governmental functions. Schmitt defines interference as "activities that disturb the territorial State's ability to perform the functions as it wishes" (2018: 45). Usurpation entails "performing an inherently governmental function on another State's territory without its consent" (Schmitt 2018: 45–6). In the context of foreign meddling in elections, usurpation is less relevant.

Whether foreign cyber interference in electoral processes meets the definition of interference depends on its impact. According to Schmitt, foreign cyber operations that alter election data or voters' registrations numbers constitute illegal interference. Cyber operations that target election machinery or private computers to prevent voters from casting their vote would also amount to interference in sovereignty. However, engaging in election propaganda does not amount to interference (Schmitt 2018).

In the 2016 election, the alleged Russian meddling did not include changing or deleting data or blocking people from casting their vote. Instead, Russia focused on releasing private information to the public, and distributing disinformation and fake news. These actions fall under the rubric of propaganda. This demonstrates that the concept of sovereignty has its limits in contributing to the debate on the legality of foreign meddling in elections.

## 3 The Principle of Non-Intervention

The principle on non-intervention forms part of international costmary law (Shaw 2008). According to the International Court of Justice (ICJ), the principle of non-intervention involves the right of every sovereign State to conduct its internal and external affairs without outside interference (Case Concerning Military and Paramilitary Activities in and Against Nicaragua 1986). The ICJ further emphasized that the prohibited intervention must be one bearing on matters in which each State is permitted, by the principle of State sovereignty, to decide freely, such as the choice of a political, economic, social or cultural system, and formulation of foreign policy (Case Concerning Military and Paramilitary Activities in and Against Nicaragua 1986). For an intervention to be wrongful, it must resort to coercive measures in relation to such choices:

> The element of coercion... is particularly obvious in the case of an intervention which uses force, either in the direct form of military action, or in the indirect form of support for subversive or terrorist armed activities within another State. (Case Concerning Military and Paramilitary Activities in and Against Nicaragua 1986: Para. 205)

Elections constitute the core of the State's *domaine reserve,*as reflected in the UNGA resolution "Respect for the principles of national sovereignty and non-interference in the internal affairs of States in their electoral process" (UNGA 1989). The resolution reaffirms that:

> [A]ny activities that attempt, directly or indirectly, to interfere in the free development of national electoral processes, in particular in the developing countries, or that are intended to sway the results of such processes, violate the spirit and letter of the principles established in the Charter and in the Declaration on Principles of International Law concerning Friendly Relations and Cooperation among States in accordance with the Charter of the United Nations. (UNGA 1989)

According to Jamnejad and Wood, it is not absolutely clear whether the principle of non-intervention prohibits, for example, the funding of political parties abroad. But the fact that States usually fund foreign parties through non-state actors suggests that States have doubts about the legality of their actions (Jamnejad and Wood 2009).

But without coercion, States interference in foreign elections does not amount to a violation of the principle of non-intervention. Coercion constitutes the essence of prohibited intervention. Only actions that intend to force a policy change in the target State can violate this principle (Jamnejad and Wood 2009). Coercion can take many forms. The Declaration on Principles of International Law concerning Friendly

Relations and Cooperation among States in accordance with the Charter of the United Nations states.

> No State may use or encourage the use of economic, political or any other type of measures to coerce another State in order to obtain from it the subordination of the exercise of its sovereign rights and to secure from it advantages of any kind (emphasis added). (UNGA 1970: Preamble)

Economic and political measures can also violate the principle of non-intervention. For example, exerting financial pressure on a State to force it to accept secessionist demands against its territorial integrity, or making the acceptance of such demands a condition for joining a regional institution violate the principle of non-intervention. In comparison, requiring a state to respect international obligations applicable to its territory (such as the requirement to respect its international human rights obligations), in order to negotiate its membership in a regional organization, does not violate the principle of non-intervention (Kohen 2012).

International law does not provide a clear definition of coercion. In Oppenheim's International Law, coercion is described as an interference that is.

> forcible or dictatorial, or otherwise coercive, in effect depriving the state intervened against of control over the matter in question. Interference pure and simple is not intervention. (Jennings and Watts 1992: 432)

Unlike lawful interference, the element of coercion embedded in the principle of non-intervention "implies massive influence, inducing the affected state to adopt a decision with regard to its policy or practice which it would not entertain as a free and sovereign state" (Ziolkowski 2013: 433). Buchan (2016) argues that the principle of non-intervention protects the metaphysical aspect of state sovereignty, i.e. the state's political integrity. Accordingly, a narrow understanding of the element of coercion provides an inadequate protection to the state's political integrity. Therefore, any conduct which "compromises or undermines the authority of the state" (Buchan 2016: 78) must be regarded as coercive.

Rule 66 of the Tallinn Manual 2 states that "A State may not intervene, including by cyber means, in the internal or external affairs of another State" (Schmitt 2017: 312). Reiterating the position of the ICJ, the Tallinn Manual 2 also defines the principle of non-intervention as prohibiting foreign intervention in a State's*domaine reserve*through the use of coercion. The Group of International Experts agreed that coercion "refers to an affirmative act designed to deprive another State of its freedom of choice, that is, to force that State to act in an involuntary manner or involuntarily refrain from acting in a particular way" (Schmitt 2017: 317). The Tallinn Manual 2 further states:

> [C]oercion must be distinguished from persuasion, criticism, public diplomacy, propaganda, retribution, mere maliciousness, and the like in the sense that, unlike coercion, such activities merely involve either influencing (as distinct from factually compelling) the voluntary actions of the target State or seek no action on the part of the target State at all. (Schmitt 2017: 318–9)

Schmitt argues that coercion entails subordinating the sovereign will of the target State (Schmitt 2018). Therefore, a cyber-operation that interferes with the ability of a foreign country to hold an election or manipulates elections' results constitutes a clear violation of the rule on non-intervention. The same could be said about cyber-attacks that aim at blocking voting (Schmitt 2018). Again, such scenarios are rare since most foreign interferences in elections do not prevent States from conducting elections, nor they block voters from casting their votes. In most cases, the dividing line between exerting influence and coercion is very blurred.

Additionally, there is a debate as to whether coercion requires direct causal nexus between the acts of the foreign State and the results of the elections. For example, The Group of International Experts who participated in drafting the Tallinn Manual did not reach a consensus on this point. The majority believed that an indirect causation of coercive effect is enough. An example of an indirect causation is denial of service attack against the party's website, email or other forms of online campaigning at a critical timing in the election or generating false messages purportedly from the party (Schmitt 2017, 2018).

Schmitt argues that coercion can take place when an electoral interference "results in the election of a candidate who otherwise would not win, the weakening of a successful candidate's political base, or the strengthening of an unsuccessful candidate's base in anticipation of future elections" (Schmitt 2018: 51). Other scholars refute this argument.

Ohlin argues that the ICJ ruling in the Nicaragua case implies that coercion "forces the target State to act by virtue of its desire to avoid the consequences that flow from a threatening State's illegal or impermissible action" (Ohlin 2016: 1589). If the State actions are permissible under international law, the interference would not violate the principle of non-intervention. Relying on the jurisprudence of the United States Supreme Court and on philosophical reflection on essence of coercion, he criticizes the approach that limits coercion only to actions that are legally impermissible. He also emphasizes that the "*sine qua non*of coercion is that the threat compelled the State to act in a way that it otherwise would not act, not that the threatened consequence was illegal" (Ohlin 2016: 1592).

Still, Ohlin believes that the Russian interference in the US elections does not amount to illegal intervention. A legal finding of coercion depends on identifying an individual or a collective as the target of the coercive action (Ohlin 2016). Applied to the Russian interference in the US election, Ohlin poses the following questions: "Was it the American voters? Were they coerced into voting for Trump and not for Clinton? If so, what were the threatened consequences?" (Ohlin 2016: 1592). Even if we assume that Hilary Clinton was the target of coercion, it is unclear whether she was threatened explicitly or even implicitly with coercive actions for refusing to adopt a more favorable attitude towards Russia (Ohlin 2016). According to Hollis, "having a target adopt or change certain behaviors willingly—implies an absence of coercion" (Hollis 2018: 41). Even if data dumps on WikiLeaks and elsewhere at a crucial election juncture involved coercion, it is hard to identify the targets of such operations or the threatened consequences thereof (Hollis 2018).

## 4 Right to Self-Determination

Some scholars have resorted to the right of peoples to self-determination and their right to control their own destiny, to argue that cyber interference in foreign elections constitutes a breach of international law. In describing the harms of the Russian interference in the 2016 US elections, Schmitt refers to the harms inflicted on American voters even without liking this harm to self-determination:

> Arguably, the covert nature of the troll operation deprived the American electorate of its freedom of choice by creating a situation in which it could not fairly evaluate the information it was being provided. As the voters were unaware that they were being manipulated by a foreign power, their decision making, and thus their ability to control their governance, was weakened and distorted. The deceptive nature of the trolling is what distinguishes it from a mere influence operation. (Schmitt 2018: 51)

Ohlin (2016) argues that once we shift the discussion from the victim State to its people, the concept of sovereignty loses its prominence to a new contender, i.e. the right to self-determination. The right to self-determination is "one of the essential principles of contemporary international law" (Case Concerning East Timor 1995: 102). This right is guaranteed in common article 1 of the International Covenant on Civil and Political Rights and the International Covenant on Social, Economic and Cultural Rights, which states that:

> All peoples have the right of self-determination. By virtue of that right they freely determine their political status and freely pursue their economic, social and cultural development. (UN 1966a, 1966b)

According to the ICJ, the right to self-determination "requires a free and genuine expression of the will of the peoples concerned" (Western Sahara Advisory Opinion 1975: para. 56). In other words, self-determination is a right held by peoples alone and not by governments.

Tsagourias (2019) argues that traditional reading of the principle of non-intervention vests all sovereign authority and will in the government, but it disregards how this authority and will are formed. He emphasizes that "a government's authority and will remains free only when its sourcing is also free" (Tsagourias 2019: 13). Therefore, it is the right to self-determination that should take a center stage in discussing the legality of foreign cyber interference in elections. Tsagourias rightly argues that the right to self-determination is broader than simply a people establishing their own State.

In 1988, UNESCO convened an international conference of experts to study the role of self-determination in preventing conflicts. The conference described the right to self-determination as:

> an **ongoing process of choice**for the achievement of human security and fulfilment of human needs with a broad scope of possible outcomes and expressions suited to different specific situations (emphasis added). (van Praag and Seroo 1998: 11)

The Conference emphasized that self-determination is "a process rather than an outcome" (van Praag and Seroo 1998: 22). At its core, self-determination means that "human beings, individually and as groups should be in control of their own destinies and that institutions of government should be devised accordingly" (van Praag and Seroo 1998: 22). The election process is the ultimate expression of a people's sovereign will and right to self-determination. Tsagourias argues that doxing and disinformation operations carried out by a foreign State to change the course of an election "distorts, undermines or inverses this process and nullifies the genuine expression of authority and will by the people" (Tsagourias 2019: 14). Such interference:

> substitutes the authentic process of self-determination with an artificially constructed process in order to generate particular attitudes and results aligned to the intervenor's will…the intervening state controls not only the peoples' cognitive environment within which authority and will are formed but also their choices. (Tsagourias 2019: 16–7)

Ohlin addresses three main criticisms against the invocation of right to self-determination in the context of foreign interference in elections. First, it could be argued that once a State is established, the right to self-determinations fades into the background shifting the discourse to State sovereignty. However, he emphasizes that State sovereignty and self-determination are not mutually exclusive. The principle of self-determination "remains an important guiding principle and runs parallel to the legal concept of State sovereignty" (Ohlin 2016: 1596).

Second, the invocation of the right to self-determination to condemn, say, the Russian interference in the US election presumes that we can identify, ex ante, the sovereign will of the American people, to be able to argue that the Russian interference distorted that will. To answer this line of criticism, Ohlin hints that the essence of self-determinations lies in the ability of the voters to engage in counterfactual thinking; this exchange was disrupted by the Russian interference, without which the election would have proceeded differently (2017). However, this argument too is of a factual nature. It requires assessing the impact that doxing and disinformation campaigns had on public debates concerning elections.

Third, if the Russian interference in the US elections constitutes a violation of the right to self-determination of the American people this entails that the US interference in other elections equally constitutes a violation of the right to self-determination. To answer such a criticism, Ohlin claims that there is a difference between "interventions that frustrate democratic self-government and interventions that support it" (Ohlin 2016: 1597). However, it is not clear whether such distinction is supported by international law. It is not Russia's preferences that are reprehensible, it is the means that Russia had employed to advance them that are reprehensible. Even if Russia's preferred candidate would consolidate even more democratic values and human rights in the US, it would still be reprehensible for Russia to resort to deception and the spread of disinformation to boost the electability of its favorable candidate.

Moreover, the US interference in support of regime or government changes was not always guided by strengthening democratic values and genuine self-determination of peoples. Just to name a few, in 1953, the democratically elected Iranian Prime Minister, Mohammed Mossadegh, was ousted and replaced by an authoritarian monarch, Mohammad Reza Pahlavi, favorable to Washington. In 1948 the US boosted the chances of Italy's Christian Democrat party to guarantee its victory over the Popular Democratic Front, a leftist coalition led by the Italian Communist Party. The US sent millions of dollars to the Christian Democrat party while CIA operative launched an unprecedented and clandestine propaganda campaign to support it. This campaign included fabricating sex scandals to tarnish the image of communist leaders, massive letter writing campaign from Italian-Americans to their relatives and friends in Italy and intensive propaganda campaigns (Tharoor 2016). Therefore, the distinction made by Ohlin is too simplistic.

Hollis tries to distinguish legitimate influence operations from illegal ones. He relies on the definition of influence operations provided by a RAND[1] study:

> Influence operations are the coordinated, integrated, and synchronized application of national diplomatic, informational, military, economic, and other capabilities in peacetime, crisis, conflict, and post conflict to foster attitudes, behaviors, or decisions by foreign target audiences that further U.S. interests and objectives. (Larson et al. 2009: 2)

This definition includes the following three elements: (a) the utilization of resources (monetary, economic, informational, human, etc.); (b) such resources are utilized to achieve cognitive effects among State leaders, elites or mass publics; and (c) the desired cognitive effects promoted by the influence campaign are designed to advance the interests of the State engaged in the operation (Hollis 2018).

Hollis identifies (2018) five criteria that could be useful in trying to distinguish between acceptable and unacceptable Influence Operations:

1. *Transparency*: Some influence operations are transparent, meaning that the State is transparent and open about its responsibility and ownership of the resources utilized. Hollis brings the example of his father, a Lieutenant in the U.S. Navy, who worked as a dentist in rural Vietnam offering villagers free dental care. As he points out, his father's work formed part of a larger influence operation "to win the "hearts and minds" of the Vietnamese population" and to foster support of the US presence in the country (Hollis 2018: 31). Conversely, some operations are clandestine, leading the State to false flag the source of the influence operations. Many influence operations fall in the gray zone between fully transparent operations and completely clandestine ones.
2. *Deception*: Some influence operations involve the dissemination of accurate information, others disseminate disinformation, and false and "fake news".
3. *Purpose*: Some influence operations aim at changing public conceptions in general terms, others aim at achieving cognitive effects in relation to a specific issue, and some aim at creating chaos and uncertainties to debilitate the target State. International law clearly prohibits influence campaigns that involve illegal propaganda, such as inciting to genocide, violence or hatred. Beyond this category, it is difficult to drew a clear line between lawful and unlawful influence. Hollis hints that narrowly tailored operations, such as those targeting a specific piece of legislation or elections, are more problematic.

---

[1]The RAND Corporation is a nonprofit institution that helps improve policy and decision-making through research and analysis.

4. *Scale*: Influence operations used to be costly, but the information age and the creation of the cyber space lowered the costs of influence operations and expanded their reach. Hollis hints that large scale influence operations could be more problematic compared to low scale operations.
5. *Effect*: Hollis suggests that the degree of loss of human agency or free will resulting from an influence campaign is an important factor in assessing its legitimacy. Influence operations that have an adverse and measurable impact on human agency are more likely to be considered illegitimate.

Pamment et al. (2018) suggest four criteria to distinguish between legitimate and illegitimate influence operations:

1. *Deception*: Legitimate influence operations are open and transparent about their source and purpose.
2. *Intention*: Legitimate influence operations generally aim at promoting constructive solutions, even if the promoted solution is contested. Influence operations that utilize informational resources raise more alarms regarding their intention.
3. *Disruption*: If the disruption to society, triggered by an influence operation, is disproportionate to or outweighs the potential benefits of the operation, it renders the operation illegitimate.
4. *Interference*: The legitimacy of engaging in an open and free public debate rests to some extent on being personally affected by the debated issue. Therefore, clandestine involvement in internal affairs of another State, including elections, is an illegitimate interference.

The criteria suggested by Hollis and Pammet et al. can help assessing whether an influence operation targeting foreign elections constitutes a violation of the right to self-determination. As highlighted by the experts convened by UNESCO, the right to self-determination is an ongoing process of choice. To be able to choose freely, the bearers of the right to choose must be able to access all available choices without these choices being misrepresented. If some choices are presented to the voters in a distorted way, the act of choosing becomes less free. Disinformation campaigns aim at distorting and misrepresenting the choices available to voters. Even leaking accurate information constitutes an attack on the ability of voters to choose freely. Information is interpreted contextually. The same piece of information could be interpreted differently or given a different weight depending on the identity of the source spreading the information. When a voter knows that a foreign State with a questionable agenda is responsible for leaking a certain piece of information, her interpretation of the leaked information is going to be influenced by that fact. Knowing that a foreign State is behind the leak would make the voter ask herself different sort of questions before making a decision.

Beyond doxing and spreading false information that distort the choices available to the American people, using social media to target specific voters and bombard them with news, false or not, confuses them and distracts them from exploring all the choices available for them as voters.

However, for such operations to constitute a violation of the right to self-determination, their impact cannot be trivial. Deceiving and confusing 10 thousand voters does not have the same effect as deceiving or targeting social media accounts of 10 million voters. The scale and effects of the illegitimate influence operation must be substantial for genuine self-determination to be frustrated. This is a factual condition, and it is a challenging one since it requires engaging in complicated inquiries. It also raises other legal issues, such as contributing influence operations to a State. Still, the right to self-determination remains an avenue worth exploring in trying to frame the harm caused by foreign interference in elections, using international law lexicon. Unlike the principle of sovereignty and the principle of non-intervention, the right to self-determination is more suited to tackle the most widespread forms of influence operations targeting elections, i.e. operations that usually fall under the rubric of propaganda.

## 5 Conclusions

Cyber interference in foreign elections are on the rise. While interference in foreign elections is not new, this particular form of interference has attracted much attention for two main reasons. First, this form of interference is cheaper, compared to traditional methods of election interference. This makes foreign interference an option for countries with fewer resources. Second, this form of interference seems to be more effective in perusing cognitive changes among large publics. However, the unanimous political condemnation of foreign election interference was not translated or paralleled with a unanimous position on their legality. Even former US president Obama labeled the alleged Russian interference as an attempt "to undermine established international norms of behavior, and interfere with democratic governance", without referring directly to international law rules (White House 2016).

This chapter attempted to analyze the legality of cyber interference in foreign elections by referring to three central principles of international law: State sovereignty, the principle of non-intervention and the right to self-determination of peoples. The chapter suggests that most common forms of cyber operations targeting foreign elections linger in a gray zone of legality. However, compared to the principle of sovereignty and the principle of non-intervention, the right to self-determination seems more promising in providing a legal framework capable of tackling one of the most elusive forms of interference, i.e. the use of doxing and disinformation campaigns to alter the results of a foreign elections.

## References

Besson, S. (2012). Sovereignty. In *Max Planck Encyclopedia of public international law* (pp. 366–391). Oxford: Oxford University Press.
Buchan, R. J. (2016). The international legal regulation of cyber espionage. *Tallinn Papers*, 65–86.
Corn, G. (2017). Tallinn manual 2.0—Advancing the conversation. *Just Security*, 15 Feb.

Corn, G. P., & Taylor, R. (2017). Sovereignty in the age of cyber. *AJIL Unbound, 111*, 207–212.
Hollis, D. (2018). The influence of war; the war for influence. *Temple International and Comparative Law Journal, 32*, 31.
International Court of Justice. (1986). Concerning military and paramilitary activities in and against Nicaragua (Nicaragua v. United States of America); Merits, International Court of Justice (ICJ), 27 June 1986.
International Court of Justice. (1995). Case concerning east Timor (Portugal v. Australia). *I.C.J. Reports*, p 90; General List No. 84.
International Court of Justice. (1975). Western Sahara, advisory opinion. ICJ GL No 61, [1975] ICJ Rep 12.
Jamnejad, M., & Wood, M. (2009). The principle of non-intervention. *Leiden Journal of International Law, 22*, 345.
Jennings, R., & Watts, A. (1992). *Oppenheim's international law* (9th ed.). Pearson Higher Education.
Kaczorowska-Ireland, A. (2015). *Public international law*. Routledge.
Kohen, M. (2012). The principle of non-intervention 25 years after the Nicaragua judgment. *Leiden Journal of International Law, 25*, 157.
Larson, E. V., Darilek, R. E., Gibran, D., Nichiporuk, B., Richardson, A., Schwartz, L. H., & Thurston, C. Q. (2009). *Foundations of effective influence operations: A framework for enhancing army capabilities*. RAND ARROYO CENTER SANTA MONICA CA.
Levin, D. H. (2019). Partisan electoral interventions by the great powers: Introducing the PEIG Dataset. *Conflict Management and Peace Science, 36*(1), 88–106.
Ohlin, J. D. (2016). Did Russian cyber interference in the 2016 election violate international law. *Texas Law Review, 95*, 1579.
Pamment, J., Nothhaft, H., Agardh-Twetman, H., & Fjällhed, A. (2018). *Countering information influence activities: The state of the art, version 1.4*. Department of Strategic Communication. Lund University.
Schmitt, M. N. (2018). Virtual disenfranchisement: Cyber election meddling in the grey zones of international law. *Chicago Journal of International Law, 19*, 30.
Schmitt, M. N. (Ed.). (2017). *Tallinn manual 2.0 on the international law applicable to cyber operations*. Cambridge University Press.
Shaw, M. N. (2008). *International law*. Cambridge University Press.
Tharoor, I. (2016, Oct 13). The long history of the U.S. interfering with elections elsewhere. *The Washington Post*. Available at: https://www.washingtonpost.com/news/worldviews/wp/2016/10/13/the-long-history-of-the-u-s-interfering-with-elections-elsewhere/.
The Permanent Court of Arbitration. (1928). Island of Palmas case (or Miangas), United States v Netherlands, Award, (1928) II RIAA 829, ICGJ 392 (PCA 1928).
Tsagourias, N. (2019). Electoral cyber interference, self-determination and the principle of non-intervention in cyberspace. *Self-Determination and the Principle of Non-Intervention in Cyberspace (17 Aug 2019)*.
UN. (2015). Report of the group of governmental experts on development in the field of information and telecommunication in the context of Int'l security. U.N. Doc. A/70/174.
UN General Assembly. (1966a). International covenant on civil and political rights. United Nations, *Treaty Ser, 999*, 171.
UN General Assembly. (1966b). International covenant on economic, social and cultural rights. United Nations, *Treaty Ser, 993*, 3.
UNGA. (1970). Declaration on principles of international law concerning friendly relations and cooperation among states in accordance with the charter of the United Nations. UN Doc. A/RES/2625(XXV).
UNGA. (1989). Respect for the principles of national sovereignty and non-interference in the internal affairs of States in their electoral processes. UN Doc. A/RES/44/147.
US White House. (2016). Press release, statement by the president on actions in response to Russian Malicious Cyber Activity and Harrasment.

van der Staak, S., & Wolf, P. (2019). *Cybersecurity in elections: Models of interagency collaboration.* International Institute for Democracy and Electoral Assistance.
van Praag, M. C. V. W., & Seroo, O. (1998, Nov). The Implementation of the right to self-determination as a contribution to conflict prevention. In *Report of the International Conference of Experts* held in Barcelona on Nov 1998, pp 21–27.
Ziolkowski, K. (2013). Peacetime cyber espionage–new tendencies in public international law. *Peacetime Regime for State Act Cyberspace, Int Law Int Relat Diplomacy*, Tallinn, 425–464.

# The Old City of Jerusalem: From the Tragedy of the Common to Ostrom's Solution

**Alberto Priego**

**Abstract** The conflict between Arabs and Israelis has many points of friction, but doubtless the most complicated to solve is Jerusalem in general, and the Old City in particular. While it is difficult to see East Jerusalem returned to Palestinian hands, the solution to this complicated issue may come from rethinking the status of the Old City. The Old City is a walled territory of 0.9 $Km^2$ where the most sacred places for the three monotheistic religions meet. While it is true that many initiatives (partition plan, Olmert, Clinton Parameters) have tried to prevent either party from being the guardian of Holy Places, none of these initiatives have succeeded in finding a way to do that. The key to achieve an agreement between Arabs and Israelis on the issue of Jerusalem is not to declare the Old City as an international zone but to declare it as a global, international and supranational resource. In other words, that the Old City should be consider a Global Common with no possibility of being dominated and or exploited by any state. Only through this way territorial claims on the Old City will be avoided and thus an insurmountable point for any peace plan for the Middle East will eliminate.

**Keywords** Old city Jerusalem · Global commons · Common pool resource

## 1 Introduction

The main purpose of this chapter is to study the Old City of Jerusalem in the context of proposing a peaceful solution between Arabs and Israelis. The general approach is to view this land that is holy for three monotheistic religions as a common-pool resource, moving away from the traditional vision that has considered it a public

In: Security in the Global Commons and Beyond, Edited by J. Martin Ramirez, and Bartolomé Bauzá-Abril. © 2021 Springer International. Submitted: September, 24, 2020; Accepted: October, 15, 2020.

A. Priego (✉)
Universidad Pontificia Comillas, Madrid, Spain
e-mail: apriego@comillas.edu



J. M. Ramírez and B. Bauzá-Abril (eds.), *Security in the Global Commons and Beyond*, Advanced Sciences and Technologies for Security Applications,
https://doi.org/10.1007/978-3-030-67973-6_11

good, a private good or even a club good. Thus, we employ a neo-institutionalist vision to outline the creation of a common property regime, based on Ostrom's eight principles as a solution to this complex issue.

The article is divided into these sections: first, we will try to clarify how we understand 'common', turning to the historical and etymological origins of this British institution to do so. Second, we analyse the international angle of the concept, or global commons, proposing the common-pool resource as the most suitable in our specific case: the Old City of Jerusalem. Third, we analyse the historical development of the Old City, using concepts such as public, private and club goods as framework references, to then succinctly set out the common-pool resource option for analysis. To conclude, we review Ostrom's eight principles to propose a common property regime as the best possibility to prevent this matter from becoming a stumbling block in future peace negotiations.

## 2 What is a Common?

The origin of the common dates back to British feudalism. It was an institution, more widespread in the north and east coast of England, by which the Crown gave land to feudal lords for them to care for and operate. In exchange, the lords had to assign a significant part of the land to commoners,[1] on which they could live and work. This created a common land that made it possible for commoners to earn extra income.[2]There are at least two stances on whether this amount was favourable or unfavourable for the commoners. On the one hand, authors including Hammond and Hammond (1989: 26–27) and Gonner (1966: 362–6) believe that the common represented a 'distinguished landmark' for its beneficiaries, whose end also caused the end of peasant farmers, or commoners, on the British Isles.

On the other, authors such as Chambers and Mingay (1966: 49–52) are much more critical of the value these lands provided to the peasants, as they claim that the institution harmed the commoners by making their survival dependent on pastures that were either not the best, or were assiduously beset by wildfires, or their cattle were infested by diseases that were regrettably often mortal.

However, it would not be these factors that put an end to the institution of the *common*, but instead the *enclosures*, legal proceedings via which common lands were transferred to private parties, with the consequent disappearance of the community nature of the property. While true that the majority of enclosures were executed

[1]According to Neeson (1993: 65) there are at least three types of commoners: landed commoners, who held rights to have livestock, cottage commoners, who ran a mill or a farm; and, the most numerous (50% of total), landless commoners, who had nothing, so when enclosure took place, they did not obtain any compensation.

[2]The common lands were divided into pasture, arable and Lammas lands, which were those harvested on Loaf Mass Day (1st August in the Northern Hemisphere and 6th February in the Southern Hemisphere).

**Table 1** Types of goods

| | Excludable | Non-excludable |
|---|---|---|
| Rivalrous | Private goods | Common-pool resources |
| Non-rivalrous | Club goods | Global public goods |

*Source* Own elaboration

between 1750 and 1850, in 2006 the British Parliament approved the Common Act, which legislated issues related to the commons, which had still not been regulated.

## 3 Different Types of (Global) Commons

The use of the term common, somewhat influenced by globalisation, has led some authors to evolve towards a more global concept of the word. While there are some differences referring to the land, the main difference between common and global common resides in the fact that commoner rights are not limited to a group of people, but instead the beneficiaries extend to all of humanity. In other words, a global common is the part of the planet outside the jurisdiction of the states that everyone has access to UN (2013: 15). There are countless examples, although the best known may be High seas, including deep seabeds beow, Antarctica and—most recently—cyberspace.

Abstractly, a good or resource is subject to two variables: the rivalry it causes and the possibility of excluding beneficiaries. On the one hand, a good is *rivalrous* when different parties compete for its control, use or enjoyment, meaning that two parties cannot enjoy it at the same time. On the other, a good is considered *excludable* when we can relegate its enjoyment to potential users, which tends to occur with people who have not paid for it. Thus, by combining these two variables, we obtain four possible types of goods (Table 1).

Global commons encompass resources and goods (common-pool resources,[3] or public goods) that—unlike private goods—cannot exclude anybody from enjoying them (*non-excludable*), which also create rivalry due to their exclusive control (*rivalrous*). However, a resource in a global common may be 'privatised' or, in other words, be subject to an enclosure process, which will cause conflict between the parties in the medium or long term.

Although the Old City of Jerusalem has not always been treated as such, in my opinion it can be considered a common-pool resource, as its enjoyment creates rivalry and, in parallel, it is almost impossible to exclude potential users from it. This is why these lands, which are sacred to the three monotheistic religions, have become one of the main obstacles to Arab–Israeli peace over the last 70 years.

[3]Our definition of common-pool resource is a 'natural or man-made resource system that is sufficiently large to make it costly (but not impossible) to exclude beneficiaries from obtaining benefits from its use' (Ostrom 2011: 30).

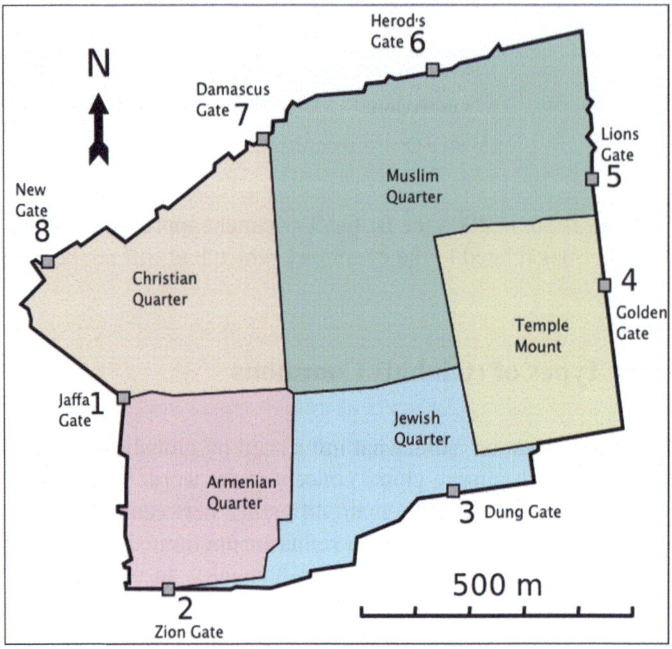


**Map 1** The old city of Jerusalem. *Source* Own elaboration

## 4 The Old City of Jerusalem as a Common-Pool Resource

The Old City of Jerusalem—*Ha'Ir Ha'Atiqah* for the Jewish and *al-Balda al-Qadimah* for Muslims—is a 0.9 $km^2$ walled complex that is home to some 35,000 people. It was built by Suleiman the Magnificent in 1516 and it represented the entire municipality of Jerusalem until the nineteenth century. Neighbourhoods were progressively added that were primarily Arabic, such as Ras al-Amud and Silwan, and primarily Jewish, such as Mishkenot Sha'ananim, which would later be integrated into the lovely Yemin Moshe neighbourhood (Goldhill 2009: 245). There are four large quarters inside of the Old City: Christian, Muslim, Armenian and Jewish. These four quarters can be accessed via seven gates,[4] although there is an eighth, the Golden Gate, which will remain sealed awaiting the arrival of the Messiah (Map 1).

This tiny area houses the largest concentration of sites of worship in the entire world. The Old City has a total of 13 mosques, 70 churches and 24 synagogues and yeshivas. The religious concentration is so high that the scant square kilometre inside its walls is holy to the three monotheistic religions, causing fierce rivalry between the commoners and an absolute impossibility of excluding anyone from enjoying it.

For Jews, the Old City is the site where the two Temples were constructed, the first (*Beit HaMikdash*) built by Solomon, and the second (*Beit HaMikdash HaSheni*)

[4]The seven open gates are Jaffa, Damascus, Lions', Zion, Dung, Herod's or Flowers, and New.

by Herod. The Temple was built as their main sanctuary, which would replace the tabernacle, which had accompanied the Jewish people since their departure from Egypt. Inside was the Holy of Holies, or *Sancta sanctorum*[5] (*Kodesh Hakodashim*), which safeguarded the Ark of the Covenant, the seven-branched menorah and the Table of Showbread. This structure was built over the Foundation Stone, to which the Jews attribute countless events set out in the Torah, such as the creation of the world, the sacrifice of Isaac at the hands of Abraham and the place where Jacob's dream occurred.

After the destruction of the First and Second Temple, the Western Wall[6] was then closest to the Holy of Holies, which is why it became the most sacred site in Judaism. Today, this is the space where a good part of the Jews' religious life takes place, who use it not only for daily prayers, but also for special celebrations, such as bar and bat mitzvahs.[7]

For Christians, the Old City is where Jesus preached, died and was resuscitated, although in the early years, they were not greatly attached to a city in which God had been murdered (Chenoll 2012: 225). However, after Constantine the Great took power, the Christians reconciled with Jerusalem, since so many episodes of Jesus' life occurred there, such as his presentation and the expulsion of the money-changers, both in the Temple, and others, like the Last Supper and his crucifixion, happened in different parts of the Old City. Perhaps for this reason—despite the fact that the Old City in general and Temple Mount in particular were the setting for important episodes in the New Testament—the Christians have never demanded exclusive use of these sites for worship, like the Muslims do with the Noble Sanctuary.

Be that as it may, for Christians the most relevant events are the death and resurrection of Jesus, which decreases the importance of Temple Mount. This is why the Via Dolorosa is the most sacred part to them, the route that Jesus walked from the Lions' Gate to his crucifixion, the location of the Church of the Holy Sepulchre today. This church, commissioned by Constantine, is built precisely on the hill where he died (Golgotha), and contains the Stone of Unction where he was anointed before his burial and the relic of the True Cross on which he was crucified.

Muslims believe that Jerusalem is the third most holy site, after Medina and Mecca. Jerusalem's importance is so great that, during the years when the Prophet lived, the city was the *qibla*, the direction in which Ummah faced to pray (Chenoll 2012: 233). The holiness of*al-Quds*, as the Muslims call Jerusalem, is essentially due to two facts.

[5]To the Jewish, this site is the spiritual union between Heaven and Earth (Axis Mundi), which is why Jews face in its direction when praying the *Amidah* or prayer of the 18 Benedictions (*Shemoneh Esreh*).

[6]The Western Wall—or Wailing Wall—remained standing because Titus decided to leave a section so that the Jews could lament, hence its name. However, the Jews interpreted it as the fulfilment of a promise God made to always keep the alliance with his people alive.

[7]The Bar Mitzvah, or Bat Mitzvah for girls, is a celebration and coming of age ritual, meaning that they are therefore ready to read the Torah. It literally means *son or daughter of the 613 commandments* (mitzvot) contained in the Torah, which all Jews must fulfil.

(1) First, Jerusalem is the site where Muhammad ascended into Heaven (*Isra* and *Miraj*) after travelling from Mecca
(2) And, second, pre-Islamic prophets and heroes lived and preached in Jerusalem, such as Abraham, Jesus and Ismael (Moghul 2017), from whom they claim that Muhammad is a direct descendent

Temple Mount, or the Noble Sanctuary (*al-Ḥaram ash-Sharīf*), is the holiest site in the entire Old City of Jerusalem for Muslims. According to Muslim tradition, after Prophet Muhammad said the fifth prayer, Archangel Gabriel (*Jibril*) appeared before him, who offered him a donkey (*Buraq*) on which to travel through the night to Jerusalem (*Isra* and *Miraj*) and pray at the furthest mosque (*Tahiyyatul*). Later, this enigmatic site was identified as the Al-Aqsa Mosque. While there is no direct allusion to it in the Koran, the Hadith identified the Foundation Stone as the point from which Muhammad ascended into Heaven. This is why the Muslims claim the Noble Sanctuary as the most suitable place to conduct their Friday prayers.

Here is one of the first places where the two religions confronted each other, making the Old City of Jerusalem a place that provokes rivalry, but at the same time a place from which nobody can be excluded. Indeed, as depicted on the Map 2, Temple Mount or the Noble Sanctuary is the site in the Old City that has caused the most clashes between different religious faiths.

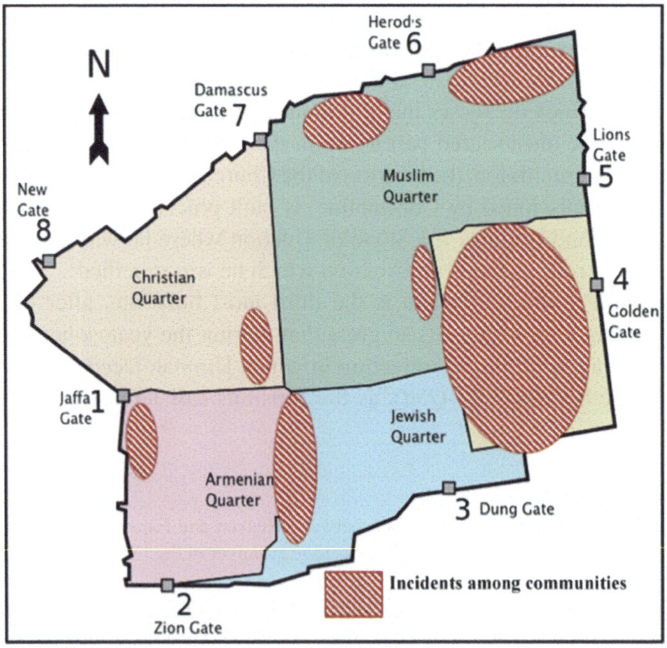


**Map 2** Places where interreligious friction occurs in the Old City of Jerusalem. *Source* Created with information from Khamaisi (Moghul 2017)

To cite only a few of the most recent episodes, it merits mention that the Camp David peace talks in 2000 did not yield results largely because of the inability of Yasser Arafat and Ehud Barak to reach an agreement on its use (Bregman 2003: 225). Only a few months later, the visit of the then opposition leader, Ariel Sharon, to the Esplanade of the Mosques unleashed the Second Intifada (Dowty 2017: 165), Al Aqsa, an event the strengthens the idea that this zone is both a rivalrous and a non-excludable good.[8]

Another incident occurred in 2014 when there was an assassination attempt on a Jewish activist, Rabbi Yehudah Glick, by a member of the Islamic Jihad Movement when he tried to enter the Dome of the Rock to pray (Dvir 2014). Yehudah Glick led the organisation HaLiba, which advocated and worked for equal rights of worship for Muslims, Jews and Christians.

Finally, in 2017, a crisis was triggered when two Israeli border police officers were killed by Palestinian terrorists. As a consequence of these events, Israel decided to enclose the area and instal metal detectors to prevent new incidents, which led to a wave of violence that lasted for eleven days and ended with eleven dead.

There are other tensions in the Old City that are not related to the use of religious sites. For example, the Armenian community has made ongoing complaints that several extremist Jews have attacked seminarians. These cases have primarily occurred at the confluence of two neighbourhoods (Sahagian 2015), although they are unfortunately not the only ones. Christians have also complained of assaults during Holy Week processions, and knife attacks against ultra-Orthodox Jews are a daily reality.

The explanation of the reason for these frictions, tensions and violent crises that erupt in holy sites is related to the concept of city as a rivalrous good, which not only cannot be shared with unbelievers, but also their multiple-faith nature makes it impossible to exclude them, regardless of what they contribute or whether they control the good. This fact makes this territory especially conflictive, as it is subject to a terrible paradox:

(a) On the one hand, the commoners want to enjoy the good exclusively and in monopoly, as they conceive of the Old City as a rivalrous good.
(b) On the other, by extending common rights to all humanity, the Old City becomes a non-excludable good to which all the faithful of the three monotheistic religions have a usage right, even if we consider them as landless commoners.

This paradox could make us think that it is impossible to find a consensual solution for the Old City. However, some research, such as the studies conducted by Ostrom, make us think that the Old City could find a balance by applying a common property regime system.

---

[8]The Mitchell Commission subsequently dismissed that this event could have caused the wave of violence.

## 5 Common Property Regime System as the Solution to the Old City Problem

We have seen that the Old City of Jerusalem suffered the majority of the woes and negativities of the commons, including what Hardin (1967) identified as the 'tragedy of the commons'. The tragedy of the commons is related to individuals' inability to act rationally to use only those resources (commons) that they need. To explain it, Hardin uses an example of a prairie to which herders take their sheep. According to Hardin, instead of taking the number of heads they are permitted to graze, the herders, upon seeing that there is abundant grass, take an increasingly larger number of sheep until the meadow starts to be degraded (Hardin 1967: 1244). The final and inevitable result is the destruction of the common good, because personal interests prevailed over collective interests. We can state in some way that the lack of cooperation among the communities in the Old City of Jerusalem also assumes the characteristics of 'the tragedy of the commons', as the parties heed the interests of their own communities more than the overall good of the Old City.

Faced with the determinism outlined by Hardin in the tragedy of the commons, some authors have suggested different solutions for overcoming the endemic wrong of the commons, which can be grouped into three broad options (Ostrom 2011: 8).

(a) The Leviathan option (Ophuls 1973: 228), which means that the state takes charge of handling the management of the common-pool resource.
(b) The option to privatise the good (Smith 1981: 465).
(c) The option to entrust management to an international institution (Ostrom 2011: 14).

These three possibilities have already been tested with little success in the Old City of Jerusalem at different times in history:

(a) The option of assigning a Leviathan to run this common-pool resource has been the situation in place since 1967, when the state of Israel started to govern the Old City (Avigad 1984: 20). While true that some issues, such as the entry of the faithful to their sites of worship, have improved significantly with regard to the previous stage, the conflicts between Muslims and Jews have just kept increasing. Further, the fact that the Leviathan is one of the parties in the conflict does not make it easy for the others to accept it as a solution. Thus, if we want to prevent the Old City of Jerusalem from continuing to be an obstacle to peace, we must rule out this model.
(b) While the privatisation of the good has not taken place as such, we could say that the management done by the Kingdom of Jordan between 1949 and 1967 is quite close (Alpert 1984: 43). During this 18-year period, non-Muslim groups were excluded from the Old City and actions were undertaken, such as destroying several synagogues and limiting access to the land in the case of Christians (Gilbert 1997: 285). These events make us think that, during the period of Jordanian control, an enclosure process of the Old City took place, which translated into managing it like a club good and not like a common-pool resource.

(c) The third and last option is entrusting the management of the common-pool resource to an institution—preferably international—as a way of overcoming the tragedy of the commons. This was the option chosen by the United Nations in November 1947 (Gilbert 1997: 179). After Resolution 181 was approved, the territory formerly under British mandate was divided into two, granting Jerusalem an exclusive international regime that prevented any of the parties from being able to govern the city. Thus, the aim was to create a neutral authority outside of the parties that would prevent conflicts. As we know, the Arab states not only rejected this, with apparent consensus, but they also started a war that lasted over two years and put an end to any option of international management of the Old City.

While true that these three solutions have all proven to be misguided, Ostrom proposes a new one that she herself considered an alternative. This winner of the Nobel Prize in Economics in 2009 set out eight principles to achieve sustainable governance of common-pool resources. The novel and innovative feature of this neo-institutionalist focus is not only that it manages to reverse the blight of the tragedy of the commons, but it also provides a framework for carrying it out, where the people responsible for putting it into practice are the beneficiaries themselves (Ostrom 1995: 40).

Before looking at the eight principles, some preliminary distinctions must be made that will allow us to better understand the principles. First, we must distinguish between a *resource system* and *resource units* (Ostrom 2011: 30). While the former is the potential of the good in and of itself or the absolute number of units the good can produce, the second is the concrete amount that individuals can appropriate or use. Ostrom uses a fishing ground as an example of a resource system and the tonnes fished by users of this common-pool resource as an example of resource unit. Another important distinction made by Ostrom (2011: 31) is between appropriators and producers/providers, where the first are defined as those who obtain the resource units, and the second are those in charge of building, repairing and conserving the common-pool resource to ensure the sustainability of this resource system.

If we transfer these distinctions to the case of the Old City of Jerusalem, we can see that the resource system would be what this good can provide as a whole to the faithful, while the resource units would be the individual enjoyment that the religious communities (appropriators) will have of these holy sites.

As mentioned above, the key so that the parties have incentives to overcome the conflict is in the eight principles on which the common property regime system are built, which let common-pool resources move past the tragedy of the commons (Ostrom 2011; Wilson et al. 2013).

1. Clearly defined boundaries
2. Congruence between appropriation, provision and local conditions
3. Collective choice arrangement
4. Monitoring
5. Graduated sanctions
6. Conflict resolution mechanism

7. Minimal recognition of rights to organise
8. For groups that are part of larger social systems, there must be appropriate coordination among relevant groups.

These eight principles are proof that reveal that it is indeed possible to manage complex situations, as Ostrom extracts them, analysing successful management cases. To do so, we believe that applying these eight principles via a theoretical-practical exercise to the case of the Old City of Jerusalem could be used to overcome the current stalemate.

The first of the principles that Ostrom establishes points to the need of *clearly defining the boundaries and the parties*, which in the case of the Old City of Jerusalem thus translates into both a geographic boundary and identification of the parties involved. While it is true that the division into quarters is useful for this point (Jewish, Armenian, Christian and Muslim), we also cannot forget that there are differences within these communities that must be born in mind, particularly in the Christian and Muslim communities.

The second principle is perhaps the most complex to apply to the Old City, since Ostrom proposes adapting the rules to local conditions, without forgetting the inherent heterogeneity of the good. Bearing in mind that we identified Israel as the provider and the religious communities as the appropriators, the relationship between them is fundamental to be able to manage the Old City. There would have to be a situation in which the parties believe that the cost of not cooperating is greater than the cost of cooperating. While the Christians and Armenians would not pose any problems, the communities with a better position (Jews and Muslims) would have to shift their current approaches.

The third principle will let us—somewhat—respond to the block described above. To this end, Ostrom (2011: 90) suggests that the individuals affected by the rules that govern the site become essential parties to modifying them. In the case of the Old City, the leaders of the religious communities have already proven they can reach agreement on issues such as COVID-19. They could, perhaps, create and manage an informal forum in which the practical matters of the Old City could be established and/or modified, such as the shared use of common sites of worship.

The fourth principle is also a consequence of the previous one, as it outlines the presence of monitors to ensure that the previously-agreed rules are fulfilled. These monitors should be mixed groups in which members of all the religious communities could participate, thus avoiding the habitual suspicions that arise in the Old City when supervising holy sites. Faced with situations like what occurred at Temple Mount in 2014 and in 2017, the presence of members of several religious faiths could prevent a provocation from ending in crisis. In other words, the members of a religious community are the only ones who can stop radicals from taking actions against people from other communities.

Fifth, she proposed a system of gradual sanctions, preventing severe sanctions from being decreed for events that are not serious. Thus, as an action becomes more serious and/or is repeated with some regularity, the sanctions would progressively increase as well. If the sanctions are established gradually, the cohesion of the community will increase, along with trust in those imposing order. This proportionality would prevent radicals from using lesser violations to cause tensions and calls for violence against members of other communities.

Sixth, informal mechanisms must be found to resolve conflicts or, at least, use existing mechanisms such as those used in Palestinian *diwans*[9] and in the Jewish *beth din.*[10] These informal, peaceful and low-cost routes for conflict resolution could be used not only to overcome disputes that arise, but also so that each community could learn from the other communities and establish common mechanisms to prevent small everyday problems from becoming large crises.

Seventh, the members of this community must be able to organise their own institutions, since—as has been proven—if the initiative comes from outside, all the hard work is headed towards failure. In the case of the Old City, Israel should transfer the power for managing religious affairs to a forum led by the leaders of the religious communities, which does involve some risk with regard to security. However, this does not mean that the forum would be in charge of public order, but would instead be responsible for issues related to worship.

The eighth and last principle states that there must be coordination between the religious communities present in the Old City, with larger religious structures to prevent the agreements from lacking validity in the long term. The explanation for the Old City would be related to the fact that the appropriators are not only the inhabitants of this small territory, but would be made up of all the faithful from the three large monotheistic religions, making the implications of their actions much broader and more widespread.

## 6 Conclusion

By way of conclusion, we can state that Jerusalem in general, and the Old City in particular, continue to be 'the insoluble problem' (Kollek 1977). Any possibility of moving beyond this situation involves changing the conception held of it and considering the option that it could be a common heritage of humanity. To do so, one option could be considering it a common-pool resource and, as such, trying to construct a common property regime based on Ostrom's eight principles (2011). The essence of this approach would have to be based on the parties' self-governance to ensure that cooperation—and not conflict—is always the preferable option, because while true that the Old City is a rivalrous good, it is also a non-excludable good, so that the path of confrontation will never be a solution.

---

[9]Palestine quasi-family communities that form groups based on their geographic origin, such as the Hebronites, Dkeidek and Qutteineh. They have their own governance and conflict-resolution systems.

[10]Tribunals used by Orthodox Jews to resolve private disputes.

## References

Alpert, F. (1984). *Getting Jerusalem together. Your historical guide to Jerusalem throughout the ages*. Jerusalem: Gefen Ltd.

Avigad, N. (1984). *Discovering Jerusalem. Recent archaelogical excavations in the upper city*. Oxford: Basil Blackwell.

Bregman, A. (2003). *Israel's wars. A history since 1947*. London: Routledge.

Chambers, J. D., & Mingay, G. E. (1966). *The agriculture revolution 1750–1880*. B.T. Batsford.

Chenoll, R. (2012). Jerusalén en la escatología Cristiana y Musulmana. *Baetica. Estudios de Arte, Geografía e Historia, 34*, 221–243.

Dowty, A. (2017). *Israel Palestine*. Cambridge: Polity Press.

Dvir, N. (2014). Right-wing activist shot during annual Temple Mount event in Jerusalem, *Ynet* (29 Nov 2014).

Gilbert, M. (1997). *Jerusalem in the twentieth century*. Pimlico-London: Chatto and Windus.

Gonner, E. C. K. (1966). *Common land and inclosure*. Abingdon: Routledge.

Hammond, J. L., & Hammond, B. (1989). *The village labourer: 1760–1832: A study in the government of England before the reform bill*. Sutton Pub Ltd.

Hardin, G. (1989). The tragedy of the commons. *Science, 162*(3859), 1243–1248.

Khamaisi, R., Brooks, R., Margalit, M., Nasrallah, R., Yunan, M, & Owais, A. (2014). *Jerusalem the old city. The urban fabric and geopolitical implications*. IPCC, Jerusalem. Available at https://www.ipcc-jerusalem.org/attachment/15/IPCC_Jerusalem_the_Old_City_Urban_Fabric_and_Geopolitical_Implications.pdf.

Kollek, T. (1977). Jerusalem. *Foreign Affairs, 55*(4).

Moghul, H. (2017). Is there room in Jerusalem for both Jews and Muslim? *Haaretz*, 24 Apr 2017.

Neeson, J. M. (1993). *Commoners: Common right, enclusure and social change in England 1700–1820*. Cambridge: Cambridge University Press.

Ophuls, W. (1973). Leviathan or oblivion. In H. E. Daly (Ed.), *Towards a steady state economy* (pp. 215–230). San Francisco: Freeman.

Ostrom, E. (1995). Designing complexity to govern complexity. In S. Hanna, & M. H. Munasinghe (Eds.), *Property rights and the environment* (pp. 33–46). Social and ecological issues. Washington D.C.: The Beijer International Institute of Ecological Economic and the World Bank.

Ostrom, E. (2011). Governing the commons. *The evolution of institutions for collective action* (29th Ed.), Cambridge: Cambridge University Press.

Sahagian, A. (2015). *Armenians under attack in the old city*. Asbarez. Available at https://asbarez.com/133798/armenians-under-attack-in-the-old-city/.

Smith, R. J. (1981). Resolving the tragedy of the commons by creating private property rights in wildlife. *CATO Journal, 1*, 439–468.

United Nations. (2013). *UN system task team on the Post 2015 UN development agency*. Available at https://www.un.org/en/development/desa/policy/untaskteam_undf/thinkpieces/24_thinkpiece_global_governance.pdf.

Wilson, D. S., Ostrom, E., & Cox, M. E. (2013). Generalizing the core design principles for the efficacy of groups. *Journal of Economic Behavior and Organization, 905*, 521–532.

**Alberto Priego** holds a Ph.D. from Complutense University (International Relations). He currently is a Senior Lecturer at the Universidad Pontificia de Comillas in Madrid, where he has been a faculty member since 2010. His research interests lie in the areas of Middle East Studies, Islam, and Diplomacy. He has collaborated actively with researchers in several other disciplines of history, economy, and political science. During 2007–2009 he was postdoctoral fellow at SOAS (The University of London).

# Beyond the Global Commons

# Personal Data: The New Black Gold

## Added Value of Personal Data in the Context of International Security

**Marcos García-Gasco Romero**

**Abstract** This chapter discusses the added value of personal data in the context of international security by analyzing the opportunities offered by the so-called new black gold in the age of digitalization: personal data. Personal data create economic and social value at an increasing pace, and personal information is used today in many different situations for numerous purposes. Inevitably, international security is not an exception. This chapter is divided into three sections: (1) it starts with a short overview of commercial aviation's relevance in the global economy and the indissoluble link between civil aviation and international security. (2) The second block analyses the legal framework regulating the processing of personal data in the European Union (EU), in particular, the General Data Protection Regulation (Regulation EU 2016/679). The essentials elements of the fundamental right to the protection of personal data will be studied. (3) The chapter ends by covering the opportunities provided by these intangible assets when moving across flows that come from sensors or machines, mainly with the increasing use of technologies such as Big Data and the Internet of Things (IoT), widely used in the field of air safety. The speed with which our information is collected and processed, however, raises fundamental questions about privacy, ownership of data, and human rights.

**Keywords** Personal data · Data protection · GDPR—general data protection regulation · Aviation safety

---

In: Security and the Global Commons, Edited by J. Martin Ramirez, and Bartolomé Bauzá-Abril.
© 2021 Springer International. Submitted: September, 03, 2020; Accepted: November, 11, 2020.

---

M. García-Gasco Romero (✉)
Madrid, Spain
e-mail: marcos.garcia-gasco-romero@airbus.com



J. M. Ramírez and B. Bauzá-Abril (eds.), *Security in the Global Commons and Beyond*,
Advanced Sciences and Technologies for Security Applications,
https://doi.org/10.1007/978-3-030-67973-6_12

# 1 Overview

Commercial aviation constitutes one of the most relevant contributors to the global economy. Traditionally, air transport has doubled in size every fifteen years (Airbus 2019) demonstrating stronger long-term resilience than other industries, even under tough circumstances. Indeed, this growth is observed despite external shocks, such as the Oil Crisis (1978), the Gulf Crisis (1990–1991), the Asian Crisis (1997), the 9/11 attacks (2001), the SARS outbreak (2002–2004) or the worldwide financial crisis in 2008.

Despite these events, air traffic has multiplied by 2,4 since 2000. In 2019 (ATAG 2019), 4,5 billion passengers were carried by the world's airlines. Over 65 million jobs are supported worldwide in aviation and related tourism. Of this, 10,2 million people work directly in the aviation industry (the amount contributed to the global economy by aviation jobs is roughly 4,4 times higher than that contributed by other jobs) and generating $704,4 billion of GDP per year (a figure comparable to the GDP of Switzerland).

Sources (Airbus 2018) show that the global civil aviation network connects all countries globally: 3,190 cities and 3,250 airports. Connectivity between these airports, which has doubled since the early nineteen-eighties, continues to grow. Most of the world's people from both emerging and mature economies use aviation as part of their lives.

The changing Covid-19 scenario continues to bring more issues and greater complexities for the civil aviation industry, but the traffic forecast pointed to 4,3% average traf-fic growth per year over the next 20 years. This means 39,210 new aircraft production units over the next 20 years (36% for aircraft replacement and 64% for growth).

All the above said, it seems appropriate to state that this is not only a matter of economic significance, but commercial aircraft shall be appreciated as a real symbol of human development and modernity: the central allegory of the consolidation of the Third Industrial Revolution.

# 2 Commercial Aviation in the Context of International Security

Since the dawn of commercial aviation and in light of commercial flights' exponential growth in the 1960s, security has been embedded by default throughout the whole aviation chain. This means that security is not only a matter of aircraft design or manufacturing but also involves airports, airlines, traffic control, authorities and regulatory bodies, aviation professionals, etc. They are all links from the same chain, close to one another and indispensable to ensure the safety of persons and properties, and thereby fostering sustainable economic development and contributing to the overall global economy.

It is unfortunate that civil aircraft have been used, over the years, as unexpected weapons by terrorist organizations, criminal groups, or individuals. This has resulted in the birth, and the subsequent continued growth, of a very comprehensive international public law output to reinforce the measures aimed at combating the abduction and unlawful detention and the hijacking of planes, the practice of hostage-taking by the illegal terrorist groups, etc. This has been the case, while not intended to be exhaustive, of the Convention on offenses and certain other acts committed on board aircraft, signed at Tokyo on 14 September 1963; the Convention for the suppression of unlawful seizure of aircraft, signed at The Hague on 16 December 1970; the Convention or the suppression of unlawful acts against the safety of civil aviation concluded at Montreal on 23 September 1971; the International Convention against the taking of hostages adopted by the General Assembly of the United Nations in New York on 18 December 1979; the Convention on the marking of plastic explosives for the purpose of detection done at Montreal on 1 March 1991; the Administrative package for ratification of or accession to the Protocol supplementary to the Convention for the suppression of unlawful seizure of aircraft (Beijing Protocol, 2010) and many others. This is without prejudice to any subsequent legislation adopted by the various countries internally in the light of these treaties.

As a result of the link between commercial aviation and international security, we shall refer to 11 September 2001. This tragic event immediately became a turning point to dramatically review the model of world air transportation, moving from a hub-and-spoke system[1] toward a point-to-point model, involving aircraft with less seating capacity.

At the Airbus universe, for instance, client companies found the A320-Family and, in particular the A319, ideal for their short-haul routes, which paired cities previously not directly linked by air. For Airbus, it meant its strategy of producing a family of *fly-by-wire* aircraft which shared commonality and provided airlines with the greatest flexibility possible had, once again, paid off. Airbus A320 Family aircrafts are perfectly suited to the new market (Airbus 2019). On the contrary, and even if, of course, this was not the only reason, the new point-to-point networks have meant a real step change in terms of aircraft fleet strategy. The point-to-point system's deployment has led the company to gradually reduce A380 production (the Airbus' iconic world's largest passenger aircraft). As a consequence of this decision, deliveries of the A380 will cease in 2021 (Airbus 2019).

This exceptional and historic adaptation effort to the new circumstances since 2001 has been accompanied by a substantial digital transformation that improved how the aircraft industry is responding to public demand for greater aviation safety. Whereas aircraft have collected many technical data, in today's era of Big Data, an activity where data play a crucial role, the industry has stepped up to mine this

---

[1] Hub-and-spoke: aircraft deployment method in which a carrier designates one or more strategically located cities as hubs to which its larger aircraft bring most of its passengers and cargo through many scheduled flights. The passengers and cargo are then taken to their respective destinations by smaller aircraft belonging to the same carrier or smaller (commuter or feeder) airlines under a code-sharing arrangement.

valuable resource to further increase aviation's sustainability and security (Airbus 2018).

Now, it has taken a further step forward with the incorporation of personal information to the soaring data analysis, entering a completely new data dimension. However, personal data exploitation could clash with certain aspects of individuals' fundamental rights, particularly the right to privacy.

## 3 The General Data Protection Regulation (EU) 2016/679

### *3.1 A Quick Snapshot of the New EU Legal Framework on the Protection of Personal Data*

The protection of individuals concerning the processing of their personal data is a fundamental right. This is laid down in Article 8(1) of the Charter of Fundamental Rights of the European Union (European Union 2000) and Article 16(1) of the Treaty on the Functioning of the European Union (European Union 2012).

The EU's data protection legal framework has a relatively recent history (EDPS 2018), but too abrupt, because of the intense pressure of the extremely rapid technological developments, which can overgrow any data protection regulatory framework.

In 2012, the European Commission proposed to strengthen online privacy rights and the digital economy. The Commission understood that the EU's 1995 data protection rules (European Parliament 1995) had become obsolete, being necessary to boost Europe's digital single market under the umbrella of a harmonized new Regulation (rather than a Directive), to avoid raising artificial barriers between the Member States.

However, the road for adopting the General Data Protection Regulation (EU) 2016/679 (European Parliament 2018) (from now on, the "Regulation" or "GDPR") was not an easy one. From the approval of the Commission's draft proposal in January 2012 to the final adoption of the GDPR in April 2016[2], the path was complicated and tortuous, facing even thousands of amendments at the EU Parliament (a record of amendments difficult to beat). That demonstrates the importance of this Regulation that would entail the world cornerstone rule for personal information processing, imposing new obligations for those operators exploiting the new black gold of the digital economy: the personal data. Without them, the new digital economy would not exist.

The adoption of the GDPR by the EU in April 2016 marked a turning point in protecting the human rights of people to privacy and intimacy not only in the EU but also worldwide, mainly to two basics elements:

[2]The GDPR was adopted in April 2016, entering into force on 25 May 2018, allowing controllers and processors to adapt themselves to the new demanding legal framework within two years.

- The GDPR has a full extraterritorial application. The Regulation applies to companies in the context of the activities of an establishment in the European Union. However, the GDPR applies also to companies not established in the Union, but the processing is related to the offering of goods or services to individuals in the Union. In this way, a company providing services from an establishment located in the US or Australia processing personal data to this end in the EU needs to comply with the Regulation.
- The fact above has spurred other countries in many regions of the world to consider follow suit. As stated by the European Commission (2020), the EU's leadership on data protection shows it can act as a global standard-setter for regulating the digital economy. The GDPR is a significant legal piece in the development of an area of freedom, security and justice in the EU. Still it is also a worldwide point of reference for many countries and regions, which have already passed their own data protection rules mirroring the GDPR, including Brazil, California (US), Chile, India, Indonesia, Japan or Kenya.

However, whereas the GDPR strengthened data protection safeguards, providing individuals with additional and more substantial rights, it is increasingly likely observing a collision between individuals' private sphere and the legitimate interests of many businesses exploiting data. This is particularly common in the context of preventing threats to public international security, where (even sensitive) personal data required to be intensively processed.

In that context, it is relevant to highlight that whether the GDPR does not apply to the processing of personal data by the Member States when carrying out activities for the purposes of the prevention, investigation, detection, or prosecution of criminal offenses[3], the Regulation still applying to private companies (e.g., aircraft manufacturers, airlines, software developers or tech companies) equally interested in incorporating an intensive use of personal data for the development of technologies more efficient security measures.

## *3.2 What We Talk About When We Talk About Personal Data? Data Protection Key Basic Concepts*

The dynamic development of information and communication technologies put individuals' privacy and personal data at the center of the legal debate. Though genuinely intensive discussions on the matter are common, data protection standard terms and fundamental principles remain relatively unknown.

To understand the obligations and responsibilities inherent under the GDPR framework, it is worth briefly reviewing some critical concepts defined by law, far away, even today, from the common general knowledge:

[3] Article 2(2)(d) GDPR.

- **Personal data**. Under the GDPR, personal data means any information relating to an identified or identifiable natural person (the **individual** or the **data subject**). An identifiable natural person is one who can be identified, directly or indirectly, in particular by reference to an identifier such as a name, an identification number, location data, an online identifier or to one or more factors specific to the physical, physiological, genetic, mental, economic, cultural or social identity of that natural person.
  Personal data notion provided in Article 4(1)(1) GDPR is extensive. We often tend to think or associate the term *personal* with *confidential*, but the abovementioned wording shows otherwise. This is because the definition reflects the intention of the EU lawmaker for a broad notion of personal data with the ultimate purpose of protecting the fundamental rights and freedoms of natural persons (EDPB 2007). By way of example, basic information from data subjects such as the name, telephone number, email or postal address, gender, face image, or voice are considered personal data, as to identify the relevant individual directly. However, information may also be linked to a data subject indirectly, e.g., thought the plate of a vehicle, the IP of a computer or the result of a blood test.
- **Processing of personal data**. Article 4(1)(2) GDPR defines processing as any operation or set of operations which is performed on personal data or sets of personal data, whether or not by automated means, such as collection, recording, organization, structuring, storage, adaptation or alteration, retrieval, consultation, use, disclosure by transmission, dissemination or otherwise making available, alignment or combination, restriction, erasure or destruction. Under such definition, it is difficult to imagine an activity related to accessing personal data outside the purview of the law.
- **The lawfulness of processing**. Under Article 6 GDPR, processing only shall be deemed lawful to the extent that at least one of the conditions included in this article applies. Whereas the consent of data subjects is the most common basis, it is not the only basis for the processing of personal data (e.g. when the processing of personal data is necessary for the performance of a contract to which the data subject is party, to comply with legal obligations).
- **Data controller and processor**. Since the first objective of the GDPR is to protect individuals concerning the processing of personal data, that objective can only be achieved and made effective in practice if those who are responsible for data processing can be sufficiently stimulated by legal and other means to take all the measures that are necessary to ensure that this protection is delivered in practice (EDPB 2010):

  - **Controller** means the natural or legal person, public authority, agency or other body which, alone or jointly with others, determines the purposes and means of the processing of personal data (Article 4(1)(7) GDPR).
  - **Processor** means a natural or legal person, public authority, agency or other body which processes personal data on behalf of the controller (Article 4(1)(8) GDPR).

These roles are crucial. The concept of data controller and its interaction with the processor plays a crucial role in the application of the GDPR by determining who shall be accountable for compliance with data protection rules and how data subjects can exercise their rights. Also, which is the applicable national law and how effective data protection supervisors and authorities can operate.

- **Special categories of personal data**[4] (also known as **sensitive data**). The Regulation laid down necessary restrictions for the processing of the special categories of personal data. Indeed, the processing of personal data revealing racial or ethnic origin, political opinions, religious or philosophical beliefs, or trade union membership, and the processing of genetic data, biometric data for the purpose of uniquely identifying a natural person, data concerning health or data concerning a natural person's sex life or sexual orientation is, in general, prohibited.
  Derogations[5] from the general prohibition for processing such special categories of personal data should be explicitly provided, *inter alia*, where the data subject gives his or her explicit consent or the processing is necessary for reasons of substantial public interest.
- **Biometric data**. Under Article 4(1)(14) GDPR biometric data means personal data resulting from specific technical processing relating to the physical, physiological or behavioral characteristics of a natural person, which allow or confirm the unique identification of that natural person, such as facial images or dactyloscopic data.
  The above prohibition referring to the processing of biometric data is fundamental, since newly developed technologies linked to aviation safety are in most cases related to the processing of biometric data. Indeed, the use of biometric data entails substantial risks for data subjects' rights, so it will be essential that biometric technologies (face, voice, fingerprint, or iris recognition) are implemented with strict respect to the principles of lawfulness, necessity, proportionality, and data minimization as outlined in the GDPR.

## 4 Personal Data as Contributors to Aviation Safety: A Practical Approach

Recent technological developments, including Big Data and the IoT, have increased the opportunities provided by personal data, these intangible assets moving across data-flows coming from sensors, cameras, or other machines, widely used in the field of air safety. However, the speed with which our information is collected and processed raises fundamental questions about privacy, ownership of information and human rights.

[4] Article 9(1) GDPR.

[5] Article 9(2) GDPR.

Supervisor authorities, such as the European Data Protection Board[6] ("EDPB"), are aware of the benefits and the inherent dangers of these technologies, having rushed to issue further analysis, guidelines and public consultations on the exploitation of biometrics data, in particular:

- **Biometrics video surveillance systems** (EDPB 2019). Collecting biometrics data (and further intelligent video analysis) is nowadays a reality[7]. These solutions, often located in public places (e.g. airports) to enhance security, have a great impact on citizen's behavior, putting pressure on the individual to prevent the detection of what might be perceived as anomalies.
  As provided by the authorities, the use of video surveillance, including biometric recognition functionality installed by private entities for their purposes (even for security) will, in most cases, require the explicit consent of all data subjects. Although exceptions pursuant to Article 9(2) GDPR may apply, the public consultation issued by the EDPB indicates in an example the following:

  > To improve its service a private company replaces passenger identification check points within an airport (luggage drop-off, boarding) with video surveillance systems that use facial recognition techniques to verify the identity of the passengers that have chosen to consent to such a procedure. Since the processing falls under Article 9, the passengers, who will have previously given their explicit and informed consent, will have to enlist themselves at for example an automatic terminal in order to create and register their facial template associated with their boarding pass and identity. The check points with facial recognition need to be clearly separated, e.g. the system must be installed within a gantry so that the biometric templates of non-consenting person will not be captured. Only the passengers, who will have previously given their consent and proceeded with their enrolment, will use the gantry equipped with the biometric system.

  According to this statement, it seems that airlines' use of facial recognition for security purposes require explicit consent; therefore, the application of other potential lawful legal basis under Article 6 GDPR (e.g. legitimate interest) is not clear. This may act as a strong disincentive for implementing such valuable biometrics technics, since an alternative recognition system for non-consenting passengers may be also available. Be that as it may, controllers using such technics must ensure that data extracted from a digital image to build a template will not be excessive and will only contain the information required for the specified purpose. Among other precautions, it shall also take all necessary measures to preserve the availability, integrity and confidentiality of the data processed. It shall proceed to the deletion of raw data and ensure the effectiveness of this deletion.

---

[6]Under Articles 68 et seq. GDPR, the European Data Protection Board has been established as a body of the EU with own legal personality. The Board is composed of the head of one supervisory authority of each Member State and of the European Data Protection Supervisor. The Board ensures the consistent application of the Regulation, among others, issuing guidelines, recommendations, and best practices on procedures related to the implementation of the GDPR.

[7]AENA tests facial recognition system for boarding at Adolfo Suárez Madrid- Barajas Airport with the new feature of registering via the app.

- **Data processing at work: the use of wearables**[8]. Another interesting example comes from the field of processing biometrics in the work environment. These may have a meaningful impact on aviation safety by providing wearable technologies to cabin crews, in particular pilots.
  The current commercial aircraft industry (Airbus 2018) uses big data technology to collect up to 24,000 parameters on a flight. This means 10 gigabytes of data per flight hour. Based on this data, new algorithms can be developed for many uses such as aircraft predictive maintenance or to improve fleet management, reducing fuel consumption and $CO_2$ emissions.
  But a real leap forward could also be achieved by exploiting personal data. The benefits of using personal information (including biometrics) through wearables technologies provided to cabin crews are enormous: the analysis of vital signs can prevent air accidents. Indeed, collecting and storing such personal data (e.g., vital signs), may also be helpful for the investigation of potential aviation accidents. The use of biometrics through wearables may be a significant advantage in the cabin to enhance machine's safety, by catching certain patterns from the data subjects on board.
  Nevertheless, imposing the use of wearables may rise important problems from a labor law perspective. In the opinion of data protection authorities (EDPB 2017), employers are increasingly tempted to provide wearable devices to their employees to track and monitor their health and activity at the workplace. However, this data processing involves the processing of health data and is therefore prohibited based on Article 9(1) GDPR. In addition, employees are not in a position, given the imbalance of power, to give free consent to the processing of their personal data by their employer, and if the data processing is not proportional, the employer does not have a legal ground.
  As a potential solution, we may think of anonymization techniques for the processing of such data. Nor should we forget that GDPR should apply to any information concerning an identified or identifiable natural person. The principles of data protection should therefore not apply to anonymous information, namely information which does not relate to an identified or identifiable natural person or to personal data rendered anonymous in such a manner that the data subject is not or no longer identifiable. However, anonymization (EDPB 2014) is technically very difficult for ensuring complete anonymization of the data. In some of the presented examples (e.g., prevent accidents by processing vital signs of the pilots) anonymization is not even desirable.
  Since employees are rarely able to freely give, refuse or revoke consent, given the imbalance of power, consent will be only lawful in exceptional circumstances. As explained in Sect. 3.2 (*Lawfulness of processing*), another legal basis under Article 6(1) rather than consent shall apply. For instance, employers' legitimate interest can sometimes be invoked as a legal ground, but only if the processing

[8]Wearables or wearable technologies are smart electronic devices with micro-sensors connecting to the Internet which, presented in various formats (including watches, glasses or clothing) may collect and process (personal) data e.g. environment data, vital signs and other biometric data.

is strictly necessary for a legitimate purpose and the processing complies with the principles of proportionality and subsidiarity. A proportionality test should be conducted before the deployment of any monitoring tool to consider whether all data are necessary, whether this processing outweighs the general privacy rights that employees also have in the workplace and what measures must be taken to ensure that infringements on the right to private life and the right to secrecy of communications are limited to the minimum necessary.

## 5 Conclusions

Collecting personal data (including biometrics and other sensitive data) has become increasingly present in many aspects of daily life. Individuals' reasonable expectation of privacy, particularly in public spaces (but also at work), appears to be progressively breaking down. Whereas biometric recognition and analog technologies demonstrated significant benefits to enhance aviation safety in the context of international security, the new scenario raises unprecedented issues from a data protection point of view, entailing potential discriminatory effects and impact on the ability to exercise individual fundamental rights.

Against this background, citizens require the implementation of strong privacy safeguards and accountability mechanisms to build individuals' trust in how public and private agents process personal data. Whereas public authorities in Europe are covered by some mechanisms such as the Law Enforcement Directive (EU) 2016/680, private actors shall make particular efforts to develop biometric tracking technologies under GDPR strict conditions, i.e.:

- by evidencing that no other less intrusive means are capable to achieve the same goals;
- with strict observance of the principle of proportionality, pursuant to the case-law of the Court of Justice of the European Union;
- deploying the principles of privacy by design and data protection by default in the development of such technologies;
- conducting prior in-deep data protection impact assessments where the processing is likely to result in a high risk to the rights and freedoms of natural persons;
- establishing communication channels with supervisory authorities under a prior-consultation scheme when the processing of personal data involves a high risk which the controller cannot mitigate by appropriate measures;
- evaluating to what extent a decision taken based solely on automated processing (including profiling), may produce an adverse effect concerning individuals; and
- implementing appropriate technical and organizational measures to ensure a level of security appropriate to the risk.

Finally, recognition technologies also raise broader issues from an ethical and societal point of view. It is not a matter of privacy only but of a global debate on ethics for a democratic society affecting many fundamental rights (including the freedom of information and expression, the freedom of assembly and association, or the freedom of thought, conscience and religion), which the EU needs to address in the short term.

## References

ATAG. (2019). *Air Transport action group*. Retrieved from www.atag.org: https://www.atag.org/facts-figures.html.

Airbus, S. A. S. (2018). *Global market forecast 2018–2037: Global network*. Blagnac Cedex, France: Global Citizens.

Airbus, S. A. S. (2018). *Big data: Airbus is mining the wealth of knowledge for aviation*. February 2018, Retrieved from Airbus Web site: https://www.airbus.com/public-affairs/berlin/en/our-topics/digitalisation.html.

Airbus, S. A. S. (2019). *Airbus and emirates reach agreement on A380 fleet, sign new widebody orders*. February 14, 2019 Retrieved from Airbus Web site: https://www.airbus.com/newsroom/press-releases/en/2019/02/airbus-and-emirates-reach-agreement-on-a380-fleet–sign-new-widebody-orders.html.

Airbus, S. A. S. (2019). *Global Market Forecast 2019–2038: Cities, Airports and Aircrafts*. Blagnac Cedex, France.

Airbus, S. E. (2019). *Airbus registration document—Annual report*.

EDPB. (2017). *Opinion 2/2017 on data processing at work, adopted on 8 June 2017*.

EDPB. (2019). *Guidelines 3/2019 on processing of personal data through video devices (version for public consultation Adopted on 10 July 2019*.

EDPB. (2007). *Opinion 4/2007 on the concept of personal data*.

EDPB. (2010). *Opinion 1/2010 on the concepts of "controller" and "processor", adopted on 16 February 2010*.

EDPB. (2014). *Opinion 5/2014 on Anonymization Techniques adopted 10 April 2014*.

EDPS. (2018). *The history of the general data protection regulation*. Retrieved from EDPS Web site: https://edps.europa.eu/data-protection/data-protection/legislation/history-general-data-protection-regulation_en.

European Commission. (2020). Communication from the commission to the european parliament and the council. *Ata protection as a pillar of citizens' empowerment and the EU's approach to the digital transition—two years of application of the general data protection regulation. Official Journal of the European Union*. 2020, June 24.

European Parliament. (1995). Directive 95/46/EC of the European parliament and of the council of 24 October 1995 on the protection of individuals with regard to the processing of personal data and on the free movement of such data. *Official Journal of the European Union*. 1995, October 24.

European Parliament. (2018). Regulation (EU) 2016/679 of the European Parliament and of the Council of 27 April 2016 on the protection of natural persons with regard to the processing of personal data and on the free movement of such data, and repealing Directive 95/46/EC. *Official Journal of the European Union*. 2018, April 27.

European Union. (2000). Charter of Fundamental Rights of the European Union. *Official Journal of the European Union*.

European Union. (2012). Consolidated versions of the Treaty on European Union. *Official Journal of the European Union*. 2012, October 26.

**Marcos García-Gasco Romero** is Data Protection Officer (DPO) for all Airbus entities in Spain, including Airbus Defence & Space, Airbus Helicopters España and Airbus Operations. He has developed his career in different international and national law firms, including Olswang LLP and CMS Albiñana & Suárez de Lezo, advising companies on privacy, data protection, technological matters, Internet and content.

Marcos García-Gasco is graduate in Law and Business Management and Administration from Carlos III University of Madrid and hold a Master Degree in European Union Law from the same university. He currently teaches at Nebrija University (Master of Data Protection, Innovation and Security).

# The Financial Perspective in the Fight Against the Crime of Human Trafficking: The Case of Spain

**Tania García Sedano**

**Abstract** Given the importance of the economic aspect of human trafficking, this chapter focuses on the financial investigation of this serious crime. It is a key to understand the financial dimension of these criminal activities, largely overlooked in the Spanish legal system.

**Keywords** Human trafficking · Modern slavery · Financial dimension · Impunity

## 1 Introduction

In 2017, the International Labour Organization (ILO) reported that 40 million people were subjected to contemporary forms of slavery in different parts of the world (ILO 2017). This situation cannot be ignored; the need to explore and consolidate new methods in the fight against this phenomenon is urgent.

Given the importance of the economic aspect of human trafficking, this article focuses on the financial investigation of this serious crime. The financial dimension of these criminal activities is largely overlooked in the Spanish legal system, but its investigation represents a useful instrument that would help to free its victims from the subjugation they are forced to endure (Ferreiro 2005).

In: Security in the Global Commons and Beyond, Edited by J. Martin Ramirez, and Bartolomé Bauzá-Abril. © 2021 Springer International. Submitted: September, 14, 2020; Accepted: November, 19, 2020.

T. G. Sedano (✉)
Provincial Court of Madrid, Madrid, Spain
e-mail: taniagarciasedano@yahoo.es



J. M. Ramírez and B. Bauzá-Abril (eds.), *Security in the Global Commons and Beyond*, Advanced Sciences and Technologies for Security Applications,
https://doi.org/10.1007/978-3-030-67973-6_13

## 2 The Economic Dimension of the Crime of Human Trafficking

Human trafficking is a lucrative business (ILO 2005) and a serious violation of the most elementary rights of human beings. However, in spite of its flagrant transgression of human rights, the abhorrence it evokes and its repercussions for the lives of the victims, the economic dimension of this crime remains below the radarscope.

The United Nations (UN) (UNODC 2009) defines human trafficking as a commercial process in which human beings are bought and sold (Gimenez-Salinas 2016). Paradoxically, its proceeds are included in the Gross Domestic Product of the member countries of the European Union (EU) by virtue of Regulation (EU) No. 549/2013 of the European Parliament and of the Council of 21 May 2013 on the European System of National and Regional Accounts of the EU, despite the fact that human trafficking constitutes a flagrant violation of basic human rights, and even though the fight against it is one of the Union's priorities. According to Europol (EUROPOL 2017), between 0.7 and 1.28% of the annual Gross Domestic Product of the EU is "related to suspicious financial activities".

Exploitation is highly relevant, for two reasons. The first is that the fundamental cause of this crime is the demand for services provided by victims; the second, linked to the first, is that it constitutes the means by which criminals obtain their profits. However, the economic perspective receives very little attention. In spite of its undeniable importance, in the policies of prevention and prosecution of this crime, the economic dimension is conspicuous by its absence (UNODC 2009).

In Spain, it was not until Organic Law 5/2010, of 22 June, that human trafficking became a crime under the country's legal system, in article 177 (bis) of the Criminal Code. This legislation enabled Spain to comply with its internationally contracted obligations (European Commission 2006). Since then, this provision has been successively modified, the last time by means of Organic Law 1/2015, of 30 March, with the declared intention of incorporating Directive 2011/36/EU into the Spanish legislation. Unfortunately, the underlying reason for the various modifications is to be found in the technical deficiencies that have undermined the purpose of the legislators.

## 3 THE GLOBAL FINANCIAL SYSTEM: A Special Global Common?

Historically, the concept of the global commons is closely linked to the concept of property as it appears in Roman law (Milun 2011). However, the exercise of the powers of ownership, *ius utendi* and *ius abutendi*, inherent in the right of property over the global commons can lead to their disappearance (Hardin 1968); so, their preservation is of vital importance to all States.

The global commons have a set of defining characteristics, among them the fact that they are not under the sovereignty of any specific State, the damage that their disruption can cause (Gómez De Ágreda 2010), their interconnectedness, and the difficulty of implementing policies for their governance. In this regard, the global financial system possesses characteristics that bear similarities to the global commons, and its great impact on the world's security qualifies it perhaps as a social common. The globalized world recognizes four global commons in constant interconnection.

Thus, the role that globalization plays in the internationalization of the capitalist economic system cannot be ignored (Skrobanek et al. 1999). In Beck's words (Beck 1998; Naim 2002), this internationalization is the "dominance of the world market that permeates all aspects of society and transforms everything" with the imposition of a global model characterized by the free circulation of capital and the development of institutional elements at the service of the free market.

At the same time, lurking in the shadows of economic globalization is the globalization of crime (UN Economic and Social Council 2011; Terradillos Basoco 1999) in the form of transnational criminal activity (Villacampa Estiarte 2013; López-Sala 2011). In this new world order, human trafficking has become an immensely attractive practice for criminal organizations (Saénz De Pipaón 2005), not just because of the enormous profits it generates (European Parliament 2016) but because it entails less risk than other types of illicit trafficking, such as the drug trade (UNODC 2010).

In any case, Europol (2011) has stressed the growing tendency of criminal groups operating in Europe to engage in multiple illicit markets at the same time. Transnational crime uses the structures of international trade to obtain illicit profits that grow exponentially and vitiates legal relationships in order to attain impunity (Zúñiga 2009).

The increasing permeabilization of borders for capital and merchandise has increased the profitability of criminal businesses, multiplying their gains and minimizing the costs (Queloz 1997).

## 4 The Fight Against Human Trafficking: The Case of Spain

UNODC defines financial investigation as

> the task of identifying, tracking and confiscating the financial resources of human trafficking networks. Financial investigation seeks to identify the accounts or sources of funding based on information provided by the criminal investigation (interviews, documents, wiretaps, etc.), to create a demonstrable causal link between the accounts and the suspects, and to detect the commercial guises used to hide money (for example, corporations, associations, etc.), to establish the most opportune moment for the seizure of the resources identified and to establish the necessary contacts to follow the money and other assets abroad and to obtain evidence that is suitable for use in court.
>
> UNODC (2009)

Indeed, in Spain, the State Prosecutor's Office (2012) states that the financial investigation of trafficking networks is a fundamental element that must be present from the very beginning of a police investigation. And this affects the actions of the

Ministry of Prosecution in two ways. The first is that it makes mandatory the effective investigation of assets in coordination with the State security forces and with official agencies specialized in the prevention of money laundering (Consejo Fiscal 2016). The second is that in the investigation phase of the crime of trafficking the Prosecutor's Office for Immigration must make a rigorous assessment of the economic profits derived from the exploitation of the victims (Consejo Fiscal 2017). So, the coordination between the Prosecutor's Office for Immigration and the Prosecutor's Office for Economic Crimes is growing ever more important (Consejo Fiscal 2016).

The European Parliament (2012) has underlined that investigations that trace, seize and recover financial assets and act against money laundering play a crucial role in combating trafficking, and has highlighted the possibility of their use even on a preventive basis. Nevertheless, the use of financial investigation measures in the field of criminal investigations relating to trafficking in human beings remains limited, and their integration into the prosecution of this crime is still a major challenge. In our view, the incorporation of financial investigation is a key step in the attempts to improve the current model. At present, the number of prosecutions for human trafficking remains "extremely low" (UNODC 2012).

In the following sections, we look at some of the factors that currently act as obstacles to financial investigation.

## *4.1 On the Criminal Liability of Legal Entities*

Traffickers often use legitimate business structures to conceal their illicit activities (European Commission 2019).

Indeed, business activity can both perpetuate trafficking in human beings and contribute to its eradication; however, most companies are unaware of the connections, and only a few Member States have prosecuted legal persons (European Commission 2019).

The Article 10 of UN Convention against Transnational Organized Crime, in virtue of paragraph 1 establishes that each State Party shall adopt: "such measures as may be necessary, consistent with its legal principles, to establish the liability of legal persons for participation in serious crimes involving an organized criminal group" and for the offences established in accordance with the Convention itself.

For its part, the International Covenant on Civil and Political Rights, in its General Comment No. 31 (2004) on the nature of the general legal obligation imposed on States Parties to the Covenant, stipulates the need for States to exercise due diligence to protect people not only against violations of Covenant rights by their agents, but also against the acts of private individuals or entities.

In 2011, the Human Rights Council unanimously approved the Guiding Principles on Business and Human Rights, which establish in Principle No. 1 that:

> States must protect against human rights abuse within their territory and/or jurisdiction by third parties, including business enterprises. This requires taking appropriate steps to prevent,

> investigate, punish and redress such abuse through effective policies, legislation, regulations and adjudication.

In the Spanish Criminal Code, the criminal liability of legal persons for the crime of trafficking in human beings is defined in paragraph 7 of article 177 *bis*. In accordance with article 31 bis 5.3 of the Criminal Code, financial activity is considered *ex lege*as an area of risk. For this reason, the legal system requires regulations aimed at preventing crimes in the context of financial resource management. At present, the liability of legal persons is not provided for in all the crimes classified in the Criminal Code—for the ones that the legislation has expressly defined. What is more, there is no explanation of how the offences are selected (Quintero Olivares 2018).

To conclude, the establishment of offences in the Criminal Code is by no means an ideal measure for enforcing liability. On the one hand, there is still no comprehensive consideration of corporate liability for human rights violations. On the other, victims of human rights violations in which transnational corporations participate face multiple obstacles with regard to gaining access to judicial remedy (European Parliament 2018).

### *4.2 The Role of the Public Sector*

Governments must act with due diligence to ensure that public employees have the necessary training to identify and take action against trafficking in human beings as well as in the fight against corruption, given its contribution to this phenomenon (European Parliament 2016).

Researchers have suggested that the main reason for the existence of modern-day slavery in many countries is the complicity or indifference of governments (Zhang and Pineda 2008; Bales 2014). According to Zhang & Pineda, corruption is

> probably the most important factor in explaining human trafficking" and "(c)ountries that make the least effort to fight human trafficking also tend to be those with high levels of official corruption
>
> UN Global Initiative to Fight Human Trafficking (2008)

So, it is quite easy to establish a link between the general levels of corruption present in a country and the extent of human trafficking in that country.

In Spain, the Law of Public Sector Contracts of 9 November 2017, article 71, prohibits those who have been convicted for the crime of trafficking in human beings from applying for public contracts. For its part, the Preamble to Law 9/2017, point IV, refers to the adoption of measures of "self-regulation"; it thus reaffirms voluntary compliance as a measure for accrediting the fulfilment of legal requirements at national and community level.

## 4.3 Non-financial Information Statements

By means of Law 11/2018 of 28 December, which modifies the Commercial Code, the revised text of the Capital Companies Law approved by Royal Legislative Decree 1/2010, of 2 July, and Law 22/2015, of 20 July, on Auditing of Accounts regarding non-financial information and diversity, Directive 2014/9/EU of the European Parliament and of the Council has been incorporated into Spain's legal system.

The law applies to companies or groups of companies that are obliged to prepare consolidated accounts, employ 500 or more staff, are considered of public interest or which, over the course of two consecutive years, meet two of the three following requirements: their consolidated assets exceed two million euros; their turnover amounts to four million euros; or their workforce exceeds 250 workers.

The most significant feature of this law is that it establishes the obligation to publish a statement of non-financial information. With regard to the matter that concerns us here, this obligation involves the establishment and application of procedures of due diligence, the prevention of the risk of human rights violations, and measures to mitigate, manage and redress possible abuses.

## 4.4 Money Laundering

It is striking that the Spanish Criminal Code, despite classifying money laundering in articles 301 to 304, does not specifically incriminate the practice in relation to the crime of human trafficking.

In our view, Organic Law 1/2015 of 30 March should have established in article 301 of the Criminal Code a harsher penalty for cases in which the assets derive from the crime of trafficking in human beings, in a form analogous to the specification in article 301, first paragraph, Sect. 2, regarding the relation of assets to any of the crimes associated with the trafficking of toxic drugs, narcotic drugs or psychotropic substances (Berdugo De La Torre and Fabián Caparrós 2011).

The justification for this proposal would be twofold. First, this is a serious offence, committed, like drug trafficking, in the context of organized crime (De La Cuesta Arzamendi and Pérez Machío 2015). Second, if trafficking in human beings has reached the level it has, it is because of the profits it generates. In fact, trafficking in human beings is the world's third most lucrative illicit business, and the assets of organized criminal groups represent between 2% and 5% of the planet's GDP (European Parliament 2016). Finally, the European Parliament itself notes that the proceeds from trafficking are reinjected into the world economy; therefore, both States and other actors have the duty to work to change trafficking from a business that is "low-risk, high-reward" to one that is "high-risk, low-reward" (European Parliament 2016).

### 4.5 The Lack of a Clear Legal Definition of Some of the Most Serious Forms of Exploitation

The crime of trafficking is conceived as a predicate crime with respect to others whose purpose it is create situations of domination or exploitation (Ontiveros Alonso 2016; Consejo Fiscal 2009). Thus, if the aim pursued by article 177 bis is fulfilled, this crime would be considered together alongside the other crimes committed or attempted.

However, in Spain the legislation has not defined the purposes of the crime of trafficking established in paragraph 1 (a) of article 177 bis. Thus, the crimes of slavery, practices analogous to it, and forced labour are not covered in Spanish law. Article 607 bis 2, paragraph 10 of the Criminal Code defines submission to slavery as a crime against humanity, the article states that the conduct must be carried out "as part of a generalized or systematic attack against the civilian population or part of it". From any perspective, our legal system presents a lacuna that is unparalleled in comparative law (Consejo Fiscal 2018).

To overcome this deficiency (see the Circular of the State Prosecutor's Office 5/2011, on the criteria for the special action unit of the Prosecutor's Office for Immigration), articles 311 and 312.2 on offences against the rights of workers are applied jointly with article 173.2 on offences of degrading treatment.

In the context of the EU, several member States have reported that trafficking in human beings for the purpose of labour exploitation is increasing, reaching 21% of the total number of recorded victims (European Commission 2016). In 2013, the GRETA (Group of Experts on Action against Trafficking in Human Beings) Report urged the Spanish authorities to develop awareness measures regarding the existence and relevance of trafficking in human beings in order to pursue the aims established in section a) of paragraph 1 of article 177*bis*.

To date, no national plan against the crime of trafficking for labour exploitation has been approved (Consejo Fiscal 2016). Despite Spain's ratification of the ILO's Protocol to the 1930 Convention on Forced Labour of 2014, it has not been created any national plan or policy to combat forced labour, as prescribed in Article 1, paragraph 2. In our view, this situation represents a failure to comply with the international obligations entered into by Spain. The European Court of Human Rights itself has established the obligation of the States Parties to the European Convention on Human Rights to protect the individual (2005, 2010, 2012a, b), proclaiming the need for the State to penalize, in proportion to the severity of the offence, the practices prohibited in article 4 of the Convention (slavery, servitude and forced labour) and to punish any act that keeps a person in such a situation or that constitutes human trafficking.

### 4.6 Seizures and Confiscations

The European Commission (2016) has reported the existence of practical problems in carrying out seizures and confiscations in cases related to trafficking in human beings. These include difficulties in detecting the proceeds of criminal activities and ineffective international cooperation when money has been sent to a country outside the European Union.

Directive 2011/36/EU establishes the obligation for the Member States to adopt the measures necessary to allow their competent authorities to seize and confiscate the instruments and proceeds of human trafficking offences. The EU also adopted Directive 2014/42/EU of the European Parliament and of the Council, of 3 April, 2014, on the seizure and confiscation of instruments and proceeds of crime in order to optimize prevention and to combat transnational organized crime and neutralize its proceeds. Financial investigations are reported to increase the number of seizures and thus lead to more confiscations.

In any case, specific international cooperation mechanisms are also required so that States can respond to requests from foreign countries to effect preventive seizures and confiscations and to decide the most appropriate way to use the proceeds confiscated.

## 5 Conclusions

Just as the growth of European wealth in the eighteenth century cannot be conceived without the monopoly on slavery that paved the way for the development of industrial capitalism in the nineteenth century, today we must address the economic dimension of human trafficking in order to fight this practice effectively.

The criminalization of human trafficking and related offences is not enough to deter organized criminal groups, because it does little to diminish their perception that this is a highly profitable activity. Instead, the strategies to combat this form of crime should be centred on the economic profits it generates. To be effective, they must focus on the monitoring, seizure and confiscation of the proceeds of crime.

The consolidation of the social commons and the awareness of their importance will help us to take on longstanding problems with renewed tools for the benefit of humanity.

## References

Bales, K. (2014). Slavery in contemporary manifestations. In J. Allain (Ed.), *The legal understanding of slavery from the historical to the contemporary*. Oxford: Oxford University Press.

Beck, U. (1998). *¿Qué es la globalización?. Falacias del globalismo, respuestas a la globalización.* Barcelona: Paidós.

Belser, P. (2005). *Forced labor and human trafficking: Estimating the profits.* Working document, International Labour Office, 2005, Geneva.

Berdugo De La Torre, I., & Fabián Caparrós, E. (2011). La emancipación del blanqueo de capitales en el Derecho Penal español. In Muñoz Conde, Lorenzo Salgado, Ferré Olivé, Cortés Bechiarelli and Núñez Paz (Dirs), *Un derecho penal comprometido. Libro homenaje al Prof. D. Gerardo Landrove Díaz*. Valencia: Tirant lo Blanch.

Consejo Fiscal (Spanish Prosecutors' Council). (2009). Report on the draft Organic Law modifying Organic Law 10/1995, of 23 November, of the Criminal Code. Madrid.

Consejo Fiscal (Spanish Prosecutors' Council). (2016). *Meeting of prosecutors on issues of immigration. Conclusions*. Madrid, 2016. Paragraph 8.

Consejo Fiscal (Spanish Prosecutors' Council). (2017). *Annual Report*. Madrid.

Consejo Fiscal (Spanish Prosecutors' Council). (2018). *Annual Report*. Madrid.

De La Cuesta Arzamendi, J. L., & Pérez Machío, A. I. (2015). La lucha económico-financiera contra la trata de seres humanos: el ordenamiento jurídico español. In M. Poelemans, M. Richard González, M. R. Gutiérrez Sanz, & I. Riaño Brun (Coords.), *El fenómeno de la prostitución: cooperación franco-española en la lucha contra la trata de seres humanos*. Aranzadi, Cizur Menor: Thomson Reuters.

EUROPOL. (2011). *Organised crime threat assessment*. The Hague.

European Court of Human Rights. (2010). Case Rantsev v. Cyprus and Russia, 7 January 2010, Demand no. 25965/04.

European Court of Human Rights. (2012a). Case CN and V. v. France, 11 October 2012. Application nº 67724/09.

European Court of Human Rights. (2012b). Case of C.N. v. the United Kingdom, 13 November 2012. Application Nº 4239/08.

European Parliament. (2016). Resolution of 5 July 2016 on the fight against trafficking in human beings in the EU's external relations. Document nº 2015/2340(INI).

European Parliament. (2018). Resolution on the EU's input to a UN binding instrument on transnational corporations and other business enterprises with transnational characteristics with respect to human rights. Document: (2018/2763(RSP).

European Commission. (2006). Report from the commission based on article 9 of the council framework decision of 28 November 2002 on the strengthening of the penal framework to prevent the facilitation of unauthorised entry, transit and residence. Document COM (2006) 770 finals. Bruxelles, 6.12.2006.

European Commission. (2016). Report from the commission to the European parliament and council. Report on the progress made in the fight against trafficking in human beings (2016) as required under Article 20 of Directive 2011/36/EU on preventing and combating trafficking in human beings and protecting its victims. Document COM (2016) 267 final.

European Court of Human Rights. (2005). Judgment in the case Siliadin vs France, 26 July 2005, Application 73316/01.

Ferreiro, X. (2005). *La víctima en el proceso penal*. Madrid: La Ley.

Gimenez-Salinas Framis, A. (2016). La trata de personas como mercado ilícito del crimen organizado. Factores explicativos y características. *Cuadernos de la Guardia Civil*, 52.

Gómez De Ágreda, A. (2010). Global commons en la era de la incertidumbre. *Boletín de Información* nº 317, 2010.

Hardin, G. (1968). *The tragedy of the commons*. Science.

Human Rights Council. (2011). Guiding principles on business and human rights. New York and Geneva.

International Covenant on Civil and Political Rights. (2004). General Comment No. 31 [80].

International Labour Organization. (2017). *Global estimates of modern slavery, forced labour and forced marriage*. Geneva.

López-Sala, A. (2011). La trata de personas: ¿su abordaje como un nuevo problema de seguridad internacional?. In M. Requena, & Díez De Revenga (Coord.), *La seguridad y la defensa en el actual marco socio-económico: nuevas estrategias frente a nuevas amenazas*. Madrid: UNED.

Milun, K. (2011). *The Political Uncommons*. Ashgate: The Cross-Cultural Logic of the Global Common.

Naim, M. (2002). Five wars of globalization. *American University International Law Review, 18*, 167.

Ontiveros Alonso, M. (2016). *El derecho penal frente a la trata de personas (problemas técnicos y político-criminales*. México: Universidad Autónoma de México.

Queloz, N. (1997). "Les actions internationales de lutte contre la criminalité organisée: le cas de l'Europe", *Revue de Science Criminelle et Droit Pénal Comparé.*

Quintero Olivares, G. (2018). Los programas de cumplimiento y el derecho penal. In E. Demetrio Crespo, & A. Nieto Martín (Dir), *Derecho Penal económico y derechos Humanos*. Valencia: Tirant lo Blanch.

Saénz De Pipaón Y Mengs, J. (2005). *Expresiones de fenomenología criminal y su etiología*. Madrid: ACPA.

Skrobanek, S., Boonpakdi, N., & Janthakeero, C. (1999). *Tráfico de mujeres: realidades humanas en el negocio internacional del sexo*. Madrid: Narcea.

Terradillos Basoco, J. M. (1999). El derecho penal de la globalización. Luces y sombras. In Capella Hernández (Coord.), *Transformaciones del Derecho Penal en la Mundialización*. Madrid: Consejo General del Poder Judicial.

UN Economic and Social Council. (2011). Ad Hoc committee on the elaboration of a convention against transnational organized crime *Report of the informal preparatory meeting of the open-ended Intergovernmental ad hoc committee on the elaboration of a Comprehensive international convention against organized Transnational crime*. Document A/AC.254/3.

UN Global Initiative to Fight Human Trafficking. (2008). Workshop: corruption and human trafficking: the grease that facilitates the crime. The Vienna forum to fight human trafficking 13–15 February 2008, Austria Center Vienna. Background paper.

UN Office on Drugs and Crime. (2009). *Manual de autoaprendizaje*. New York.

UN Office on Drugs and Crime. (2010). *Organized crime involvement in trafficking in personas and smuggling of migrants, passim*. New York.

UN Office on Drugs and Crime. (2012). The international legal frameworks concerning trafficking in human beings, ICAT paper series – Issue 1, October 2012 c).

Villacampa Estiarte, C. (2013). La trata de seres humanos como manifestación de la delincuencia organizada. Especial referencia al derecho positivo español. In C. Villacampa Estiarte (Coord.), *La delincuencia organizada: un reto a la política criminal actual*. Cizur Menor: Aranzadi.

Zhang, S. X., & Pineda, S. L. (2008). Corruption as a causal factor in human trafficking. In *Organized crime: Culture, markets and policies*. New York: Springer.

Zúñiga Rodríguez, L. (2009). *Criminalidad organizada y sistema penal*. Comares, Granada: Contribución a la determinación del injusto de organización criminal.

**Dr. Tania García Sedano** is Deputy Magistrate at the Provincial Court of Madrid, Associate Professor at the Carlos III University of Madrid, and Associate Professor at the Universidad Pontificia de Comillas.

Her research work focuses mainly on the study of the human rights of people who are particularly vulnerable, immigrants and victims of trafficking in human beings.

She is Secretary of the CICA International Foundation.

# Food Security: The Sea and the Sustainable Fight Against Global Hunger

## Combining the Sustainable Development Goals Life Below Water and Zero Hunger: The Sea as a Great Ally in the Sustainable Fight Against Global Hunger

**Pablo Morón-Elorza**

**Abstract** One of the main challenges that humanity faces is to meet the growing demand of food linked to the rapid increase in global population in a secure way. As human population rises, overfishing, water stress related mainly to agriculture, livestock and industry, together with marine pollution and global warming are dangerously reducing marine biodiversity and natural resources. In this challenging landscape, ensuring food security by finding a sustainable and high-quality food source has become a priority. In this sense, fish should be considered as a preferred food, being an important source of digestible proteins, beneficial fatty acids and vitamins, with a low content of saturated fats. However, overfishing of wild populations, together with marine pollution, have been linked to a significant biodiversity loss and have contributed to a downward trajectory in wild caught fishing. Within this framework, a great opportunity arises for an efficient productive sector: aquaculture. Aquaculture provides a great opportunity to fight global hunger, as it is the food sector and one of the productive sectors experiencing the fastest growth, which currently supplies more than half of the fish consumed worldwide. Aquaculture is considered a sustainable alternative, since it allows the efficient use of natural resources, guaranteeing food hygiene, security and promoting economic growth, with a minimal environmental impact.

**Keywords** Food security · Aquaculture · Sustainability · Ocean conservation · Nutrition

---

In: Security and the Global Commons, Edited by J. Martin Ramirez, and Bartolomé Bauzá-Abril.
 Submitted: August, 18, 2020; Accepted: October, 24, 2020.

---

P. Morón-Elorza (✉)
Biodomo Zoo and Aquarium, Science Park of Granada, Granada, Spain
e-mail: p-moron@hotmail.com

 
J. M. Ramírez and B. Bauzá-Abril (eds.), *Security in the Global Commons and Beyond*, Advanced Sciences and Technologies for Security Applications,
https://doi.org/10.1007/978-3-030-67973-6_14

# 1 Introduction

As any other species, we, humans must eat to live. One of the main challenges that humanity faces is meeting the growing food demand linked to the rapid increase in global population, which is estimated to exceed 9.8 billion people by 2050 (FAO 2014; APROMAR 2018).

This challenge is directly affected by our environmental impact (Ji-Zhong et al. 2018). Human impact on the environment, or anthropogenic impact, includes changes such as: global warming, environmental degradation, mass extinction and biodiversity loss (Leu et al. 2008; Doney 2010; Nickel et al. 2020).

Different studies concluded that, based on extensive evidence, human activities, especially emissions of greenhouse gases, are the dominant cause of the observed warming since the mid-twentieth century (Wuebbles et al. 2017), being climate variability and extremes one of the main threats to progress in food security, which undermines efforts to end hunger and malnutrition (FAO 2020a). World's current food system and dietary patterns are responsible for around 21–37% of total greenhouse gas emissions (FAO 2020a).

But climate change is not the only environmental effect of human activities: carbon dioxide is added to the atmosphere whenever fossil fuels are burnt. As the amount of carbon dioxide in the atmosphere rises, it is absorbed by the ocean. In the ocean, carbon dioxide reacts with seawater to form carbonic acid which causes the acidity of seawater to increase. This, and the rising sea temperatures, are the main cause of coral bleaching and further coral degradation, which results in the habitat loss for many of the aquatic species which depend entirely on coral reef ecosystems. Thus, coral bleaching together with ocean pollution and overexploitation show the necessity of an appropiate management in order to ensure the long-term persistence of marine ecosystems (Pratchett et al. 2008).

One example of an anthropogenic impact and marine pollutant which directly affects food security are microplastics. Microplastics are emerging pollutants produced during plastic degradation and which are found mainly in the marine environment (Andrady 2011). They are ingested by marine biota accumulating in the trophic chain, and have been found in many animal species consumed by humans and in humans, as they are found in large quantities in bivalves cultured for human consumption (Van Cauwenberghe and Janssen 2014). Microplastic have shown to affect the physiology of some marine animals, decreasing their energy reserves and metabolism (Wright et al. 2013).

Modifying the environment to fit the needs of the society is causing severe effects, which become worse as the problem of human overpopulation amplifies (Butler 2004). Biodiversity loss has profound impacts on human health, as it is linked to the rise of zoonotic pathogens and the exacerbation of the risk and incidence of infectious diseases. Zoonotic diseases caused by the West Nile Virus and Lime disease are good examples of this process, whilst a high diversity in the community of vertebrate hosts for arthropod vectors strongly reduces human risk of infection (Ostfeld 2009). Investing in preserving rich ecosystems with a high biodiversity could protect us against future pandemics such as the COVID-19 outbreak we are experiencing (Morand et al. 2014).

FAO 2020 reports show that the COVID-19 pandemic, together with the worst locust outbreak in decades which has affected Eastern Africa, are obscuring global food security prospects in an unprecedented way.

As the main conclusion, human activities should be regulated so that their impact on the environment is reduced and food systems should be transformed to deliver affordable, healthy and sustainable diets for all. What people eat and how that food is produced, not only affects their health, but also has major effects in the state of the environment (FAO 2020a).

## 2 Food Security and Global Hunger

The abovementioned anthropogenic impacts, together with a surge in the number and complexity of conflicts in African and Near East nations, intensified by the economic slowdowns taking place at an international level, are putting significant pressure on food security. The concept of food security implies the physical, social and economic access to safe and nutritious food for consumers worldwide, in order to obtain the energy and nutrients necessary to develop a healthy and active life. In addition, this situation must be stable and continuous over time (FAO 2018a).

After many years of international advances in food security, with a slow but steady decrease in global hunger, food insecurity and malnutrition, the last two years show a reversal in the progress achieved, with a progressive increase in the number of undernourished people, reaching the figures found in 2010 with 821 million undernourished people worldwide. The Sustainable Development Goal number 2 (No Hunger) seeks to "end hunger, achieve food security and improve nutrition and promote sustainable agriculture" (UN 2019), yet the goal stablished at the United Nations Millennium Development Goals, to reduce hunger worldwide by fifty percent before 2015, has not been yet achieved in many regions worldwide (WHO 2020).

While 1.5 billion people are nowadays affected by one or more forms of micronutrient deficiency, other forms of malnutrition are also experiencing a progressive increase: four out of every ten adults are affected by obesity and overweight, which is leading to a significant increase in the occurrence of diet related disease in both the developed and developing world (FAO 2018a). In addition, child malnutrition remains a global threat, as "in 2019, 21.3% (144 million) children under the age of 5 were estimated to be stunted, 6.9% (47 million) wasted and 5.6% (38.3 million) overweight, while at least 340 million children suffered from micronutrient deficiencies" (FAO 2020a). Food security regarding child malnutrition is influenced by the irregular trends mentioned, as they affect diet quality and quantity, including children's and women's diet, and people's health in many different ways.

FAO projections reflect that the world is not on track to meet nutrition targets and to achieve Zero Hunger Sustainable Development Goal by 2030, being food security and global hunger greatly affected by the socio-economic and health impacts of the COVID-19 pandemic (FAO 2020b).

An important factor in food insecurity is its unequal distribution, as "out of the 2 billion people suffering from food insecurity, 1.03 billion are in Asia, 675 million in Africa, 205 million in Latin America and the Caribbean, 88 million in Northern America and Europe, and 5.9 million in Oceania". In addition, at a global level, food insecurity prevalence is higher among women than men (FAO 2020a), as another form of inequality.

In this challenging landscape, finding a sustainable and high-quality protein source has become a priority; we should see not only healthy, affordable and nutritious food, but also food whose production has the lowest impact on the environment.

One measure of this impact is the **feed conversion ratio**, an estimate of the feeding amount required to produce one kilogram or pound of product. As shown in Fig. 1, chicken meat production is more efficient than pork and beef meat production, but less efficient than farmed fish. Farming salmon is about seven times more efficient in terms of feed-conversion than raising beef.

In addition to the feed conversion ratio, another objective measure we can use to evaluate the sustainability of the food we eat is the **water footprint**. While water covers 70% of the earth's surface, only 2.5% is freshwater (School 2018). It is estimated that by 2050 the demand for this freshwater in food production will be 2.5–3.5 times greater than it is today. With agriculture already using an estimated 70% of freshwater (Fox and Fimeche 2013), water usage and management will clearly become an important issue in the near future.

The vegetable water footprint varies significantly between different crops. In order to produce one kilogram of wheat, only nine hundred liters of water are needed; to

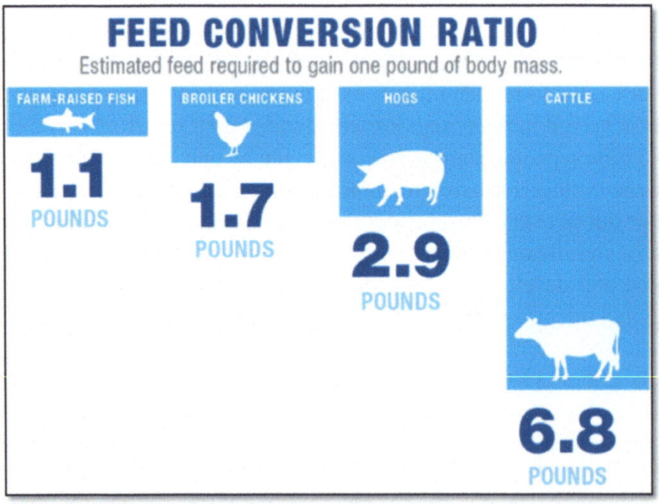


**Fig. 1** Feed-conversion ratio of the main animal protein sources (GAA 2018)

produce one kilogram of corn, one thousand liters of water are required. In order to produce one kilogram of nuts, we need nine thousand liters of water. Cotton requires ten thousand liters per kg (Hoekstra 2014). Curiously, the food which requires the highest amount of water per kilogram is not of animal origin, it is chocolate, which requires seventeen thousand liters to produce one kilogram (Fox and Fimeche 2013).

When it comes to water footprint in animal production, fish production in aquaculture farming systems results again the most efficient. Of those, the aquaponic production system, which requires four hundred liters per kilogram of fish meat, has proven to be the most optimal so far. On the contrary, the most inefficient meat source in terms of water usage is beef, which requires fifteen thousand liters per kilogram produced, followed by pork meat, which requires almost five thousand liters per kilogram of meat. Poultry is again more efficient than the aforementioned two protein sources, with a water footprint of less than four thousand liters per kilogram. During the last years, an increase in the usage of insects as a novel protein source has taken place, with cricket production having a water footprint slightly larger than four thousand liters per kilogram of meat (Joyce et al. 2019).

Taking all these results into account, fish should be considered as a preferred food, being an important source of digestible proteins, with a low content of saturated fats and a high content of essential micronutrients, beneficial fatty acids omega-3, minerals (calcium, phosphorus, iodine, zinc, iron and selenium) and vitamins A, D, E, B6 and B1 (Tacon and Metian 2013).

Over one billion people worldwide rely on fish as their primary source of animal protein; people living in poverty and in lower socio-economic households do not have access to sufficient nutritional food in order to ensure a healthy lifestyle, often relying on low-cost cereals and being unable to purchase meat, fruit or vegetables. Fish, particularly when produced in aquaculture systems, is commonly cheaper than any other animal meat. In addition, fish protein bioavailability is approximately 5–15% higher than that of plant sources. Due to their highly beneficial nutritional properties mentioned, containing several essential amino acids such as lysine, methionine and a unique lipid composition, they are a mean of providing greater nutrition for poorer households (including pregnant, breastfeeding mothers and your children).

An increased fish availability could lead to a better global health and a more diverse diet (FAO 2019). Globally, wild caught fishing and aquaculture are essential for food security and sustenance of millions of people, decreasing poverty rates in developing states (FAO 2018b). However, overfishing of wild populations and the use of non-sustainable fishing methods together with pollution of the seas and oceans, have been linked to a significant loss of biodiversity (FAO 2020b). As represented in Fig.2, in orange, world marine fish stocks are becoming increasingly overfished.

## 3 Aquaculture as a Possible Ally Against Global Hunger

Within this framework, a great opportunity arises for an efficient and sustainable productive sector: **aquaculture**. According to the Food and Agriculture Organization

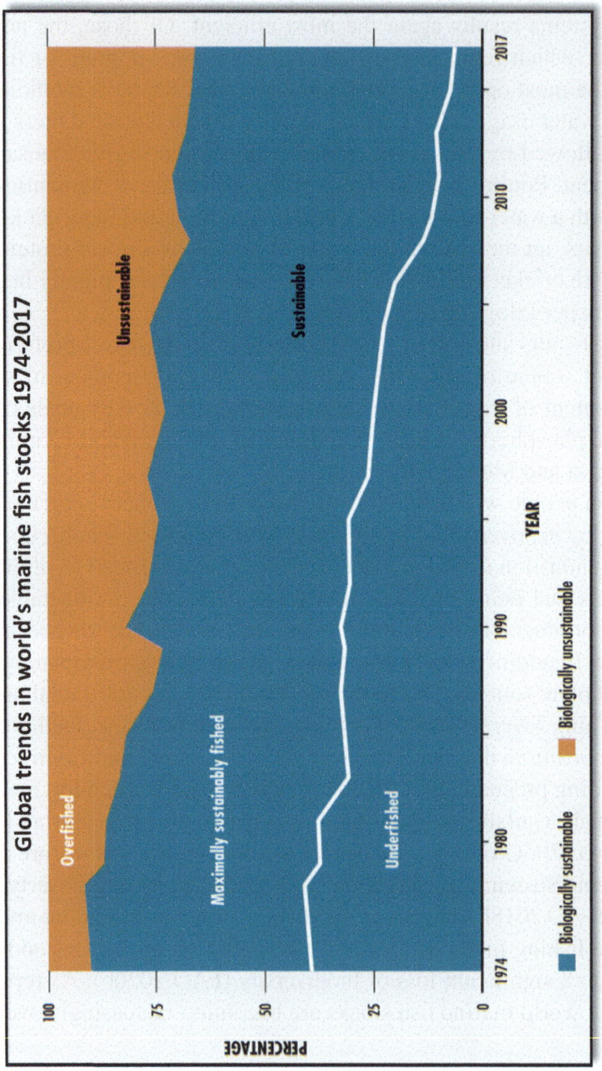


**Fig. 2** Global trends in the state of the world's marine fish stocks, 1974–2017 (Ji-Zhong et al. 2018)

of the United Nations (FAO), "aquaculture is the breeding, rearing, and harvesting of fish, shellfish, algae, and other organisms in all types of water environments" (FAO 2019).

A key reason why millions of people globally suffer from hunger and malnutrition is the impossibility to afford healthy diets. Food supply disruption and lack of income as a result of COVID-19 are also producing an increase in the difficulties for poorer and more vulnerable households to access nutritious foods (FAO 2020a).

There is a need to look throughout the food system to address the factors that are increasing the cost of nutritious foods and having negative environmental impacts, mainly due to the greenhouse gas emissions associated with the current dietary patterns. This could mean supporting food producers, especially local and small scale ones, that can bring nutritious foods to local markets at low cost and with a reduced impact in the environment (FAO 2020a).

Aquaculture provides a great opportunity to fight global hunger, as it is the food sector and one of the productive sectors which is experiencing a fastest growth. It is recognized as a possible sustainable solution for food security and increase dietary nutrition in developing regions. As we have seen in section two of this chapter, we are clearly facing the challenge of transforming food systems to ensure that no one is constrained by the high prices of nutritious foods in order to afford a healthy diet, while ensuring that food production and consumption contributes to environmental sustainability (FAO 2020a).

As represented in Fig. 3, aquaculture production has increased compared to wild caught fishing, currently supplying more than half of the fish consumed worldwide

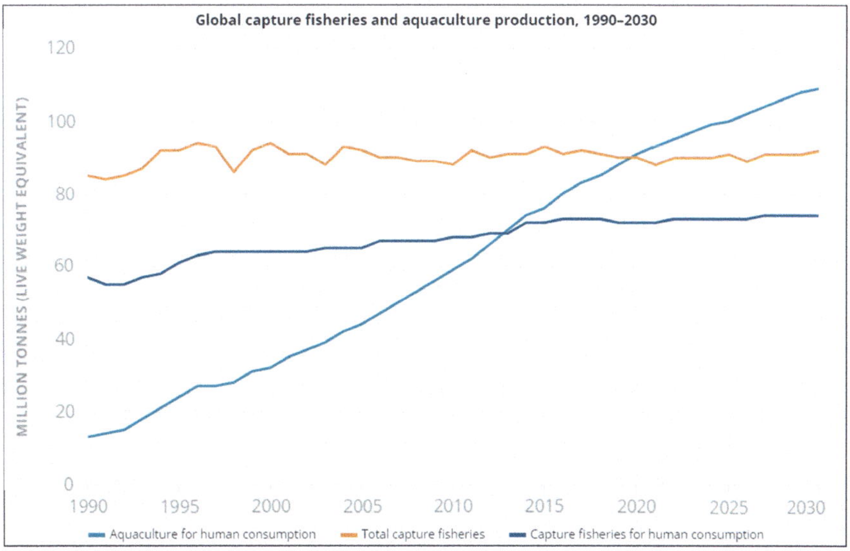


**Fig. 3** Fish production 1990–2030. Please note the much faster increase in fish production linked to Aquaculture compared to wild-caught fishing (FAO 2018c)

(53%) and is responsible for the global increase in fish consumption, which has doubled in the last 50 years (FAO 2020a, b). Furthermore, it is estimated that by 2050, 62% of all the fish consumed worldwide will come from Aquaculture (Kobayashi et al. 2015; World Bank Report 2013).

Aquaculture is considered a sustainable alternative, since it allows the use of natural resources in an efficient manner, guaranteeing food hygiene and security, while promoting economic growth with a minimal impact on the environment, thus facilitating the recovery of the natural balance in the marine ecosystem (Mahfuzuddin and Lorica 2002).

When it comes to purchasing a fish-product, the prevalence of misinformation polarizes the public opinion. A high percentage of the population believes that eating fish caught in the wild is better, since it's natural and therefore allegedly healthier and friendlier with the environment. Fish in their natural habitat tend to consume a more varied diet than fish raised on a fish farm, which can be beneficial because nutrients are more varied, but can also increase the risk of having parasites, toxic substances from harmful algae, bacteria, viruses or chemical pollutants in the meat, which are problematic in several parts of the world. Several inorganic and organic compounds can be present in fish, being heavy metals such as methylmercury, cadmium and organic tin the compounds that represent the most significant health hazards (Dickey and Plakas 2010). Furthermore, there are many species of wild caught fish that are on decline and even close to extinction because of overfishing (Coll et al. 2008). For those reasons, there is another big sector in the population that view consuming wild caught fish as unsustainable and prefer purchasing farm raised fish as a more sustainable and controlled source in terms of food security.

To make healthy diets more affordable, costs of nutritious foods must come down. One of the biggest challenges to ensuring that people have enough nutritious food to eat is the current cost and affordability of healthy diets, as the cost of the diet increases incrementally in relation to the diet quality (FAO 2020a). Aquaculture can end with this tendency, making high quality fish more affordable. The average price of 5.18 euros/kg for European seabass produced in Spain in 2017, greatly under the price of wild caught European seabass (APROMAR 2018) is a good example. The price of nutritious food is determined by many factors: from food production and supply chain to food environment. Costs could be reduced by addressing low productivity and insufficient diversification towards production of nutritious foods, which result in higher market prices. Food and agricultural policies can also directly or indirectly affect the cost of food; trade policies also affect costs and affordability of healthy diets as they alter relative prices between imported and import-competing products. A reorientation of food priorities towards more nutrition-sensitive food production must be performed, and policies that penalize food and agricultural production should be avoided in order to ensure that nutritious foods are made abundantly available (FAO 2020a).

## 4 Future Challenges in Aquaculture

Unfortunately, some fish farms have proven to be lax in their quality control, using practices that are inefficient, unsustainable and that can ultimately be harmful to both consumers and the environment, producing some important challenges for aquaculture such as contamination and environmental impact (Tacon and Metian 2009). That's why it is very important when buying fish to check the sources and make sure the fish come from a sustainable source with stringent quality control procedures. As aquaculture fish is frequently less expensive than wild-caught fish of the same species (APROMAR 2018), a psychological feeling of poorer quality towards farm raised fish may be induced in the consumer. The truth is that aquaculture is continuously improving (FAO 2018b), and the quality of the fish produced has simultaneously increased, providing fish rich in quality proteins and beneficial fatty acids in a sustainable way today.

Nutrition is an important factor that directly affects the response of fish against disease (Blazer 1992) and therefore a correct dietary management can help reducing the production losses through improvement in fish health management. Every vertebrate species requires fatty acids for their optimal development, growth, reproduction and health, lipids being the main source. Some fatty acids are synthesized in the body, while essential fatty acids must be obtained through diet. There must be a correct correlation in the fatty acid intake, due to the competitive interactions that take place during digestion. In marine fish, essential fatty acids are: eicosapentaenoic acid 20:5 n-3 (EPA), docosahexaenoic acid 22:6 n-3 (DHA), and arachidonic acid 20:4 n-6 (ARA) (Sargent 1997). If they drop, the incidence of disease increases (Sargent et al. 1997). Health status of the aquatic species produced through aquaculture is essential for the success of aquaculture activity, with infectious diseases being the main cause of economic losses in this sector throughout the development of aquaculture (Blazer 1992). If fish have a good nutrition, disease incidence will decrease, reducing the treatments required and therefore making aquaculture production more sustainable (Blazer 1991).

There is still a need for research and improvement in the aquaculture field. One of the main problems in aquaculture is the environmental impact, largely due to the fact that the feeding of carnivorous fish traditionally depends on the use of oils and meals of small pelagic fish, which contributes to the loss of biodiversity (Sargent and Tacon 1999). Therefore, we need to find sustainable alternatives to these products.

One of the alternatives uses terrestrial raw materials such as rapeseed oil (Bell 2001) but several studies have shown negative consequences, as the tissues of fish on this diet have lower amounts of highly unsaturated omega-3 fatty acids, beneficial for human health (Izquierdo et al. 2003). In addition, omega-6 fatty acids increase, producing an alteration in the omega-6/omega-3 ratio. This decompensated ratio and the increase of omega-6 fatty acids are correlated with an incidence of vascular, inflammatory and neurodegenerative disorders, together with some types of cancer (Riediger et al. 2009; Simopoulos 2016).

The second alternative consists of using transgenic terrestrial plants, such as genetically modified cameline (*Camelina sativa*), to which synthetic algae-like genes have been added (Betancor et al. 2017). The result is a terrestrial plant rich in long-chain omega-3 fatty acids, which are highly beneficial for human health (Izquierdo et al. 2003). These fatty acids can be extracted and supplied in the feed of aquaculture fish, thus reducing the tremendous pressure that the fishing industry places on the oceans.

Recent studies have proven that European sea bass (*Dicentrarchus labrax)*fed with an experimental diet in which fish oil was completely replaced with genetically modified cameline oil, showed no statistically significant differences in terms of weight gain during the four months of the study (Morón et al. 2019; Betancor et al. 2020), proving that oil from genetically modified cameline can effectively replace fish oil in seabass nutrition. In this study, a total of 450 European sea bass were separated in nine groups of 50 animals and fed by triplicate with three different diets: diet 1 was a commercial diet with a 5.72% content of fish oil and 7.16% rapeseed oil, diet 2 replaced fish oil with genetically modified cameline oil, while diet 3 was supplemented with fish oil and poorer in rapeseed oil. This study showed that the fish blood serum and the white blood cells of European sea bass contained the essential fatty acids EPA, DHA and ARA in a proportion equivalent to the concentration found in the diet used, and with no significant differences between the three diets. Essential fatty acids mentioned, are required by marine fish for their correct development, as they are indispensable for the development of an optimal immune response and bactericidal activity of the fish immune cells (Blazer 1992). In addition, there were no significant differences in the omega-6/omega-3 ratio of the fish lymphocytes obtained from the fish fed from the three different diets. These results support the use of genetically modified cameline oil as a substitute supplement of fish oil for aquaculture fish diets, as growth and feed efficiency observed were equivalent between the different groups, resulting in fish rich in omega-3, highly beneficial for human health (Izquierdo et al. 2003) and with a compensated omega-6/omega-3 ratio. However, the use of raw materials from genetically modified plants needs more studies regarding the production of highly unsaturated fatty acids, especially DHA, and will require societal acceptance of consuming fish fed with products from transgenic origin. Nevertheless, due to its high cost, environmental impact, and the rise in novel alternatives to fish oil used in fish nutrition, fishmeal production (obtained from wild caught fish) peaked in 1994 and has followed a fluctuating but declining path since then. Fishmeal and fish oil are still considered the most nutritious and digestible ingredients in compound feeds for aquaculture, but their inclusion rates show a downward trend, being used in an increasingly selective manner (FAO 2018b). Studies above mentioned are only a small part of the large group of aquaculture studies which are constantly improving its efficiency, thus decreasing the global impact and enriching the nutritional properties of cultured fish.

## 5 Conclusions

a. Regarding food security, fish should be considered a priority food and aquaculture is a key tool in providing high quality cultured fish products in a more healthy and sustainable way; strict controls should be implemented for aquaculture products, in order to guarantee food security and promote sustainability.
b. Aquaculture can aid in the reduction of anthropogenic pressures on the marine ecosystem and help them recover.
c. Aquaculture will be an important food industry in the fight against global hunger linked to the fast increase in global population.
d. Fish production has proven more efficient in terms of feed-conversion ratio and water-footprint than most of the animal protein sources.
e. Further research is needed in many of the fields in aquaculture, to increase its efficiency, decrease its environmental impact and increase the nutritious properties of farmed fish.

## References

Andrady, A. L. (2011). Microplastics in the marine environment. *Marine Pollution Bulletin, 62*(8), 1596–1605. Cited 5 Mar 2020. Available from: https://www.sciencedirect.com/science/article/pii/S0025326X11003055.

APROMAR Asociación Empresarial de Acuicultura en España. (2018). Cádiz. Cited 15 Feb 2020. Available from: http://www.apromar.es/sites/default/files/2018/APROMAR_Informe_ACUICULTURA_2018.pdf.

Bell, J. G., McEvoy, J., Tocher, D. R., McGhee, F., Campbell, P. J., & Sargent, J. R. (2001). Replacement of fish oil with rapeseed oil in diets of Atlantic salmon (Salmo salar) affects tissue lipid compositions and hepatocyte fatty acid metabolism. *Journal of Nutrition, 131*(1), 1535–1543. Cited 26 Apr 2020. Available from: https://pubmed.ncbi.nlm.nih.gov/11340112/.

Betancor, M. B., Li, K., Sprague, M., Bardal, T., Sayanova, O., Usher S., Han, L., Måsøval, K., Torrissen, O., Napier, J. A., & Tocher, D. R. (2017). An oil containing EPA and DHA from transgenic Camelina sativa to raplace marine fish oil in feeds for Atlantic salmon (Salmo salar L.): Effect on intestinal transcriptime, histolofy, tissue fatty acid profiles and plasma biochemistry. *Plos ONE, 12*(4). Cited 30 Apr 2020. Available from: https://pubmed.ncbi.nlm.nih.gov/28403232/.

Betancor, M. B., MacEwan, A., Sprague, M., Gong, X., Montero, D., Han, L., Napier, J. A., Norambuena, F., Izquierdo, M. & Tocher, D. R. (2020). Oil from transgenic Camelina sativa as a source of EPA and DHA in feed for European sea bass (Dicentrarchus labrax L). *Aquaculture, 530*, 735–759. Cited 30 Apr 2020. Available from: https://www.sciencedirect.com/science/article/pii/S0044848620315544?via%3Dihub.

Blazer, V. S. (1991). Piscine macrophage function and nutritional influences: A review. *Journal of Aquatic Animal Health, 3*, 77–86. Cited 23 Apr 2020. Available from: https://afspubs.onlinelibrary.wiley.com/doi/abs/10.1577/1548-8667%281991%29003%3C0077%3APMFANI%3E2.3.CO%3B2.

Blazer, V. S. (1992). Nutrition and disease resistance in fish. *Annual Review of Fish Diseases*, 309–323. Cited 22 Apr 2020. Available from: https://www.sciencedirect.com/science/article/abs/pii/0959803092900689?via%3Dihub.

Butler, C. D. (2004). Human carrying capacity and human health. *PLoS Medicine, 1*(3), e55. Available from: https://www.ncbi.nlm.nih.gov/pmc/articles/PMC539046/.

Coll, M., Libralato, S., Tudela, S., Palomera, I., & Pranovi, F. (2008). Ecosystem overfishing in the ocean. *Plos One, 3*(12):e3881. Cited 16 Apr 2020. Available from: https://journals.plos.org/plosone/article?id=10.1371/journal.pone.0003881.

Dickey, R. W., & Plakas, S. M. (2010). Ciguatera: A public health perspective. *Toxicon, 56*(2), 123–136. Cited 26 Mar 2020. Available from: https://pubmed.ncbi.nlm.nih.gov/19782098/.

Doney, S. C. (2010). The growing human footprint on coastal and open-ocean biogeochemistry. *Science, 328*(5985), 1512–1516. Cited 10 Feb 2020. Available from: https://science.sciencemag.org/content/328/5985/1512.

FAO [Food and Agriculture Organization of the United Nations]. (2014). *El estado de la inseguridad alimentaria en el mundo—Fortalecimiento de un entorno favorable para la seguridad alimentaria y la nutrición*. Roma: Food and Agriculture Organization. Report No. 978-92-5-308542-2. Cited 10 Mar 2020. Available from: http://www.fao.org/3/a-i4030s.pdf.

FAO. (2018a). *Help eliminate hunger and malnutrition*. Report No. CA3923EN/1/3. Available from: http://www.fao.org/3/ca3923en/ca3923en.pdf.

FAO. (2018b). *The state of world fisheries and aquaculture; meeting the sustainable development goals*. Roma: Food and Agriculture Organization of United Nations. Report No. 978-92-5-130562-1. Cited 5 Mar 2020. Available from: http://www.fao.org/documents/card/es/c/I9540EN/.

FAO. (2018c). *The state of world fisheries and aquaculture (SOFIA)*, Rome. Cited 10 May 2020. Available from: http://www.fao.org/fileadmin/templates/SOFIA/2018-l/src/images/charts/figure50.pdf.

FAO. (2020a). *The state of food secutrity and nutrition in the world: Transforming food systems for affordable healthy diets*, Rome. Cited 12 Sept, 2020. Available from: http://www.fao.org/3/ca9692en/CA9692EN.pdf.

FAO. (2020b). *Aquaculture newsletter* [The state of world fisheries and aquaculture], Roma. Cited 31 Jul 2020. Available from: http://www.fao.org/3/ca9229en/ca9229en.pdf#page=20.

FAO. (2019). Cited 3 Feb 2019. Available from: http://www.fao.org/aquaculture/en/.

Fox, T., & Fimeche, C. (2013). *Global food waste not, want not*. London: Institute of Mechanical Engineers, Energy and environment. Cited 24 Apr 2020. Available from: https://www.imeche.org/policy-and-press/reports/detail/global-food-waste-not-want-not.

GAA [Global Aquaculture Alliance]. (2018). Cited 12 May 2020. Available from: https://www.aquaculturealliance.org/what-we-do/why-it-matters/.

Hoekstra, A. Y. (2014). Water for animal products: a blind spot in watre policy. *Environmental Research Letters, 9*(9). Cited 20 Apr 2020. Available from: https://iopscience.iop.org/article/10.1088/1748-9326/9/9/091003.

Izquierdo, M., Obach, A., Arantzamendi, L., Montero, D., Robaina, L., & Rosenlund, G. (2003). Dietary lipid sources for seabream and seabass: Growth performance, tissue composition and flesh quality. *Aquaculture Nutrition, 9*(6), 397–407. Cited 28 Apr 2020. Available from: https://onlinelibrary.wiley.com/doi/abs/10.1046/j.1365-2095.2003.00270.x.

Joyce, A., Goddek, S., Kotzen, B., & Wuertz, S. (2019). Chapter 2, Aquaponics: Closing the cycle of limited water, land and nutrient resources. In S. Goddek, A. Joyce, B. Kotzen, G. M. Burnell (Eds.), *Aquaponics food production systems-combined aquaculture and hydroponic production technologies for the future* (pp. 19–33). Cham, Switzerland: Springer International Publishing. Cited 20 Apr 2020. Available from: https://link.springer.com/chapter/10.1007%2F978-3-030-15943-6_2.

Ji-Zhong, W., Ching-Jing, W., & Fei-Hai, Y. (2018). Human footprint and climate disappearance in vulnerable ecoregions of protected areas. *Global Planet Change, 170*, 260–268. Cited 10 Feb 2020. Available from: https://www.sciencedirect.com/science/article/abs/pii/S0921818118300055?via%3Dihub.

Kobayashi, M., Msangi, S., Batka, M., Vannuccini, S., Dey, M. M., & Anderson, J. L. (2015). Fish to 2030: The role and opportunity for aquaculture. *Aquaculture Economics & Management, 19*(3). Cited 7 Mar 2020. Available from: https://www.tandfonline.com/doi/abs/10.1080/13657305.2015.994240?journalCode=uaqm20.

Leu, M., Hanser, S. E., & Knick, S. T. (2008). The human footprint in the west: A large-scale analysis of anthropogenic impacts. *Ecological Applications, 18*(5). Cited 10 Feb 2020. Available from: https://pubmed.ncbi.nlm.nih.gov/18686576/.

Mahfuzuddin, A., & Lorica, M. H. (2002). Improving developing country food security through aquaculture development—Lessons from Asia. *Food Policy, 27*(2), 125–141. Cited 25 Mar 2020. Available from: https://econpapers.repec.org/article/eeejfpoli/v_3a27_3ay_3a2002_3ai_3a2_3ap_3a125-141.htm.

Morand, S., Jittapalapong, S., Suouttamongkol, Y., Abdullah, M. T., & Huan, T. B. (2014). Infectious diseases and their outbreaks in Asia-Pacific: Biodiversity and its regulation loss matter. *Plos One, 9*(2). Cited 7 Mar 2020. Available from: https://journals.plos.org/plosone/article/authors?id=10.1371/journal.pone.0090032.

Morón, P., Montero, D., Torrecillas, S., Betancor, M. B., Bravo, J., Vega, B., et al. (2019). In vitro study of the serum effect on the supplementation of sea bass (Dicentrarchus labrax) head-kidney macrophage culture medium: Effect on the immune response. *Fish & Shellfish Immunology, 91*, 409–410. Cited 30 Apr 2020. Available from: https://www.sciencedirect.com/science/article/abs/pii/S1050464819303638?via%3Dihub.

Nickel, B. A., Suraci, J. P., Allen, M. L., & Wilmers, C. C. (2020). Human presence and human footprint have non-equivalent effects on wildlife spatiotemporal habitat use. *Biological Conservation, 241*. Cited 5 May 2020. Available from: https://www.sciencedirect.com/science/article/pii/S0006320719313837?via%3.

Ostfeld, R. S. (2009). Biodiversity loss and the rise of zoonotic pathogens. *Clinical Microbiology and Infection, 15*(1). Cited 7 Mar 2020. Available from: https://www.sciencedirect.com/science/article/pii/S1198743X14604122.

Pratchett, M. S., Munday, P. L., Wilson, S. K., Grahan, N. A. J., Cinner, J. E., Bellwood, D. R., Jones, G. P., Polunin, N.V., & McClanahan, T. R. (2008) Effects of climate-induced coral bleaching on coral-reef fishes—Ecological and economic consequences. In R. N. Gibson, R. J. A. Atkinson, J. D. M.Gordon (Eds.), *Oceanography and marine biology. An annual review*, vol. Milton Park: Taylor & Francis Group. Cited 4 Mar 2020.

Riediger, N. D., Othman, R. A., Suh, M., & Moghadasian, M. H. (2009). A systemic review of the roles of n-3 fatty acids in health and disease. *Journal of the American Dietetic Association, 109*(4), 668–679. Cited 30 Apr 2020. https://pubmed.ncbi.nlm.nih.gov/19328262/.

Sargent, J., McEvoy, L., & Bell, J. (1997). Requierements, presentation and sources of polyunsaturated fatty acids in marine fish larval feeds. *Aquaculture, 155*, 117–127. Cited 22 Apr 2020. Available from: https://www.sciencedirect.com/science/article/abs/pii/S0044848697001221?via%3Dihub.

Sargent, J. R., & Tacon, A. G. (1999). Development of farmed fish: a nutritionally necessary alternative to meat. *Proceedings of the Nutrition Society, 58*(2), 377–383. Cited 28 Apr 2020. Available from: https://pubmed.ncbi.nlm.nih.gov/10466180/.

School, W. S. (2018). *U.S. Geological Survey (USGS)*. Cited 18 Apr 2020. Available from: https://water.usgs.gov/edu/earthwherewater.html.

Simopoulos, A. P. (2016). An increase in the omega-6/omega-3 fatty acid ratio increases the risk for obesity. *Nutrient, 8*(3), 128.

Tacon, A. G., & Metian, M. (2009). Fishing for aquaculture: Non-food use of small pelagic forage fish. A global perspective. *Reviews in Fisheries Science, 17*(3), 305–317. Cited 21 Apr 2020. Available from: https://www.tandfonline.com/doi/full/10.1080/10641260802677074.

Tacon, A. G., & Metian, M. (2013). Fish matters: Importance of aquatic foods in human nutrition and global food supply. *Fish Science, 1*(21), 22–23. Cited 20 Apr 2020. Available from: https://www.tandfonline.com/doi/abs/10.1080/10641262.2012.753405.

UN [United Nations]. (2019). *Sustainable development goals*. Goal 2: Zero Hunger. Cited 26 Aug 2020. Available from: https://www.un.org/sustainabledevelopment/hunger/.

Van Cauwenberghe, L., & Janssen, C. R. (2014). Microplastics in bivalves cultured for human consumption. *Environmental Pollution, 193*, 65–70. Cited 7 Mar 2020. Available from: https://pubmed.ncbi.nlm.nih.gov/25005888/.

WHO [World Health Organization]. (2020). *Millennium development goals (MDGs)*. Cited 26 Aug 2020. Available from: https://www.who.int/topics/millennium_development_goals/about/en/.

WORLD BANK. (2013). Washington, DC: The World Bank, *Agricultural and Environmental Services*. World Bank Report No. 83177-GLB. Cited 6 Mar 2020. Available from: http://documents1.worldbank.org/curated/en/458631468152376668/pdf/831770WP0P11260ES003000Fish0to02030.pdf.

Wright, S. L., Rowe, D., Thompson, R., & Galloway, T. S. (2013). Microplastic ingestion decreases energy reserves in marine worms. *Current Biology, 23*(23), R1031–R1033. Cited 7 Mar 2020. Available from: https://pubmed.ncbi.nlm.nih.gov/24309274/.

Wuebbles, D. J., Fahey, D. W., Hibbard, K. A., Dokken, D. J., Stewart, B. C., & Maycook, T. K. (2017). *Climate science special report: Fourth national climate assessment* (Vol. I). Executive summary. Washington, DC: U.S. Global Change Research Program. Cited 5 May 2020. Available from: https://science2017.globalchange.gov/chapter/executive-summary/.

**Pablo Morón-Elorza** graduated with a degree in Veterinary Medicine from the Complutense University of Madrid in 2019 as first in his Class. With a career focused on the fields of wildlife medicine and the study and conservation of marine species, he has collaborated with many prestigious organizations, nature parks, zoos and NGOs. He is currently completing a Ph.D. on Shark Pharmacology at the Oceanografic Marine Park of Valencia and the Complutense University of Madrid. He is also working as head veterinarian at the Biodomo Zoo and Aquarium, at the Science Park of Granada, Spain. He is passionate about biodiversity and ecology as means to promote the Sustainable Development Goals.

# Coexistence in School: A Proposal for Preventing Violence

**Valentín Martínez-Otero**

**Abstract** In this study, the serious global phenomena of violent and antisocial behavior in school are addressed, mainly those happening among students or between students and teachers. School should be an environment in which everyone coexists and gets along with each other; however, occasionally this interpersonal harmony is disrupted and the educational process becomes an impossible task. Given how difficult it is to fully analyze the complex phenomenon of school violence and antisocial behavior, we approach the problems of coexistence in school in order to better know the reality and, at the same time, to study the path that may lead us to its solution. In summary, some of the most frequent types of school violence and antisocial behavior in school environments are described herein, as well as some of the ways it can be prevented and the most used solutions in other countries, such as discipline, mediation, social competence, etc.

**Keywords** School violence · Antisocial behavior · Coexistence · Prevention · Resolution

## 1 Introduction

When speaking of coexistence, we are referring to life in the company of others. The social nature of human beings does not prevent social relationships from weakening, breaking or being considerably upset. This is precisely what happens when we speak of conflict in human relationships, be they family, work, school or relationships of any other type. Interpersonal tensions are not necessarily negative, but there are times

In: Security and the Global Commons, Edited by J. Martin Ramirez, and Bartolomé Bauzá-Abril.
© 2021 Springer International. Submitted: August, 18, 2020; Accepted: September, 21, 2020.

V. Martínez-Otero (✉)
School of Education, Universidad Complutense de Madrid, Madrid, Spain
e-mail: valenmop@edu.ucm.es



J. M. Ramírez and B. Bauzá-Abril (eds.), *Security in the Global Commons and Beyond*,
Advanced Sciences and Technologies for Security Applications,
https://doi.org/10.1007/978-3-030-67973-6_15

when intra- and inter-group disagreements and confrontations get violent or destructive, which overshadow the coexistence and put people's integrity, both emotional and physical, at risk.

In this study we focus on negative conflicts occurring at school, above all on those among students or between students and teachers. Even though school should be an environment of coexistence, this peace is frequently broken to the point that teaching-learning becomes impossible. Such a conflictive environment makes educational impossible.

Aware of the difficulty of fully addressing the phenomenon of school conflict, we approach the problems of coexistence in schools in order to better know this reality and, at the same time, to see possible paths leading us to a solution. We trust, in summary, that research and critical reflection will help us deal with this problem which every day is more present in schools and which is transcending borders. As stated by Zurita (2018), the serious consequences of school violence, not only in those individuals and institutions directly involved, but also in democratic life and in the exercise of human rights, make prevention a pressing task. In a word, it has an ultimate impact upon human security.

As defended by Caireta (2013), from the closest levels to those furthest away, a pedagogy for coexistence that gives people the tools to hold healthy relationships is necessary, both in their immediate environment as well as in the world, founded in values and human rights, a type of education that fights to prevent and overcome violence, promoting the individual's capacity to critically analyze problems, to act and participate responsibly, as well as to promote the positive dimension of the conflicts and favor harmonious and cooperative relationships among individuals, enhancing security.

## 2 Causes of School Violence

Violence is the force (from the Latin *vis* = force) exerted against another or others. These intentional actions directed toward hurting others are found in degrees. At school, for example, we have physical aggression toward classmates and teachers that vary in intensity, including theft, material damage, insults, cruel jokes, threats, bullying, etc. This behavior upsets the educational process of everyone to the point school security has become an object of international concern. From UNESCO-IICBA (2017), for example, it is affirmed that safe schools with positive climates contribute to the students' physical, social, emotional and cognitive development, as well as the health and well-being of teachers and staff.

Why do we have school violence? This problem is due to a group of intermingled, pluricausal factors of a social/environmental, communicational and relational, scholastic, family and personal nature (see Martínez-Otero (2018)):

2.1 *Society.* Social inequalities, with significant sectors affected by poverty and unemployment in contrast to the opulence of some groups. This structural imbalance acts as a breeding ground for lack of adaptation and antisocial behavior. It is known that, in general, children from poor families, as well as children of immigrants, are most vulnerable to bullying and cyber bullying (UNESCO 2019). Even though the school, in some cases, counteracts the negative effects of exclusion, it can do little by itself. If we look at this current pandemic caused by the coronavirus, Cabrera (2020) shows for example, that the closing of schools in Spain, with the differential assumption, e-teaching and learning has seen and increased the inequality of educational opportunities due to the lack of electronic devices in poorer homes.

2.2 *Means of communication and technology.* Mass media and the generalized use of digital devices influence students considerably, frequently in the production of negative behavior. In this regard, the research conducted with adolescents by Den Hamer and Konijin (2015) revealed that high levels of exposure to media with antisocial and risky content contributed significantly to cyber bullying, above all in males.

2.3 *Fragility of relationships.* The impoverishment of communication and the increase in relationships dominated by competition, to which rampant individualism should be added. Strategic pedagogic action in the face of school violence must take into account the existence of groups and communities more vulnerable to environmental influences that weaken relationships and the associative dimension (Dalcin et al. 2016).

2.4 *Family.* Family is the first and foremost community in the formation of personality; and family problems may have a great impact on development. Among the factors that may increase aggressiveness in children and adolescents are broken families, the absence of a parent or lack of attention, mistreatment or the use of violence—since the child learns to solve conflict through physical damage or verbal aggression—, educational methods based on permissiveness, indifference or excessive punishment, the lack of affection between spouses and the resulting insecurity of the child, the family example of "survival of the fittest" and the lack of communication. To this regard, Garcés-Prettel et al. (2020) have concluded that open communication of the parents with school-age teens contributes to the decrease and prevention of school violence. And Estévez et al. (2018) found that aggressive behavior in couples is significantly related to high scores in offensive communication and family conflict, as well as to low scores in open communication with parents, general expressiveness and family cohesion.

2.5 *School.* The educational institution is based on an internal hierarchy and organization that in itself may cause conflict. The scholastic seeds of violence may be traced to crisis and diversity of values of the school itself, to discrepancies in the distribution of spaces, organization of time, patterns of behavior, etc., to the emphasis on students' results and their comparison with the norm, as well as to the inattentiveness of people and the educational processes, to the presence of a hegemonic school culture which may clash with others that are at a disadvantage, to the relational and communicative asymmetry between teachers and students, to the elevated numbers of students and to the difficulty in giving personalized attention. One aspect that acquires growing interest is that regarding the school climate, a multidimensional concept dealt with in PISA 2018 (OECD 2019) from four interrelated aspects: safety, teaching-learning, school coexistence and school environment. In general, the scientific literature underlines the importance of the school climate in reducing violence and creating a safe school environment (Espelage and Hong 2019). A study of adolescents by Estévez et al. (2018) found that aggression is associated with low scores in the scholastic dimensions of attitude toward school and the teachers, academic commitment, friendliness in the classroom and support received from the teacher.

2.6 *Personality.* The aspects associated to personality that contribute to the activation of school violence include axiological misdirection which leads to an "anything goes" attitude and legitimizes the use of violence to reach one's own goals, the inability to accept responsibility for actions carried out, occasionally, without true awareness of its negative effects, the lack of empathy, the need for intense and constant stimulation, prejudices, the tendency to cheat and manipulate others, the use of alcohol and other drugs, low self-esteem and superficial relationships. Jara et al. (2017) showed the relevant role of immorality in bullying. Regarding some variables of personality, it is noted in the same study, upon establishing comparisons, that extraversion is greater in aggressors, while ethical awareness is more present in those who do not participate in bullying.

Most authors agree that school violence is attributable to a group of causes in which the interaction of all of them allows its interpretation and possible models for intervention and prevention (Gázquez et al. 2015). In as much as the factors corresponding to the mentioned areas converge, it is more probable that the student show antisocial behavior.

Experience gathered in the prevention and overcoming of school violence emphasizes some general considerations that are synthesized into the enrichment of interpersonal communication and in the real inclusion of students in the activities of the educational community. It is necessary to advance in the construction of humanized schools, erected on rationality, the social dimension, emotion and ethics, in which family participation should fulfill a fundamental role.

We find ourselves in societies with a large presence of violence, and school is not isolated from that. If there is violence in the family, on the street, and in content available on digital devices, it would be strange for there not to also be violence in schools. This asseveration is not a justification, but rather a confirmation of the interdependence of the various environments, as described by the systemic model, as well as the complexity of the violence that, *stricto* sensu, would need a macroscopic analysis, although for practical reasons we focus mainly on schools.

School violence, in any of its expressions, is a worldwide problem. UNESCO (2019) warns that school violence negatively impacts in education, health, wellbeing and in the quality of life of children and adolescents. In this report, it is noted, for example, that the students bullied have more probabilities of feeling alone, of having sleep problems, of considering suicide and of participating in risky behavior, such as early sexual activity, smoking and use of alcohol and marijuana, than those not bullied.

## 3 Types of School Violence

School violence, besides being the result of a tangled web of causes, includes behaviors of a diverse nature, among which is bullying, which we put forward and describe below, from the types recognized by UNESCO (2019) and conceptually enriched by other sources:

3.1 *Bullying*. This is an aggressive behavior that implies unwanted negative actions. It is repetitive over time and allows an imbalance of power or strength between the perpetrators and the victim. Molina and Vecina (2015) highlight some characteristics of bullying, which are the victim's defenselessness, the absence of provocation, the imbalance of power between aggressor and victim, the complicity, passivity or ignorance of the surroundings and persistence. We can distinguish the following types of bullying:

  3.1.1 *Physical bullying*. This is not to be confused with a fight or physical attack. This type of bullying includes repeated aggressions, such as being hit, hurt, kicked, pushed or locked in. It may also be characterized by the theft of or damage to the victim's belongings, which may force him or her to do something against his or her will.

  3.1.2 *Psychological bullying*. This includes verbal and emotional abuse, as well as social exclusion. It may be exerted as insults, cruel jokes, belittlement, lies and negative rumors about the victim, etc.

  3.1.3 *Sexual bullying*. This is a form of sexual violence, characterized by gestures, jests, jokes or intimidating sexual comments, which may be accompanied by threats or provocations. According to UNESCO (2018), sexual bullying is the second most frequent type of school bullying. Sexual cyber bullying is increasingly more present and is most experienced by girls. Recent research by Garaigordobil and Larrain (2020) reveals that bullying and cyber bullying affect more students with a non-normative sexual identity or orientation than heterosexual students.

  3.1.4 *Cyberbullying*. This includes intimidation through messages, publications, images, e-mails, websites, etc. without permission and improperly or hurtfully. As we highlighted in previous research (Martínez-Otero 2017), cyber bullying is a type of harassment that does not let up, it is difficult to evade and its effects may be more devastating than in the case of bullying, although they frequently happen together. The aggressors, often anonymous, invisible, have more difficulty empathizing with their victims since they do not see them. Precisely since they lack information about the damage they inflict on the victim, the aggressors' cruelty may increase. This lack of feedback hinders the activation of self-control mechanisms of the aggressiveness; therefore, the cyber bully's lack of inhibition, frequently situated at a comfortable position, with a sense of impunity, reaches very serious levels.

3.2 *Fights.* This is a form of physical violence among classmates. For Paulín (2015), the beginning of the fight is frequently associated with challenging looks, cruel jokes and insidious comments or explicit insults interpreted as lack of respect and constitute a valued way in some school environments and areas in which there are young people to maintain honor since they define the conflict through a winner and a loser. Research carried out by Gaspar et al. (2019) from more than 5000 Portuguese adolescents revealed, among other results, that 21.3% of the students reported at least one fight, 61.1% of the fights were fought in school, fights are related to the use of alcohol and other drugs.
3.3 *Physical attacks.* These are actions carried out by one or more individuals to hit or harm a student, sometimes through the use of a weapon (stick, knife, switchblade or gun). For this type of behavior, the establishment of preventive programs is fundamental. Although many variables come into play upon explaining this violent behavior, it is fundamental to implement universal or general prevention strategies, designed for all the students, complemented by specific interventions allocated to the disadvantaged students, students at risk or students with recent involvement in problematic behavior (Hawkins et al. 2015).
3.4 *Sexual violence.* This refers to forced sexual relations or any other non-consensual sexual act or contact. It includes attempts at non-consensual sexual acts, threats of sexual violence, exhibitionism and verbal sexual harassment. Sexual violence and sexual harassment may be overlaying. Levine (2015) states that this sexual violence in school is rarely dealt with in specialized literature and that, when dealt with, focuses above all on violence of adults towards minors more than in the victimization of students by classmates. The Department of Education of the United Kingdom (2018) shows from evidence that girls have higher probabilities of suffering sexual violence than boys, and that boys have higher probabilities of committing such violence.
3.5 *Physical violence carried out by teachers.* This is the intentional use of physical force with the potential to cause death, disability, injury or harm, even if it is used as a form of punishment. Ferrara et al. (2019) argue that violence from teachers is more probably directed toward children and adolescents from stigmatized and excluded populations.
3.6 *Corporal punishment inflicted by teachers.* Corporal punishment is the use of physical force with the intention of causing a certain degree of pain or discomfort, no matter how mild; for example, hitting with their hand or an instrument, kicking, shaking, pushing or scratching the children. Ogando and Pells (2015) indicate that corporal punishment occurs in the context of other structural inequalities and in the framework of a broader culture of school violence. These authors acknowledge the importance of legislation to eradicate its use,

although they themselves state that it is insufficient; therefore, it is also necessary to have preventive measures in policies and programs, accompanied by changes in the structures, norms and practices of the school environment.

Together with these types of school violence, other antisocial behavior can be mentioned with which the norms of coexistence are violated, as are the rights of others; for example, aggression toward the teacher, vandalism, classroom disruption, etc. which disrupt in greater or lesser degree the academic environment.

3.7 *Violence toward the teacher.* As Berlanda et al. (2019) show after a thorough review of the literature, this can be seen as a serious worldwide phenomenon, traditionally underestimated, but which every day is getting greater attention since a good number of teachers have to face the violence committed by students and parents, in the form of insults and cruel jokes, inappropriate comments and insolence, screaming, intimidation and verbal threats, cyber harassment, damage and theft of personal property and even physical aggression.

3.8 *Vandalism.* Torner (2016) defines school vandalism as a group of behaviors, often carried out in groups, through which material property of the institution is destroyed or damaged, such as windows, locks, fires, graffiti, tables and chairs, computer equipment, etc. Vilalta and Fondevila (2017) have found an association between school vandalism and membership in gangs, drug use, intimidation, lack of adherence to school rules and unequal treatment given by teachers to their students.

3.9 *Disruptive behaviors.* These are actions that disrupt the class rhythm. Generally, the disruptions have upset students as protagonists who, with their comments, laughter, games, movements, etc. unrelated to the teaching-learning process, impede or make teaching difficult. Närhi et al. (2017) emphasize that disruptions in the classrooms threaten the teaching-learning process, put academic performance at risk and is an important source of the teachers' work-related stress.

In general, it can be said that there is growing evidence that antisocial behavior, such as that above described, carried out by some students, may serve as negative behavioral reference for their classmates (Alimardany and Alimardany 2014). The research also suggests that students with antisocial behavior run the risk of becoming involved, with the passing of time, in other antisocial behavior (Nasaescu et al. 2020).

## 4 School Safety and Preventive Guidance

School safety occupies a prominent place in the public sphere, mainly due to the alarm that violence generates in the media, although, unfortunately, sometimes the proposed solutions are simple and narrow. Hence, it is appropriate to emphasize collaboration and transdisciplinary knowledge to better understanding violent behavior in institutions and promote school safety without resorting exclusively to psychology or pedagogy (Mayer and Jimerson 2019).

In general, and from an international perspective, school safety and violence prevention require the convergence of disciplines and agents. Theoretical models and research from fields, such as law, health, anthropology, sociology, etcetera, enrich the strictly psycho-pedagogical approach, even more, if it has the governmental sensitivity and the political and legislative adequacy, as well as the synergistic citizen, police, journalistic and judicial collaboration.

To create and maintain a safe school environment, support student learning, health, and well-being, and prevent violence in school, policymakers as well as education officials and professionals, in addition to reviewing robust research and relevant literature (May 2018), have to promote close coordination of agents at different levels and to have sufficient resources. There is no single solution for schools to be safe places, especially if we consider that many neighborhoods are not. The complexity of the issue encourages us to say, on the one hand, that it seems more effective to prevent than to react (Afkinich and Klumpner 2018) and, on the other hand, from a systemic perspective, that it is necessary a continuous effort that requires, in one way or another, the interrelation of sectors and the involvement of the entire society.

Everything we have said about violence and antisocial behavior in schools leads us to become aware of the complexity of these phenomena, as well as of the need to continue researching to have explanatory models and appropriate preventive interventions that allow us to promote security in schools.

The cancellation of school violence is no simple task, since there are many causes, and people involved. In general, it can be affirmed that preventing and addressing violence in the school have been carried out from scientific and humanistic foundations in a congruent political and legislative context, with interventions of an individual, group, family, institutional and community scope. It is fundamental that reflection, involvement of the parts, agreement, responsibility and personal and social development are worked. This is the psychopedagogical framework that may guide any educational planning directed toward preventing and solving school violence. The solely punitive interventions or dangerous proposals, such as giving the teachers weapons (Rajan and Branas 2018), must give way to rational, contextualized and integrative actions that take into account the interrelationship of scenarios, the characteristics of the individuals involved, the shared establishment of norms and objectives, as well as the alternatives to conflict.

Fernández (2014) proposes a model of preventive intervention in the problems of coexistence that include various channels of action: raising awareness, curricular approach, individualized attention, participation and organization. Together with this outline, we cite three complementary paths of action that may be combined to favor coexistence in schools:

4.1 *Discipline.* In general, scientific literature reveals that there is broad gap in disciplinary practices used in schools, very conditioned for the action by directors and by the teachers themselves in the management of the classroom, of interactions between students and teachers, as well as the cultural mishaps (Galés and Little 2018). The review by these authors has allowed us to see the tendency to establish, faced with the discipline of exclusion, alternative disciplinary strategies and programs aimed at keeping students in schools and oriented toward improving the school culture and climate, promoting intercultural skills in teachers to manage students' behavior, as well as positive behavioral interventions and support, restorative justice practices, social and emotional learning, etc.

In personalized school environments, it is preferable to reinforce correct behavior rather than to punish incorrect behavior. It is also advisable for students to have good learning models, which leads us to emphasize the importance of teacher training and, of course, it should favor reflection and communication as ways of knowing the motive and the scope of the problem, while guiding the student in what should be the correct action. In the entire positive and educational disciplinary process, the involvement of parents and the community as a whole plays a critical role (Joseph 2013) although unfortunately many schools remain isolated.

4.2 *Mediation.* Mediation has had a growth in recognition at a worldwide level in many environments as well as in school. Within the complex framework of human relationships, conflicts happen and, in the search for solutions, legal systems are sometimes rejected for their sluggishness and depersonalization, which makes mediation more popular. It is a work of approximation and harmonization of individuals and groups, an alternative and extrajudicial professional activity promoting understanding which, from the prevention or solution of conflicts, coexistence is situated. In our pedagogical field, it is, therefore, a harmonizing, balancing and unifying action. Through the neutral and impartial mediator help is given to two or more persons or distinct groups so they improve their relationship, avoid conflict or solve their existing problems. García-Raga et al. (2019) show that mediation having students' support is a useful tool for prevention of school violence and construction of coexistence by its promotion of personal development, of relationships and of the positive institutional climate. Together with mediation carried out by professionals, mediation among duly prepared peers is also effective in cases of school violence (Mic et al. 2013; Eisenkraft 2015). The research done by Karakiozis and Papakitsos (2018) in secondary schools revealed that the school mediation programs activate assistance among students as well as favor responsibility and social/communication skills of the participants.

4.3 *Social competence.* This refers to cognitive and positive affective processes that are translated into behavior valued by the community. It may also refer to social skills, that is, adaptive behaviors that allow people to begin and maintain healthy relationships with others. The promotion of social competence/skill helps to overcome isolation, insecurity, shyness and antisocial behavior. Its training is one of the proper ways to prevent and solve violent behavior in school since it has been found, for example, that deficits in social skills are associated to the participation in episodes of bullying in school (Mendoza and Madonado 2017). In line with the recommendations by the World Health Organization (2019), many of the skills promoted to prevent and respond to school violence, such as communication, emotion management, the resolution of conflicts and of daily problems constructively, are the same that can help students be successful in school, which may equally protect them from other risks derived from the use of drugs and alcohol; therefore, its promotion may be combined with the training of parents and teachers.

## 5 Conclusions

In this study, we have focused on some relevant questions corresponding to violence and antisocial behavior in schools. We have summarily reviewed some of the solutions that have been most followed or used in the concerning environment of violence and school unrest, for example, discipline, mediation and promotion of social competence. Antisocial behavior and violence are realities that are very present in educational institutions and, as has been gathered in this study, are due to multiple causes. This plural etiology makes it difficult to find definitive and fully satisfactory answers upon suggesting an effective intervention. In this field, the affirmation 'an ounce of prevention is better than a pound of cure' holds a great truth, which leads us to suggest a *pedagogy of coexistence* erected on the following pillars:

- The empowerment of communication and of positive interpersonal relationships. They are being educated for peace from coexistence, respect and participation, that is, from healthy and pro-social interaction.
- Special attention to the most vulnerable students. To this regard, an inclusive pedagogical design must be developed, which prevents discriminatory and exclusive practices.
- Inter-institutional collaboration which allows synergies to be established and efforts to be taken advantage of which are carried out from different environments, particularly school, family and community (Fig. 1).

The construction of coexistence in school must begin in childhood, based on attention to the students' cognitive and socio-affective development. The school must open the doors to give help, solidarity, empathic understanding, inclusion, etc., all actions we can label as pro-social and which constitute the best vaccine against its opponent, which is antisocial behavior.

The review carried out in this study and experience allows us to affirm that, in general, any strategy or intervention aimed at preventing, reducing or solving school violence must take into account four interrelated dimensions:

1. The *cognitive* dimension refers to the need to offer positive and realistic information to the members of the educational community with the objective of fighting prejudice or irrational beliefs about individuals or groups.
2. The *affective* dimension has to do with the need to cultivate emotional education in scholastic institutions. Basically, it is to give value to empathy, as well as to the identification, expression and government of the affective phenomena.

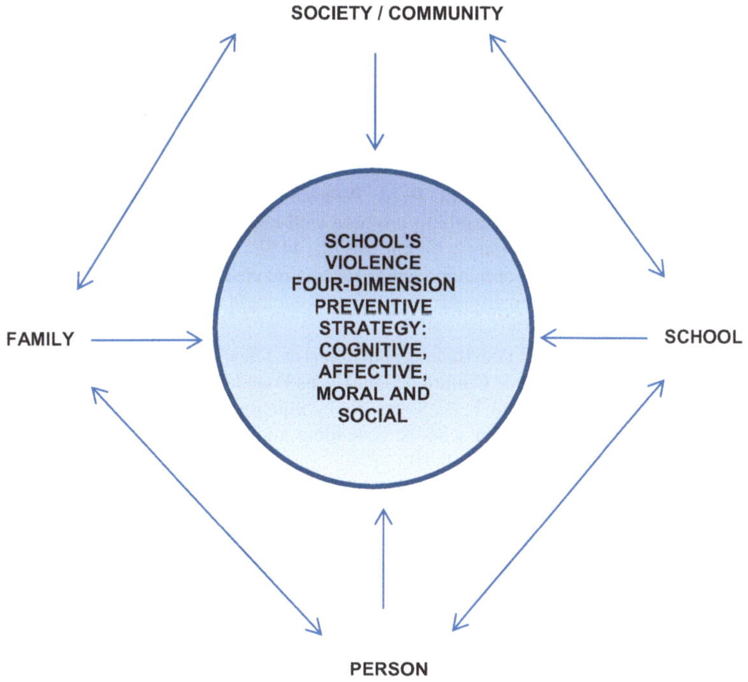


**Fig. 1** Graphic representation of school's violence four-dimensional preventive strategy (cognitive, affective, moral, and social) through the junction of efforts at four interrelated levels: society/community, school, family, person *Source* own elaboration

3. The *ethical* dimension is directed toward promoting the moral development of the students, the discussion of dilemmas, the classroom and the school environment, etc.
4. The *social* dimension makes reference to the importance of communication, positive relationships and, in sum, to the climate of the classroom based on cordiality, trust and effort.

These four dimensions (cognitive, affective, ethical and social) allow one to systematize the psychopedagogical intervention in the cases of school violence. This four-part distribution does not break the unit of violent or antisocial behavior, but rather it helps to organize the educational action in the complex structural constellation of violent behavior. This four-dimensional work perspective is equally useful to assess the different proposals, models, strategies and programs for conflict prevention and resolution in schools. The approach presented helps to select the forms and instruments that best adjust to the needs and the objectives, that in our case are summed up as *educate for coexistence.*

## References

Alimardany, A., & Alimardany, A. (2014). School, a place to learn social and antisocial behavior. *International Journal of School Health, 1*(2), 1–5.

Afkinich, J. L., & Klumpner, S. (2018). Violence prevention strategies and school safety. *Journal of the Society for Social Work and Research, 9*(4), 637–650.

Berlanda, S., Fraizzoli, M., de Cordova, F., & Pedrazza, M. (2019). Psychosocial risks and violence against teachers. Is it possible to promote well-being at work? *International Journal of Environmental Research and Public Health, 16*(22), 4439.

Cabrera, L. (2020). Efectos del coronavirus en el sistema de enseñanza: aumenta la desigualdad de oportunidades educativas en España. *Revista de Sociología de la Educación-RASE, 13*(2), 114–139 (Especial, COVID-19).

Caireta, M. (2013). *Peace and coexistence education in school settings: A teacher training perspective.* Barcelona: Escola de Cultura de Pau-Evens Foundation.

Dalcin, C. B., Backes, D. S., Zanatta, F. B., Sousa, F. G., Siqueira, H. C., & Oliveira, A. M. (2016). Factors associated with violence in schools: Extending knowledges and practices for nursing. *Texto y Contexto-Enfermagem, 25*(4), 1–10.

Den Hamer, A. H., & Konijn, E. A. (2015). Adolescents' media exposure may increase their cyberbullying behavior: A longitudinal study. *Journal of Adolescent Health, 56*(2), 203–208.

Department for Education. (2018). *Sexual violence and sexual harassment between children in schools and colleges.* Advice for governing bodies, proprietors, headteachers, principals, senior leadership teams and designated safeguarding leads, London. https://assets.publishing.service.gov.uk/government/uploads/system/uploads/attachment_data/file/719902/Sexual_violence_and_sexual_harassment_between_children_in_schools_and_colleges.pdf.

Eisenkraft, K. O. (2015). *Intervening in school-based youth conflict: Violence reduction, positive youth development, peer mediation, and conflict resolution education.* Boston: Massachusetts Office of Public Collaboration, John W. McCormack Graduate School of Policy and Global Studies, Boston, University of Massachusetts.

Espelage, D. L., & Hong, J. S. (2019). School climate, bullying, and school violence. In M. J. Mayer, & S. R. Jimerson (Eds.), *School safety and violence prevention: Science, practice, policy* (pp 45–69). Washington, DC: American Psychological Association.

Estévez, E., Jiménez, T. I., & Moreno, D. (2018). Aggressive behavior in adolescence as a predictor of personal, family, and school adjustment problems. *Psicothema, 30*(1), 66–73.

Fernández, I. (2014). *Prevención de la violencia y resolución de conflictos.* Madrid: Narcea.

Ferrara, P., Franceschini, G., Villani, A., & Corsello, G. (2019). Physical, psychological and social impact of school violence on children. *Italian Journal of Pediatrics, 45*(76), 141–158.

Galés, R. O., & Little, S. (2018). The school discipline dilemma: A comprehensive review of disparities and alternative approaches. *Review of Educational Research, 88*(5), 752–794.

Garaigordobil, M., & Larrain, E. (2020). Acoso y ciberacoso en adolescentes LGTB: Prevalencia y efectos en la salud mental. *Comunicar, 62*(v. XXVIII), 79–90.

Garcés-Prettel, M., Santoya-Montes, Y., & Jiménez-Osorio, J. (2020). Influence of family and pedagogical communication on school violence. *Comunicar, 63*(XXVIII), 73–82.

García-Raga, L., Grau, R., & Boqué, M. C. (2019). School mediation under the spotlight: What spanish secondary students think of mediation. *Journal of Educational, Cultural and Psychological Studies, 19*, 41–60.

Gaspar, S., Guedes, B. F., Cerqueira, A., Oliveira, R., & de Matos, G. M. (2019). Physical fights involvement in school setting and adolescents' behaviours: highlights from health behaviour in school-aged children (HBSC/WHO)—fights in school setting and adolescent's behaviours. *Primary Care Epidemiology and Global Health, 1*, 1–7.

Gázquez, J. J., Barragán, A. B., Pérez-Fuentes, M. C., Molero, M. M., Garzón, A., & Martos, Á. (2015). Factors associated with school violence: A systematic review. *British Journal of Education, Society & Behavioural Science, 11*(3), 1–12.

Hawkins, J. D., Jenson, J. M., Catalano, R., Fraser, M. W., Botvin, G. J., Shapiro, V., Brown, C. H., Beardslee, W., Brent, D., Leslie, L. K., Rotheram-Borus, M. J., Shea, P., Shih, A., Anthony, E., Haggerty, K. P., Bender, K., Gorman-Smith, D., Casey, E., & Stone, S. (2015). *Unleashing the power of prevention* (Discussion Paper). Washington, DC: Institute of Medicine and National Research Council.

Jara, N., Casas, J. A., & Ortega-Ruiz, R. (2017). Proactive and reactive aggressive behavior in bullying: The role of values. *International Journal of Educational Psychology, 6*(1), 1–24.

Joseph, P. (2013). The role of parents in the dynamics of school discipline. *International Journal of Independent Research and Studies, 2*(1), 45–50.

Karakiozis, K., & Papakitsos, E. C. (2018). School mediation programmes and incidents of in-school violence and bullying. *Research Journal of Education, 4*(3), 44–50.

Levine, E. (2015). Sexual violence among middle school students: The effects of gender and dating experience. *Journal of Interpersonal Violence, 32*(14), 1–24.

Martínez-Otero, V. (2017). Acoso y ciberacoso en una muestra de alumnos de Educación Secundaria, Profesorado. *Revista de currículum y formación de profesorado, 21*(3), 277–298.

Martínez-Otero, V. (2018). Condicionantes de la violencia en la escuela. In J. M. Ramírez, & V. Martínez-Otero (Eds.), *Violencia y educación* (pp. 18–21). Madrid: Universidad Nebrija.

May, D. C. (2018). Introduction to the special issue on school safety: increasing understanding/decreasing misunderstandings in the realm of school safety. *American Journal of Criminal Justice, 43*, 1–5.

Mayer, M. J., & Jimerson, S. R. (2019). The importance of school safety and violence prevention. In M. J. Mayer, & S. R. Jimerson (Eds.), *School safety and violence prevention: Science, practice, policy* (pp. 3–16). Washington DC, USA: American Psychological Association.

Mendoza, B., & Madonado, V. (2017). Acoso escolar y habilidades sociales en alumnado de educación básica. *Ciencia ergo-sum, 24*(2), 109–116.

Mic, E., Mic, V., & Rădulescu, D. M. (2013). The role of mediation in school. *Social Economic Debates, 2*(1), 1–5.

Molina, J. A., & Vecina, P. (2015). *Bullying, ciberbullying y sexting ¿Cómo actuar ante una situación de acoso?*. Madrid: Pirámide.

Närhi, V., Kiiski, T., & Savolainen, H. (2017). Reducing disruptive behaviours and improving classroom behavioural climate with class-wide positive behaviour support in middle schools. *British Educational Research Journal, 43*(6), 1186–1205.

Nasaescu, E., Zych, I,, Ortega-Ruiz, R., Farrington, D. P., & Llorent, V. J. (2020). Longitudinal patterns of antisocial behaviors in early adolescence: a latent class and latent transition analysis. *The European Journal of Psychology Applied to Legal Context, 12*(2), 85–92.

OECD. (2019). *PISA 2018 Results (Volume III): What School Life Means for Students' Lives*. Paris, PISA: OECD Publishing.

Ogando, M. J., & Pells, K. (2015) *Corporal punishment in schools: Longitudinal evidence from Ethiopia, India, Peru and Viet Nam, Florence, UNICEF*.

Paulín, H. L. (2015). Ganarse el respeto. Un análisis de los conflictos de la sociabilidad juvenil en la escuela secundaria. *Revista Mexicana de Investigación Educativa, 20*(67), 1105–1130.

Rajan, S., & Branas, C. C. (2018) Arming schoolteachers: What do we know? Where do we go from here? *American Journal of Public Health, 108*(7), 860–886.

Torner, M. (2016). *Investigación sobre la incidencia del vandalismo en los centros de educación secundaria*. Doctoral Dissertation. Alcalá de Henares, Universidad de Alcalá.

UNESCO. (2018). *School violence and bullying: Global status and trends, drivers and consequences*. París: UNESCO.

UNESCO. (2019). *Behind the numbers: Ending school violence and bullying*. París: UNESCO.

UNESCO-IICBA. (2017). *School safety manual. Tools for teachers*. Addis Ababa: UNESCO-IICBA.

Vilalta, C. J., & Fondevila, G. (2017). School vandalism in Mexico. *Journal of School Violence, 18*, 392–404.

World Health Organization. (2019). *School-based violence prevention. A practical handbook.* Geneva: World Health Organization.
Zurita, Ú. (2018). Violencia escolar, Eunomía. *Revista en Cultura de la Legalidad, 14*, 299–309.

**Valentín Martínez-Otero** is Doctor of Psychology from the UCM and Doctor of Philosophy and Education Sciences from the UNED, with an extraordinary award; specialist in Clinical Psychology at the UCM; and with Master's Degree in Psychopathology and Health, Expert in Community Mental Health Professional and Trainer of Trainers; Research professor in the Department of Educational Studies (UCM). Lecturer, researcher and visiting professor at academies and universities in Spain, Europe and Iberoamerica. Author of numerous publications on topics of his specialty. Director of the Complutense Research Group on Psychosociobiology of Violence: Education and Prevention.

# Epilogue

From the readings above it is apparent that the first decades of the twenty-first century are and will be characterized by strategic ambiguity and hybrid threats. A chemical reaction between information, perception, interpretation and decision-making …, between non-attribution and asymmetry …, deception and persuasion …, and all these ingredients are particularly conspicuous when related to the Global Commons, areas differentiated by unimpeded access and weak regulation and enforcement.

The reader may have noticed that some aspects of the Global Commons have been approached from different perspectives: security, condition or even a model to address or characterize international conflicts. They are welcome as they show how the Global Commons are relevant in a globalized world. Globalized? Funny, this globalizing word it is not encompassing at all the course of the world in its entirety. The SARS-CoV-2 pandemic has propitiated a shift of the interests of the citizens and Governments, as they get more local, gradually focusing narrowly to the pandemic and the counting of infected or deceased persons. As a consequence, governmental policies and concerns are becoming parochial, especially in those countries that have been most affected by the virus, and geopolitical events are being systematically dismissed or simply ignored, hopefully temporarily. A form of geopolitical blindness.

As a paradox, this pandemic has contributed significantly to the resurgence of some form of Geopolitics: this virus is rearranging some parts of the world, again. And it will probably change the concept and practice of Globalization as it has been understood until now. To the tensions resulting from the trade wars between China and the United States, the BREXIT, or the ones derived from the use or abuse of the Global Commons, we have to tally the ones derived from the restrictions to the movement of people caused by the pandemic. In the EU, some borders have been closed resulting in a form of international lockdown, widening the gap between healthy and wealthy northern countries and struggling plague-ridden southern EU countries; the subsequent political and economic alignment is happening right now.

An ambiguous world, as ever.



J. M. Ramírez and B. Bauzá-Abril (eds.), *Security in the Global Commons and Beyond*, Advanced Sciences and Technologies for Security Applications,
https://doi.org/10.1007/978-3-030-67973-6

But this book also deals with security beyond the Global Commons. A few chapters refer to them. All of them significant and providing insight on human activities not usually dealt in Security books. But Security is multi facetious and permeates all layers of society. We hope you have found them relevant. We hope you have found the book interesting.

Bartolomé Bauzá-Abril
J. Martín Ramírez

The manufacturer's authorised representative in the EU is Springer Nature Customer Service Centre GmbH, Europaplatz 3, 69115 Heidelberg, Germany. If you have any concerns regarding our products, please contact ProductSafety@springernature.com

Printed and bound by CPI Group (UK) Ltd, Croydon, CR0 4YY
30/09/2026
02225692-0004